PRAIRIE STATE POLITICS

PRAIRIE STATE POLITICS

Popular Democracy in South Dakota

By ALAN L. CLEM

Professor of Government, University of South Dakota

Public Affairs Press, Washington, D. C.

FOR MARY

JK
6525
1967
.C4

PREFACE

Scholarly and popular works about public affairs focus so much attention on national issues and international crises that many an American citizen is better informed about events in Washington, Moscow, and Saigon than about matters in his own state. This is unfortunate because state politics deeply influences our national affairs. Our national leaders are, almost without exception, products of state political systems; of all our elected officials, only the President and Vice President are chosen by the national constituency. Further, states are important as laboratories for political experimentation, where new ideas can be tested and refined.

The true test of democratic government occurs, of course, at the state and local level, where the citizen is closest to his government. For a people who believe they can continue to govern themselves sensibly, fairly, and democratically — in a word, successfully — the study of state politics is, then, of critical importance.

This study should be useful not only for what it says about South Dakota, but also for what it says about state political systems as integral parts of the national community. Political scientists will find something of value in an understanding of how the people of South Dakota behave within their constitutional, ideological, geographical, cultural, economic, and social environments — how they are affected by these environments, and how in turn they seek to change them.

My affection for the state and its people has undoubtedly biased some of the things I say in these pages. It is possible that I have expected too much and that I have been more impatient than a completely objective scholar should be with certain inadequacies, inconsistencies, and timidities. The reader will have to judge for himself; I content myself with the thought that my service is better performed by demanding too much, rather than too little, of the citizens and officials of my state.

Systematic research into state politics owes much to the writings of the late V. O. Key, Jr., and to subsequent studies by Leon Epstein, John Fenton, Herbert Jacob and Kenneth Vines, Frank Jonas, Duane Lockard, Theodore Mitau, Frank Munger, and Austin Ranney. It is hoped this book will build on their groundwork and suggest patterns for comparative studies of other state political systems.

For general materials on South Dakota government and history,

v

I am especially indebted to W. O. Farber and Herbert S. Schell. The Populist, Progressive, and Nonpartisan movements and related midwestern political developments have been richly portrayed by John D. Hicks, Russell B. Nye, and Robert L. Morlan. Those interested in Dakota territorial politics should consult the work of Howard Roberts Lamar. For particular South Dakota aspects, I have relied on C. Perry Armin, Clarence Berdahl, Gilbert Fite, T. C. Geary, Charles O. Jones, and George Platt. The references indicate additional specific obligations. Moreover, I have benefited considerably from the willingness of politicians to discuss with candor their craft and their problems; those I have consulted include Senators, Congressmen, Governors, members of the legislature, state administrative officials, county commissioners, mayors, and aldermen, as well as party officials from both sides of the political fence.

I am also grateful for the assistance of the University of South Dakota Computer Center, the State Geological Survey, my colleagues in the Governmental Research Bureau, and other members of the university family. Michael Pieplow, Carole Muchmore, Patricia Quenzer, Douglas Hale, and Jean Eckert tabulated and processed much of the statistical data. Patricia Quenzer, Jean Eckert, Nancy Wissink, Julie Rehder, and Gail Manning typed the manuscript. William Willroth helped with the maps, Kay Wastlund with proofreading, and Lois Schnell with the index. I should not overlook my students, both the few who actively contributed insights and information to my awareness of politics and the many who merely listened passively to embryonic versions of much of what is written here.

Finally, and with deep gratitude, I must mention my wife and my parents, whose contributions have been less specific and academic but certainly most essential. I alone, of course, bear full responsibility for any shortcomings in this study.

ALAN L. CLEM

Vermillion, South Dakota

CONTENTS

I

Introduction: People and Politics   1

II

Comparative State Politics: Neighbors and Nation   9

III

Historical Politics: The Shifting Tide   21

IV

Party Politics: Agencies of Participation   47

V

Electoral Politics: Voter Variations   65

VI

Administrative Politics: The Focus of Leadership   86

VII

Legislative Politics: Every Man A Policy-Maker   98

VIII

Congressional Politics: The Washington Scene   115

IX

Conclusion: The Past, Present, and Future   134

References   147

Appendix: Winning Candidates in Major Elections   165

Index   167

MAP OF SOUTH DAKOTA SHOWING COUNTIES, PRINCIPAL CITIES, AND RIVERS

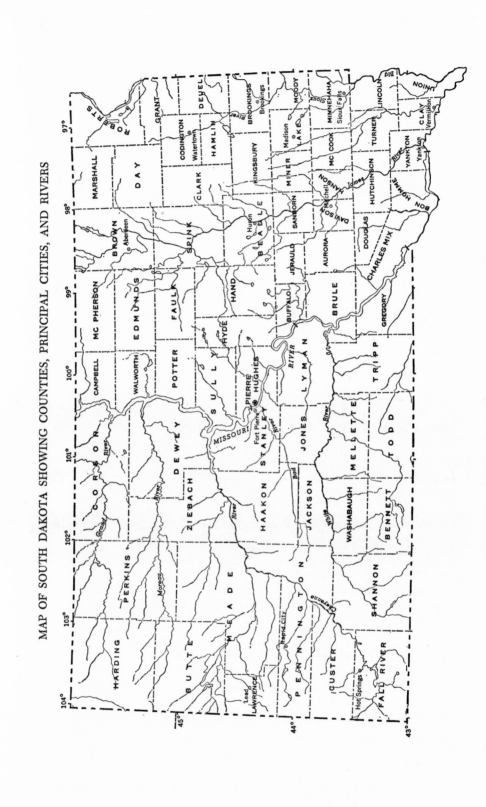

I

INTRODUCTION: PEOPLE AND POLITICS

Political power in South Dakota, as elsewhere, involves the organization, regulation, and administration of government and includes the management and direction of the affairs of public policy. In a formal sense, politics is concerned with the constitutional and statutory distribution of governmental power; such power is associated more with an office than with a particular individual holding it. Less formally, politics is concerned with the application of power or influence to the process of determining public policy; in this sense the personality, intellect, and force of character of the individual in office are the focus of attention. Thus the study of politics must involve both the study of an official's formal authority to act and his personal ability to control or influence the actions of others.

The difference between the formal and informal in politics might be made more apparent by considering the office of the nation's chief executive. All Presidents of the United States have had generally equivalent powers, given the differing circumstances of their own times, but each has behaved in a distinctive way in response to the problems he faced. The formal sources of authority give the President a number of options to follow in responding to a particular situation; the option he chooses necessarily depends on his personal proclivities.[1] To understand the American Presidency requires an appreciation of the formal, constitutional powers available to the office and of the personal characteristics of the incumbent that conditioned what he accomplished or failed to accomplish during the course of his administration. In the same way, to understand the politics of South Dakota demands an appreciation of the potential legal authority to act as well as of the individual official's action.

Politics Takes Many Forms. The citizen commits a political act when he complains of a high property appraisal, delinquent mail service, shoddy street repair work, or a basement full of sewer water. He performs a crucial role when he casts his vote and thus indicates his personal preferences on questions such as whether or not his community should build a new high school or whether Lyndon Johnson or Barry Goldwater would be the better President.

1

Citizens may join together in groups to make their protests against or recommendations for governmental action more effective. Special interest pressure groups such as the National Farmers Organization, the National Association of Manufacturers, the Birdwatchers Club of Lincoln County, and the East Main Street Citizens Association encourage controlled farm marketing, tighter restrictions on labor organizations, reservation and protection of virgin woods, and widening and surfacing of city streets.

Party officials are, of course, deeply involved in politics; their characteristic actions include recommending persons for appointive positions, planning fund-raising dinners, and finding candidates to run for national, state, and local office.

Local officials of government act politically when they vote on a zoning ordinance, a building permit, or a water rate increase.

At the level of state government, legislators write the laws politically and public executives, from the Governor far down into the administrative bureaucracy, administer those laws politically. Whether to support or oppose measures to increase the sales tax, to reclassify agricultural property for tax purposes, or to raise the bounty on foxes and thus help the pheasant population are actions conditioned by the political background and the political ambitions of the legislators and administrators.

U. S. Senators and Representatives from South Dakota, even though they are national officers, are elected by and responsible to the state's people, and consequently the politics of the state is foremost in the Congressional mind.

In short, politics is a very broad topic. It is all around us every day, quite visible to the eye and audible to the ear. But the very ubiquity of politics compounds the problem of the person who desires to reduce politics to an observable form. The study of politics in so broad an arena as an American state, albeit a comparatively underpopulated midwestern prairie state, is a difficult process which can best be handled by systematic analysis of the component institutions of government, with particular attention to political parties, the state administrative organization, the legislature, and the Congress. We must ask not only what the laws provide regarding the location and use of power, but what individuals do as a result of the laws. We must study both the formal apparatus of government—legislative bodies, administrative agencies, judicial courts—and the human behavior that occurs within the formal framework.

Wisdom, Democracy, and Responsibility. A wide array of value preferences resulting from the political, economic, social, and religious experiences of many generations in America and Europe have produced our governmental system. They conditioned our basic charters of government and continue to condition the policies we adopt to meet the circumstances of contemporary society. Citizens and public officials alike behave within the framework of specific statutes, more general constitutional mandates, and even more general and less tangible theories of government. Some citizens are active; they vote at every opportunity and are vocal in praise of or opposition to a particular official or action. Most citizens are moderately active, perhaps voting more often than not but seldom attempting to influence the actions of officials or fellow citizens. Some citizens are inactive, neither voting nor concerning themselves at all about their political surroundings. This study will of necessity be largely concerned about the behavior of the active citizen.

Political officials can be similarly classified as active or passive. Some are eager to use the power of government to solve every problem that arises, and are imaginative in their efforts to find and use power. At the other extreme are those who are decidedly pessimistic about the good that can come from governmental action, and accordingly use their ingenuity to avoid involving the public and the government in settling problems. Most officials fall somewhere between these extremes. This study will be concerned about all types of public officials.

Relationships between popular preferences and wisdom in a democratic system ought to be of major concern to the people. However, a little reflection is sufficient to indicate that wisdom in government is almost impossible to define in such a way as to meet with the agreement of all observers. What objective and authoritative tools are available to help determine whether John F. Kennedy was a better President than Richard M. Nixon might have been or that an aggressive policy in Viet Nam in 1966 advanced American interests more effectively than would have a more passive role? Thus another aspect of politics can be more fruitfully and confidently pursued, and that is the degree to which government is held responsible for its actions.

Officials are held responsible to the people through the election system. But this check, while significant, is one of gross dimensions and has little capacity for careful discrimination. For example, a given citizen does not, when he enters the voting booth, have a clear choice before him between one candidate with whose stands he is totally agreeable and another candidate with whose stands he is in total disagreement. Recent issues may have involved expansion of the state game, fish, and parks department; improving farm-to-market roads; requiring stricter loyalty affidavits of state personnel; requiring all land to be within a 12-year school district; more equitable legislative apportionment; and a broadened sales tax. It is unlikely that the individual voter will entirely agree with either candidate on these matters, and yet his vote is in effect a preference for one candidate's total position.[2] No matter whether the citizen votes for one candidate or the other, with such cross pressures he is incapable of voting in absolute agreement with his own perceived interests.

One of the functions of governmental, party, and pressure group structures should be to sift the elements in the course of political events in such a way as to throw in sharp relief the officials and interests responsible for a given governmental action. In this way, government can become visible and meaningful to its public. Without this sort of public responsibility, the political process becomes meaningless and perhaps positively dangerous to the average citizen who has taken no significant part in that process. Parties exist for the purpose of enhancing the role of the individual citizen in political decisions by reflecting his desires to the government and by making clearer to him the responsibility for the ensuing official action. A recent general commentary deserves attention:

"The circumstances and character of democracy created two needs. First, as the circle of political participants broadened, some means was required of organizing their relationships and imparting to their actions a pattern of purpose and coherence. The recording of millions of votes, without some common focus of policy and program, would only yield chaos. It could not serve as the durable basis for a government founded on the consent of the governed. Second, the institutions of the democratic state had to provide in some crucial place for the representation of the voting public and the reflection of its cross-pressures. . . .

"The party system evolved to meet both needs and provided the link, otherwise missing, between their solutions. It has been the vehicle for organizing millions of citizens and it has lent substance and direction to the work of the legislative assembly. Elections are the mechanism for ascertaining the wishes of the former about the membership and product of the latter. The parties make up the core and center of politics. Everything which is politically relevant — be it social, institutional, or ideological — converges here. A party system serves democracy as a bridge, uniting society and the state."[8]

This study is concerned with the probem of whether or not political structures in the state perform the elementary but crucial functions of linking citizen with state and of defining responsibility for governmental action.

The Setting. South Dakota is located in the upper middle west, bounded on the north by North Dakota, on the east by Minnesota and Iowa, on the south by Nebraska, and on the west by Wyoming and Montana. The only large city within 100 miles of its borders is Sioux City, Iowa. To a remarkable degree South Dakota has an introspective nature, looking inward and tending to view its problems as if unique and unrelated to problems in its sister states.

The state is home to about 700,000 inhabitants who live in an area of 76,378 square miles, within a nearly perfect rectangle 200 miles from north to south and 400 miles from east to west; the population density is only 8.9 per square mile, ranking forty-fourth among the fifty states in this respect. One in seven South Dakotans lives in the state's two largest cities, Sioux Falls and Rapid City, both growing commercial and residential centers. Another one-seventh of the state's population lives in six cities with populations over 10,000. There are four cities larger than 5,000 and twelve more with populations greater than 2,500. Over sixty percent of the population live in smaller towns and in the residual rural area.

Except for the northeastern corner, the state is part of the vast Missouri River basin. The great American corn belt extends into the southeastern corner, and much of the eastern half is indistinguishable in land use and occupation from the general farming land to the east. Toward the west, as the annual rate of rainfall steadily diminishes, greens turn to browns, shimmering humidity turns to arid dustincrs, and the wind blows; compact, neat farms gradually give way to sprawling, rolling range land stretching lazily to the far horizons, broken only by two geological marvels, the Badlands and the Black Hills. The area has been civilized for less than one hundred years. Its political history is comparatively brief. But there is a permanence about South Dakota now that perhaps was missing as recently as a generation ago, when the population diminished as disappointed thousands sought relief elsewhere from the state's economic anxieties.

There remains on the American prairie a feeling of isolation from the main currents of national life. The recent comments of a psychologist are pertinent here; he points to a syndrome observed by prac-

ticing clinical psychologists that does not conform to standard
psychiatric classifications:

". . . The behavior pattern in question, which is fairly common in
this part of the country [presumably including South Dakota as well
as North Dakota: author's note], involves the following symptoms:
apathy, depression, listlessness, withdrawal, and inhibition of both
speech and action. . . . For want of a better term and perhaps partially
facetiously and partially with pride, local psychologists have informally
labelled this syndrome as the North Dakota Depressive Reaction.

"The development of this behavior pattern can be related to several
converging environmental presses. The primary cultural pattern and
the dominant religious philosophy are compatible in their emphasis
on: inhibition of emotional responsiveness; maintenance of interper-
sonal distance even among members of the same family; and denial of
pleasure in this life in order to be properly prepared for the next life.
An important stress in the physical environment involves the relative
isolation that is produced by long, cold winters in a primarily rural
state . . . The above comments should not be taken as an attack on
any particular way of life, for others could argue with some justifica-
tion that it requires a repressive, sacrificing, other-world oriented
approach to life in order to sustain the hardships inherent in a rugged
existence. However, one can also argue that when problems in living
do develop, the form that symptoms of maladjustment take will be, to
a large extent, a function of the behavior patterns that have received
constant reinforcement of environmental agents."[4]

Readers of novels concerning the South Dakota frontier—works such
as Ole Rolvaag's *Giants in the Earth*, Rose Wilder Lane's *Let the
Hurricane Roar*, J. Hyatt Downing's *A Prayer for Tomorrow*, Hamlin
Garland's *Main-Travelled Roads*, and Herbert Krause's *The Thresher*
(set in neighboring Minnesota)—may recall the endless parade of
blizzards, grasshopper plagues, droughts, and dust storms, not to mention the spaciousness and loneliness, and will appreciate more fully
the numbing effects thereof on the primitive prairie psychology.[5]

Political Heritage: A Capsule Survey. The most significant aspect of
South Dakota's political development is its involvement in the agrarian
radicalism and popular democracy that were characteristic of the
prairie states at the turn of the century, their period of greatest national influence. As Schell has put it, "The early history of South
Dakota may be viewed as a series of protest movements against external forces."[6]

The Populist movement was strong in the first decade of statehood and Populist candidates, running under the Fusion banner with the Democratic party, won major elections in 1896 and 1898. The Populist-Democratic alliance did not last, and after 1900 the radical elements split badly, some going into the progressive wing of the Republican party, some into the struggling Democratic party, and some into minor parties. Progressivism was a major factor in South Dakota throughout the first quarter of the new century, its influence being strong in the Republican party due to the leadership of Coe Crawford and Peter Norbeck. The state ventures of the Progressive period proved to be a serious burden on the taxpayers in the depression of the 'Thirties; the experience sobered the electorate and probably contributed to a lack of enthusiasm for ambitious state programs in the 'Forties and 'Fifties. The state has paid its debts and is today providing at least a modicum of the state services to which American citizens have become accustomed.

With maturity, South Dakota's early tendencies toward radicalism have moderated considerably. In recent decades, as Schell points out, the state "has been politically conservative. Differences between political parties over state issues have been more imagined than real: the distinction has been one of degree rather than a matter of basic principles." [7]

Both major parties had become distinctly conservative by 1925. Subsequently, the New Deal caused a re-orientation of the Democratic party in South Dakota toward the national norm, but attracted so little support in the state that Democratic control lasted only four years. The post-New Deal Republican supremacy in South Dakota, mildly conservative by national standards, was broken by Democratic victories in 1956, 1958, and 1962. In the contemporary period elections have been relatively close and the state appears to be in the midst of a competitive political period.

Closely connected with the agrarian radicalism of the Populist and Progressive movements were a number of reforms which had the effect of heightening the independence of office holders and voters alike from political party or state governmental restraints. South Dakota pioneered in the initiative and referendum movement, and retains the system today at some expense to the power and dignity of the legislature. Nominations to major office are by popular primary election rather than party endorsement. Judicial, educational, and municipal elections are nonpartisan, further diminishing the potential influence of the political party organizations.

The state's two most notable political figures have been Peter Norbeck and Karl Mundt. Norbeck was a Progressive Republican who served as Governor from 1917 to 1921 and as U. S. Senator from 1921 until his death in 1936. His influence led the state to adopt a number of socialistic state ventures and left the modern Republican party with the somewhat embarrassing problem of explaining how a state-owned cement plant squares with the party's private enterprise ideals. Mundt, a Congressman for 10 years and Senator since 1949, is the state's master politician. He is probably best known nationally for his reluctant chairmanship of the McCarthy hearings in 1954.[8] He is virtually the prototype of the midwestern Republican conservative, as often attacked from the South Dakota right as from the left.[9]

A few other of the state's political leaders, notable for their relative independence of party control, applied more than the ordinary degree of imagination to their responsibilities. These include Richard F. Pettigrew, the Silver Republican Senator, 1889-1901; James H. Kyle, the clergyman turned Populist Senator, 1891-1901; the Populist Governor Andrew E. Lee, 1897-1901; the reformer Coe I. Crawford, Republican Governor 1907-1909 and Senator 1909-1915; William McMaster, Progressive Republican Governor 1921-1925 and Senator 1925-1931; William J. Bulow, a conservative Democratic Governor, 1927-1931, and Senator, 1931-1943; Tom Berry, Democratic Governor 1933-1937; war hero Joe Foss, Republican Governor 1955-1959; and liberal Democrat George McGovern, Congressman 1957-1961 and Senator since 1963. Except for Kyle and McGovern, each saw his political career ended by an election defeat.

The summary judgments made in the previous paragraphs will find supporting evidence in the chapters that follow; they are entered here to acquaint the unfamiliar reader with some of the high points of the state's political experience and to enrich his comprehension of the more detailed analysis that follows.

II

COMPARATIVE STATE POLITICS: NEIGHBORS AND NATION

An obvious starting point for analyzing a state's political system and experience is to relate them with systems and experiences in neighboring states and in the nation as a whole. It is in the national and regional contexts that the state's distinct political philosophies and practices have developed.

State Political Trends and National Politics. The major events in the state's political history are a part, in some cases a most significant part, of regional or national developments.[1] When statehood was achieved in 1889, South Dakota was distinctly Republican. The territorial legislature of Dakota was dominated by Republicans, even though the next-to-last territorial Governor, Louis L. Church, who served until March of 1889, was an appointee of Democratic President Grover Cleveland.[2] However, opposition quickly developed to the Republican state administration. Agrarian agitation grew during the 1890's and flowered in victories for Independent, Populist (or People's party), and Fusionist candidates through the entire decade. Republicans lost control of the Senate in the 1896 election. An Independent was elected to the U. S. Senate as early as 1890, William Jennings Bryan carried the state as a Populist Presidential candidate in 1896, the People's party elected two Congressmen, a Senator, and a Governor in 1896, and the Fusion ticket won the governorship in 1898.[3]

The first decade of the twentieth century saw the Republican Party re-establish its primacy in state politics. That control was to be maintained with but one interruption until the New Deal a generation later. But the fact that the Republican Party held a monopoly on major election victories did not mean that politics was not competitive and exciting. What was happening, very simply, was that the state was fighting out its major political controversies within the framework of the then dominant majority party. Indeed, it may be said that one of the state's most crucial political eras was the long period of Republican domination stretching from 1900 to 1926. For out of the Populist revolution of the 1890's developed a realignment of political forces that both contributed to and then threatened to shatter the Republican's new hegemony.

In short, progressive forces challenged the traditional, more conservative leaders of the Republican party and, in the persons of Coe I. Crawford and Peter Norbeck, re-shaped both the party and the state as well. Both Crawford and Norbeck consistently and effectively went to the people over the heads of the leaders of the Stalwart faction in the Republican party. It was precisely this eagerness by Crawford and Norbeck to base their policies on popular support that helped to make South Dakota a notably democratic and progressive state, particularly in terms of broadened political decision-making and of government intervention in the economy, and a remarkably dependable state from the standpoint of the Republican party. For in emphasizing his willingness to do what the people (especially the farmers) seemed to want done, Norbeck effectively diminished the appeal of the Nonpartisan League to South Dakota voters during and after World War I. By and large, the progressive orientation of Crawford and Norbeck allied South Dakota Republican politics with the progressive wing of the national party; it was the Bull Moose candidate Theodore Roosevelt rather than the regular Republican candidate William Howard Taft who received the state's five electoral votes in the 1912 election.

By 1920 Norbeck had completed his two terms in the Governor's chair and was ready for his first successful campaign for election to the U. S. Senate. When he moved to Washington to take his Senate seat in 1921, the guiding inspiration of the progressive movement was weakened in its ability to directly affect state policy. In the 1920's, South Dakota joined her sister states in a retreat to normalcy, and, though Norbeck remained in the Senate until his death in 1936, the Republican party had lost his strong and direct leadership of the political affairs of the state. In 1926 and 1928, a conservative old-line Democrat, William J. Bulow, won elections and served four years as Governor. Following this he successfully challenged Republican Senator William H. McMaster in the 1930 Senate election. There Bulow was to spend two full terms, fighting liberal Democrats as vigorously as he fought his more obvious political foes in Washington and South Dakota.

The Republicans, with the notable exception of Norbeck, were rocked back by the New Deal victory of 1932 and shattered by even more general Democratic victories at the state elections of 1934, when the Republicans failed to win a single state-wide election and lost control of both houses of the legislature. But the 1936 election, in which Franklin Roosevelt crushed his Republican opponent Alf Landon in South Dakota as well as in the entire nation save Vermont and Maine, saw the Republicans make substantial advances in South Dakota. Leslie Jensen defeated the incumbent Democratic Governor, Tom Berry, and Francis Case won the second Congressional district election over T. B. Werner. These two close victories were an earnest of the new Republican dominion in South Dakota which was firmly established in the 1938 elections, wherein the GOP took complete control of state offices, the legislature, and the two Congressional districts.

In the developments of the late 1930's leading to two decades of Republican hegemony can be seen two attitudes that explain in general terms the state's reaction to the national political environment. Isolationism and a distrust of big government both depended largely on the isolated and grim nature of life on the prairies.[4] The tendency was for South Dakota voters to favor political leaders of both parties who stood for a diminished (as opposed to an expanded) role for the federal government, and for withdrawal from (as opposed to increased involvement in) the affairs of the world beyond. The marked preference for Republican candidates in the period 1938-1954 was due substantially to two factors, the militantly liberal orientation of national Democratic candidates and the lack of appeal possessed by most state Democratic candidates, the latter no doubt conditioned by the difficulties encountered by any minority party attempting to generate leadership.

While many of the state's Republican leaders supported Senator Robert Taft's candidacy for the GOP Presidential nomination in 1952, the organization swung easily (and the voters enthusiastically) behind Dwight Eisenhower after the latter was nominated. Eisenhower and Governor Sigurd Anderson led the party to the biggest electoral margins ever rolled up in the state's history, so that 1952 marks the modern highpoint of Republican strength in South Dakota. But the Eisenhower-Benson policies engendered increasing opposition among the farmers, Republican Congressional and gubernatorial candidates saw their percentages diminish, and under the leadership of George S. McGovern the Democrats welded together a relatively permanent and cohesive organization which produced significant victories in 1956, 1958, and 1962. And thus in the 1960's the state found itself in a competitive political situation with the Republicans controlling most of the offices and registering most of the voters, but with the Democrats in a position to provide serious competition up and down the ticket.

Political Strength as Measured in Elections. That South Dakota is basically a Republican state is suggested by cursory investigation of the number of Republicans and Democrats elected to public office in the state. A few examples will suffice to support the hypothesis that, over the years and at all levels of government, the state has shown a marked preference for Republican candidates. Republican candidates have won more than three out of every four South Dakota elections involving the executive and legislative branches of the national and state government. The pattern of Republican superiority is substantially even for all categories of public office, as shown in Table 1. The GOP predominance is also evident at the county level; in the forty-four East River counties in the period 1940-1960, Republican candidates won 3,173 of the 4,285 partisan county officer elections, or 74.0 percent.[5]

TABLE 1

PARTY VICTORIES IN SOUTH DAKOTA ELECTIONS, 1889-1964

Office	Republican Victories	Democratic Victories	Other Victories	Percent Republican Victories
President	15	3	1	78.9
U. S. Senator	20	4	2	76.9
U. S. Representative	79	10	2	86.4
Governor	32	5	2	82.1
Lieutenant Governor	36	3	0	92.3
Secretary of State	35	4	0	89.8
State Auditor	34	4	1	87.2
State Treasurer	36	3	0	92.3
Attorney General	34	4	1	87.2
Superintendent of Public Instruction[a]	22	3	0	88.0
Commissioner of School and Public Lands	36	3	0	92.3
Railroad or Public Utilities Commissioner[b]	36	2	3	87.8
State Senator	1233	329	107	73.9
State Representative	2915	559	190	79.6
Totals	4563	936	309	78.6

[a] Office became non-partisan in election of 1938 and has remained so.

[b] Railroad Commission through election of 1938, Public Utilities Commission thereafter. First commission election held in 1894. There are three commission districts, ordinarily with one vacancy to be filled at each biennial state election.

Sources: Clem, *South Dakota Political Almanac, op. cit.,* pp. 15-27, supplemented by election returns for 1962 and 1964.

While the three-out-of-four Republican predominance is general for offices at the national, state, and county level, there is considerable variation over time. Periods of substantially complete GOP control include the first few elections after statehood, the post-Populist period, 1900-1924, and the post-New Deal period, 1938-1954. The People's Party had a virtual monopoly in the 1896 election, as did the Democrats in 1932, 1934, and 1958.

An obvious and no less useful means of assessing South Dakota's political disposition is to compare the state's election results with those of her neighboring states.

It needs to be emphasized first of all that geographical proximity is no guarantee of political similarity between or among states. Morlan, in commenting on the failure of the Nonpartisan League movement in South Dakota, makes an interesting conclusion about the lack of communication between the two Dakotas: ". . . the two states had then [in 1918], as they have now, almost no contact with each other and relatively little in common. Moreover, the existing political situation in South Dakota was appreciably different. South Dakota had experienced a greater degree of 'insurgency and progressivism' than had North Dakota, discontent was far less prevalent, and in the governor's chair sat Peter Norbeck, who described himself as a 'Theodore Roosevelt Republican'." [6]

In terms of support for the Republican Presidential tickets in the period 1928-1964, South Dakota ranks second behind Nebraska among the eight neighboring states and is followed in order by Iowa, Wyoming, North Dakota, Wisconsin, Montana, and Minnesota. In these ten Presidential elections, South Dakota voters supported the Republican candidate seven times, the Democratic candidate three times (1932, 1936, and 1964). South Dakota ranked first among the eight states in Republican percentage support in both 1936 and 1940 and second in 1944, 1952, 1960, and 1964, so that her Republican disposition with respect to the neighboring states is a current as well as a long-term condition. The highest Republican Presidential percentage was recorded by South Dakota voters in 1952 when Dwight D. Eisenhower received 69.3 percent of the vote; the highest Democratic mark was reached in 1932 when Franklin D. Roosevelt received 64.9 percent of the vote. Iowa, Montana, Nebraska, and North Dakota, like South Dakota, also recorded their highest GOP percentage in the first Eisenhower election; Wisconsin's high figure came in 1956 and Minnesota's and Wyoming's in 1928 for Herbert Hoover.

The partisan ranking of states based on Presidential elections, 1928-

1964, undergoes some change when gubernatorial elections in the period 1946-1964 are considered. Averaging the Republican gubernatorial percentages since 1945, one arrives at the following rank order:

North Dakota	59.3	Minnesota	52.2
South Dakota	57.7	Wyoming	51.4
Nebraska	54.5	Montana	50.6
Wisconsin	53.0	Iowa	50.2

South Dakota remains in the second position, but following the lead of its northern rather than of its southern neighbor. In relation to its sister states, North Dakota is more Republican in gubernatorial than in Presidential elections, while the converse holds for Nebraska. Of course, methodological problems abound in such a summary comparison. For one thing, Montana and Wyoming have quadrennial rather than biennial gubernatorial elections, Montana holding gubernatorial contests in Presidential election years and Wyoming in non-Presidential years.[8] To the extent that the national ticket helps or hurts the state ticket, such data have severe limitations. More to the point, these data involve different candidates in every state, whereas the Presidential comparisons involve the same national tickets from state to state. It must be emphasized that in this gubernatorial analysis the personal impact of individual politicians is affecting what might be called the underlying political disposition of a given state. At any rate, there are some significant differences in the Presidential and gubernatorial partisan rank orders of states.

Analysis of Senatorial and Congressional elections sheds further light on partisan differences from state to state. In U. S. Senate and House of Representatives elections since World War II, one finds the ranking in Table 2. Here, Iowa exhibits considerably more Republican strength than in the gubernatorial elections. Republican strength is notably more apparent in the Congressional than in the Senatorial races, perhaps partially due to gerrymandered Congressional districts.

To carry the state comparisons one step further, consider the partisan composition of the eight state legislatures since World War II. A methodological problem here is that Minnesota and Nebraska elect their legislatures on a non-partisan basis, so these two states cannot be analyzed with the rest. Table 3 ranks the other six regional states on the basis of the percentage of seats held by Republicans in the postwar era. North Dakota tops the list, as it did the gubernatorial list, followed in order by South Dakota, Iowa, Wisconsin, Wyoming, and Montana. South Dakota is the only state in the group where the Republican party held a majority of state legislative seats in every session since 1946.

Table 4 summarizes for each state the data just discussed and more precisely illustrates the variable electoral patterns from office to office and from state to state. Among the generalizations that can be made from Table 4 are these: that the firmest bases of major

TABLE 2

PARTY VICTORIES IN CONGRESSIONAL ELECTIONS, 1946-1964

State	SENATE Republican Victories	Democratic Victories	HOUSE Republican Victories	Democratic Victories
Nebraska	8	0	34	4
South Dakota	5	1	18	2
Iowa	5	1	64	14
North Dakota[a/]	6	2	18	2
Wyoming[a/]	4	4	9	1
Wisconsin[a/]	4	4	72	28
Minnesota	2	5	50	38
Montana	1	6	8	12
Total	35	23	273	91

[a/] Data includes non-cyclic Senate elections caused by the deaths of William Langer of North Dakota in 1959, Joseph R. McCarthy of Wisconsin in 1957, and Keith Thomson of Wyoming in 1960.

TABLE 3

PARTISANSHIP IN SIX STATE LEGISLATURES, 1947-65[A]

State	Republican Members	Democratic Members	Percent Republican
North Dakota	1296	313	80.5
South Dakota	840	256	76.6
Iowa	1166	438	72.7
Wisconsin	875	441	66.5
Wyoming	514	317	61.9
Montana	738	742	49.9
Totals	5429	2507	68.4

[a/] Omitting Independents, vacancies, etc. Data compiled from the biennial editions of The Book of the States (Chicago: Council of State Governments, several editions).

Table 4: CONTROLLING PARTY IN NATIONAL AND STATE ELECTIONS, 1946-1964, BY STATES

IOWA

	1946	1948	1950	1952	1954	1956	1958	1960	1962	1964
President	-	D	-	R	-	R	-	R	-	D
Senate	-	D	R	-	R	R	-	R	R	-
House of Representatives	R	R	R	R	R	R	*	R	R	D
Governor	R	R	R	R	~	D	D	R	D	D
State Legislature	R	R	R	R	R	R	R	R	R	D

MINNESOTA

	1946	1948	1950	1952	1954	1956	1958	1960	1962	1964
President	-	D	-	R	-	R	-	R	-	D
Senate	R	D	-	R	D	-	D	D	-	D
House of Representatives	R	R	R	R	D	D	R	R	*	±
Governor	R	R	R	R	D	D	D	R	D	-
State Legislature				non-partisan						

MONTANA

	1946	1948	1950	1952	1954	1956	1958	1960	1962	1964
President	-	D	-	R	-	R	-	R	-	D
Senate	R	D	-	D	D	-	D	D	-	D
House of Representatives	*	*	*	*	*	D	D	*	*	*
Governor	-	D	-	R	-	R	-	R	-	R
State Legislature	R	D	R	R	R	D	D	D	R	D

NEBRASKA

	1946	1948	1950	1952	1954	1956	1958	1960	1962	1964
President	-	R	-	R	-	R	-	R	-	D
Senate	R	R	-	R	R	-	R	R	-	R
House of Representatives	R	R	R	R	R	R	*	R	R	R
Governor	R	R	R	R	R	R	D	D	D	D
State Legislature				non-partisan						

NORTH DAKOTA

	1946	1948	1950	1952	1954	1956	1958	1960	1962	1964
President	-	R	-	R	-	R	-	R	-	D
Senate	R	-	R	R	-	R	R	D[1]	R	D
House of Representatives	R	R	R	R	R	R	*	R	R	*
Governor	R	R	R	R	R	R	R	D	D	D
State Legislature	R	R	R	R	R	R	R	R	R	D

[1] special election caused by death of William Langer. (R)

SOUTH DAKOTA

	1946	1948	1950	1952	1954	1956	1958	1960	1962	1964
President	-	R	-	R	-	R	-	R	-	D
Senate	-	R	R	-	R	R	-	R	D	-
House of Representatives	R	R	R	R	R	*	*	R	R	R
Governor	R	R	R	R	R	R	D	R	R	R
State Legislature	R	R	R	R	R	R	R	R	R	R

WISCONSIN

	1946	1948	1950	1952	1954	1956	1958	1960	1962	1964
President	-	D	-	R	-	R	-	R		D
Senate	R	-	R	R	-	D[1]	D	-	D	D
House of Representatives	R	R	R	R	R	R	*	R	R	*
Governor	R	R	R	R	R	R	D	D	D	R
State Legislature	R	R	R	R	R	R	D	R	R	R

[1] special election caused by death of Joseph McCarthy (R).

WYOMING

	1946	1948	1950	1952	1954	1956	1958	1960	1962	1964
President	-	D	-	R	-	R	-	R	-	D
Senate	D	R	-	R	D	-	D	R	R[1]	D
House of Representatives	R	R	R	R	R	R	R	R	R	D
Governor	D	-	R	-	R	-	D	-	R	-
State Legislature	R	R	R	R	R	R	R	R	R	R

[1] special election caused by death of Keith Thomson (R).

Note: For President, Senate, and Governor, letter indicates party winning the election. For U. S. House of Representatives and State Legislature, letter indicates party controlling at least half of the seats. Asterisk (°) indicates evenly split delegation. Years in which no election was held for President, Senator or Governor are indicated by a hyphen. Minnesota and Nebraska legislatures are elected on a non-partisan basis.

office strength for the Republican party in both Minnesota and Wisconsin are the Congressional districts; that Montana Republicans have much more success winning gubernatorial than other major elections; and that Iowa Republicans are similarly successful when seeking Senatorial seats as compared to other major offices.

The foregoing data with their vagaries from state to state and from electoral level to electoral level help develop a better understanding of South Dakota's immediate political background in relation to her neighboring states, and they also suggest the great difficulties and serious limitations inherent in any attempt to locate, develop, and supply empirical data with which to test general hypotheses concerning aggregate political behavior. But whatever the shortcomings of the data, it seems amply demonstrated that South Dakota is one of the most staunchly Republican states in the Upper Midwest.

The Political Culture. A contemporary study by Daniel Elazar has made pertinent and imaginative comparisons of state political cultures.[10] He distinguishes three types, individualistic, moralistic, and traditionalistic.

The individualistic political culture, stemming from the pluralistic immigrants from England and interior German states who settled in the middle Atlantic states, sees political parties as agents of accomodation, by which individuals can advance themselves socially and economically. Politics is a specialized vocation for professionals, of whom is expected party regularity and loyalty. The public tends to believe that politics is a dirty business, "better left to those who are willing to soil themselves by engaging in it."[11] Public officials want above all else to keep the citizens quiet and satisfied, and are not willing to initiate new programs on their own.[12]

The moralistic culture, related to the Yankee Puritan stock originating in New England and spreading across the northern part of the nation, sees politics as one of the great activities of man. It is the duty of every man to participate in politics and thus to help the community achieve the public good, whether by nongovernmental or governmental action. There is a great deal of amateur participation in politics, and party loyalty is comparatively unimportant.

The traditionalistic culture, based on the plantation economy of the Old South and its antecedents in the European landed gentry, has a paternalistic and elitist conception of the commonwealth, accepting a hierarchical society as part of the natural order. Politics is for the elite few who inherit their "right" to govern through family ties or social position. "Political parties are of minimal importance in T political cultures, since they encourage a degree of openness that goes against the fundamental grain of an elite-oriented political order." [13]

Elazar has studied immigration and cultural patterns and produced a map showing the dispersion of the three cultures across the United States.[14] The T culture is almost entirely limited to the South and Southwest, with fingers of traditionalism stretching into eastern Pennsylvania, central Ohio, southern Illinois, northern Missouri, and central California. The M culture is strong in New England, the Midwest, the upper plains, and the West. The I culture is strongest from the middle Atlantic states to Missouri and is scattered throughout the West.

South Dakota, Iowa, and Montana are classified by Elazar as MI states, indicating that the M culture is stronger than the I in these areas. North Dakota, Minnesota, and Wisconsin are viewed as pure M types, while Nebraska and Wyoming are IM states, the I dominating the M influence.

What this seems to say is that North Dakota, Minnesota, and Wisconsin are more likely to encourage open and democratic politics, and more progressive and ambitious govermental action, than the states to the south.[15] Nebraska and Wyoming are at the other extreme for the region, viewing politics with less relish. South Dakota is in the transitional zone, showing a stronger moralistic than individualistic tendency.

The gross state measurements of electorial behavior presented earlier in this chapter and of political culture suggested by Elazar do not lend themselves to comparison. If anything, there is a slight tendency for strong Republicanism to exist in the most "moralistic" states of this immediate region; a similar point could be made for the nation as a whole. Elazar's comments are useful if for no other reason than the fact that they attempt to describe political culture and thereby provide the observer with tools by which much of the state's political behavior can be related to its cultural setting.

Summary. South Dakota in the mid-1960's is considerably less Republican than it had been in the first or fifth decades of the Twentieth Century when the GOP won all major elections, but considerably more Republican than it had been at times in the fourth and sixth decades when the Democrats won a majority of the major offices at stake.[16] The situation subsequent to the 1964 elections might be compared to the state's political orientation of the two decades beween 1910 and 1930 when a complete Republican monopoly was prevented much of the time by at least one major Democratic officeholder—Senator E. S. Johnson (1915-21), Congressman Harry Gandy (1915-21), and Governor William J. Bulow (1927-31). Then as now, a shift in general party control from Republicans to Democrats, had it happened or should it happen, would not be a complete revolution but would rather be traceable to an earlier if isolated challenge to major party hegemony.

If the Republican party maintains its general control over political office in South Dakota, it will be due largely to the power and prestige presently being wielded by major GOP figures such as Senator Karl Mundt, Governor Nils Boe, and Congressmen Ben Riefel and E. Y. Berry. Similarly, if the Democratic party should in the near future further break down the Republican predominance, it will most likely be due to the efforts of Senator George McGovern, at this writing the only successful Democrat in a position to build his party at the expense of the Republicans; other Democrats are faced with the necessity to first build a place for themselves in the political picture at the expense of other Democrats.

Table 4 suggests some revisions that might be made in Schlesinger's typology of states based on inter-party competition.[17] That study based its categorizations on the results of gubernatorial elections, 1870-1950. In the period between 1950 and 1966, in the eight states of particular concern here, certain summary facts should be noted with respect to gubernatorial contests. Iowa, a Republican-party predominant state according to Schlesinger, has seen the Democrats win four of the last five gubernatorial elections, and no Republican candidate for Governor since the 1950 election has achieved as much as 53 percent of the two-party vote. Minnesota, a Republican-party cyclical state, has also witnessed four Republican defeats in the last five elections. Montana, a Democratic-party predominant state, has had four consecutive Republican victories. Nebraska, a Republican-party cyclical state, has seen four consecutive Republican losses. North Dakota, a Republican-party cyclical state, has witnessed three consecutive Democratic victories. South Dakota, a Republican-party predominant state, had a Democratic breakthrough in 1958, but otherwise has maintained its status at the Governor level. Wisconsin, a Republican-party dominant state, has had Democratic victories in three of the last six elections, and in no election since 1952 has the GOP gubernatorial candidate achieved as much as 52.0 percent of the two-party vote. And in Wyoming, a competitive state, Republicans have won three and the Democrats one of the four gubernatorial elections since 1950.

In short, of these eight states, only South Dakota and Wyoming re-

main in the same category in which they were placed by Schlesinger's
1955 study. This suggests that, while drastic changes are occuring in
most of her neighboring states, something unique is happening in
South Dakota. It should also be kept in mind that Schlesinger's study
concentrated on the governorship. The Presidential, Senatorial, Congressional, and legislative political situations also need to be considered, for the briefest examination of Table 4 indicates that a state's
partisan orientation is not necessarily consistent from office to office.

Considering everything, this chapter concludes with the obvious and
yet important summarization that South Dakota has maintained its
Republicanism to a greater degree than have its neighbor states.

III

HISTORICAL POLITICS: THE SHIFTING TIDE

Understanding of contemporary state politics is difficult without considerable knowledge of the historical background. The function of this chapter is to summarize the major forces, events, and personalities that constitute South Dakota's political heritage, and thus to set the stage for the chapters that follow.[1]

The Situation at Statehood. South Dakota's first election took place several weeks prior to the state's admission to the Union on November 2, 1889.[2] The October 1 election, in which the Republican party returned heavy majorities, thus enabled the state to begin immediately upon its sovereign responsibilities without waiting for its political leaders to qualify for their respective offices.

For their first Governor, the voters elected Arthur C. Mellette. They chose Republican Oscar S. Gifford of Canton and John A. Pickler of Faulkton for the two at-large Congressional seats, and gave Mellette a completely Republican cast of supporting state administrative officials. Mellette received 53,964 votes, his Democratic opponent P. F. McClure 23,840, and this margin was about the same in the other statewide partisan elections. The legislature was also in Republican hands, the GOP winning a 37-8 majority in the Senate and a 108-16 margin in the House.[3] In the same election, the voters overwhelmingly supported the proposed state constitution, 70,131 to 3,267, and more narrowly adopted prohibition, 40,234 to 34,510. Prohibition failed to carry five of the western counties. A provision for minority representation, pushed by the Democratic minority, was rejected 45,297 to 23,309.

At the time of the 1889 election, the state was divided into 51 counties, of which the Republican gubernatorial ticket carried 47.[4] Mellette ran strongest in Deuel, Roberts, Clay, Moody, Campbell, Brookings, Lake, and Sanborn counties, in each of which he received more than 80 percent of the vote. Athough he carried all six West River counties, his percentage in none of them equaled his statewide average. His principal strength lay in the east, along the Minnesota and Iowa borders. Comparatively speaking, he did poorly in seven southeastern counties, in Brown county (Aberdeen), Hughes county

21

(Pierre), and in Fall River and Meade counties in the west. He failed to carry Brown, Hughes, and Hutchinson counties, the latter heavily populated by German-Russian immigrants and later to become a Republican stronghold.

The legislature subsequently elected two Republicans, Richard F. Pettigrew of Sioux Falls and Gideon C. Moody of Deadwood, to the U.S. Senate. Moody's selection constituted a sop to the western part of the state, and became the focus of subsequent "agrarian" efforts to upset Republican domination of the state offices.[5]

Agrarian elements made impressive advances in the first year of statehood. Under the "Independent" banner, Populists held their first convention in Huron on June 7, 1890,[6] and in the subsequent fall election outpolled the Democratic ticket to become the state's largest opposition party. Governor Mellette won re-election, receiving 34,497 votes compared to the 24,591 received by Independent Henry L. Loucks, state president of the Farmer's Alliance, and the 18,484 received by Democrat Maris Taylor. Again the Republicans carried the two Congressional elections and the slate of state administrative officers. Their legislative dominance was seriously challenged; they retained slim majorities, winning 63 of 123 House elections and 23 of 45 Senate elections. Democrats won only 8 Senate and 14 House seats, and had definitely been replaced as the primary opposition party. While the Democrats received a plurality in the gubernatorial race in three southern counties, the Independents led in votes received in 15 counties, most of them in the northeastern part of the state. The Republican ticket ran strongest in the cities; except for Brown and Brookings counties, where the GOP ran a close second to the Independent ticket, the Republican candidates carried the larger counties.

For Congress, Pickler was re-elected and was joined in the House of Representatives by John R. Gamble of Yankton. Gamble's death necessitated a special election in November of 1891 in which a Vermillion attorney, John L. Jolley, defeated Independent Henry W. Smith, a Minnehaha county farmer, by less than three thousand votes. The Democratic candidate ran a poor third, receiving less than half the number of votes polled by the Independent.

Senator Moody's term expired in 1891, and the struggle in the legislature for the new term was one of the most drawn out legislative elections in the state's history. The legislature met in joint session on January 29 and the electoral weakness of the incumbent western Senator was quickly made apparent when in the first ballot he received only 25 of the 153 votes cast. Alonzo Wardell, who had been a prom-

inent Alliance-Republican candidate for one of the two Senate seats
in the first election, took a commanding first ballot lead with 55 votes.
Bartlett Tripp received 22 votes, A. B. Melville 19, and H. A. Goddard
11, with 21 votes scattered among a number of other candidates.[7] Before the third ballot held on the following day, Wardell dropped
out, and Moody took a slight lead with 30 votes to his credit against
23 for Tripp, 20 for Melville, 14 for Charles X. Seward, 12 for George
G. Crose, and 43 scattered.[8] In ballots Four through Seventeen (January 31-February 10) Moody, Tripp, and Melville maintained a strong
representative showing as booms for J. W. Harden (Ballots Four
through Eight) and then H. J. Campbell (Ballots Nine through Seventeen) gave them strong pluralities. Governor Mellette entered the picture with 12 votes on the seventeenth ballot, but his candidacy did
not become a serious factor.[9]

Strenuous steps were taken after the seventeenth ballot to break
the deadlock, and on the eighteenth and subsequent ballots the struggle was between two camps, a Populist group backing the new candidacy of State Senator James H. Kyle of Aberdeen and the Republican
group now throwing the main part of its weight behind Moody in a
belated attempt to hold the Senate seat. Moody received 67 votes
on the eighteenth ballot, 12 short of the necessary majority of 79.
Kyle attracted 59 votes, with 24 remaining with Tripp and seven scattered. Tripp's Democratic supporters could have given Kyle the victory on this and the subsequent four ballots taken February 11 and 12;
be that as it may, Moody was unable to get more than 69 votes and
Kyle's total fell no lower than 57.

On the twenty-third ballot, held on Friday, February 13, Moody's
candidacy was dropped and his votes went to Thomas Sterling; now
the count stood Sterling 68, Kyle 62, Tripp 17, Campbell 1, and
Sterling was only six short of the majority of votes cast.[10] Two more
ballots were taken Friday and one more Saturday, without resolution.
The decisive break came Monday, February 16, when on the twenty-
seventh ballot Kyle achieved a clear majority, attracting 74 votes
against Sterling's 56, Tripp's eight, and Campbell's loyal one.[11] Most
of Tripp's former supporters went to Kyle on the deciding ballot; all
of the legislators supporting Tripp on the final vote had voted for
Sterling in Saturday's balloting.[12]

Agrarian Successes in the 1890's. In spite of their failure in 1890
to maintain major status, the Democratic organization held aloof
from overtures to merge their efforts with the Populist revolt. Therefore, until the 1896 elections, South Dakota political struggles were

tripartisan, the principal immediate result being that the Republican party was able to win the lion's share of major elections. In the face of the Democrats' reluctance to join forces, the Populists continued to add converts to their cause. Their state convention in 1892 attracted a large and enthusiastic attendance.[13] The leaders of the drive in South Dakota gained important recognition from the national movement of which they were a part. Henry Loucks, the gubernatorial candidate of 1890, became chairman of the national convention held at Omaha in 1892, and Senator Kyle became the major alternative to James B. Weaver of Iowa as the party's Presidential nominee, the latter winning the designation by a vote of 995-275.[14]

But the time was not yet ripe for the ambitious opponents of the Republican machine. To replace Governor Mellette, the GOP had nominated Charles H. Sheldon of Day county, who had served in the territorial legislature as a member of the Farmers' Alliance.[15] Sheldon's 1892 victory over Independent candidate A. L. Van Osdel and Democrat Peter Couchman was slightly more impressive from a statistical standpoint than had been Mellette's second-term victory two years before. The Republicans again elected the full slate of constitutional officers and two Congressmen, the incumbent Pickler and W. V. Lucas of Hot Springs. In the first Presidential election participated in by South Dakota, the state supported Benjamin Harrison with 35,000 votes, while the Independent (Populist) slate received 26,000 votes and the Democratic slate only 9,000.

The 1892 election led to major shifts in the composition of American political parties, but whereas in many states the reshuffling occurred prior to the 1894 election, in South Dakota political fusion between the Democratic and Populist organizations was not achieved until the 1896 campaign. If the results of 1890 and 1892 failed to convince the reluctant Democrats of the necessity to re-align themselves, the results of 1894 were more difficult to ignore.[16] Governor Sheldon, up for re-election, increased his margin over Isaac Howe, the Populist candidate. In the presidential election year of 1892, Sheldon had received 33,414 votes; in the off-year of 1894, he received 40,381, while his two major opponents saw their combined total decline slightly. Sheldon's 1894 victory was the only one of the 1890's in which the Republican gubernatorial candidate achieved a majority of the votes cast. In both 1892 and 1894 elections, the Republicans won control of the legislature.

The year 1896 must be considered one of the most crucial in the state's political history. Senator Pettigrew was becoming more and more disenchanted with the national Republican stand on the currency system. He had been advocating the unlimited coinage of silver as early as 1890, and many Populists in 1895 were anticipating his adoption of their cause.[17] Fusion of the minority elements under the banner of the People's Party was facilitated by the Presidential nomination of William Jennings Bryan by both the Populists and the Democrats, but it involved something other than a mechanical fitting together of two monolithic political machines. The People's Party included Silver Republicans as well as Populists and Democrats; conversely, some former Democratic supporters of the conservative persuasion swung their allegiance over to the Republican party.[18]

The 1896 election resulted in the first major defeat of the Republican party in South Dakota. Except for a minute Prohibitionist ticket, the newly-formed People's Party constituted the only opposition to the entrenched Republicans. The Fusion achieved a narrow gubernatorial victory (41,187 to 40,868) for Andrew Lee of Vermillion over Republican A. O. Ringsrud of Elk Point. All state elections were almost unbearably close. In the presidential race between the McKinley/Republican and Bryan/Populist slates, less than one hundred votes separated the bottom Populist elector from the top Republican elector.[19] Freeman Knowles of Deadwood and John E. Kelley of Flandreau won narrow victories over Republicans Coe I. Crawford of Huron, the incumbent attorney general and future Governor and Senator, and Robert J. Gamble of Yankton, the future Senator.[20] Republicans held six of the state administrative offices, losing the attorney general's office and all three railroad commission positions to People's Party candidates; in no case did the margins of victory exceed 800, and in two of these statewide elections they were less than 50. As for the legislature, the Republicans for the first time since statehood lost their status as the largest party group. The 1896 election resulted in 23 Fusionist, 18 Republican, and 2 Democratic state senators, and in 39 Fusionist and 39 Republican state representatives (a swing group of five fell into neither party category).

The mid-1890's witnessed two changes of allegiance in the state's U. S. Senate delegation. Pettigrew, completing his first term March 4, 1895, had been re-elected to a second term by the legislature but by 1896, though a member of the state delegation to the Republican National Convention in St. Louis, he was publicly declaring himself to be a Populist.[21] Then, in the closely-divided 1897 legislature, with Senator Kyle's alienation from Governor Lee disrupting the Populist legislators, and with the Republicans unable to elect former Congressman John Pickler, Kyle was re-elected after "a month of monotonous balloting" on the strength of 54 Republican, 10 Populist, and three Democratic votes.[22]

The Populist victory of 1896 in South Dakota was part of a Fusionist tide that "swept everything before them" in Kansas, Nebraska, Montana, Idaho, and Washington. But the Republicans held on to complete control in two neighboring states, Minnesota and North Dakota.[23]

As it turned out, 1896 marked the high point of Populism in South Dakota, and, for that matter, in the nation as a whole. In the elections of 1898, the Fusionist movement held its own only in Nebraska. It did manage to elect governors in Minnesota and South Dakota, where Lee was re-elected in another close contest, 37,319 to 36,994, over Republican Kirk G. Phillips.[24] The effect of Lee's second victory was seriously compromised by the fact that the Republicans re-established firm control of both houses of the legislature for the 1899 session.[25] Republican candidates won clear majorities in all the state administrative elections. Republicans Gamble and Charles H. Burke of Pierre were elected to Congress where they replaced the one-term Populists Knowles and Kelley.

If the agrarian victories of the 1890's in South Dakota were short-lived and unproductive in terms of a permanent political apparatus, they did at least constitute a major challenge to the previously existing political order and they generally tended to force the state branches of the national political parties, most notably the Republicans, to appreciate the necessity for conforming their governmental policies more or less to the aspirations of the people. Among the more important, concrete, and permanent governmental innovations of the Populist period in South Dakota were constitutional amendments approved by the voters in the 1896 election to increase the local debt limit and render monopolies illegal, and in 1898 to provide for the initiative and referendum. As noted above, failure of the Fusionists to control the legislature in 1899 made it impossible for Governor Lee to carry through a coherent and positive program. The isolated farmers of the endless plains of South Dakota, "far from markets, burned by drought, beaten by hail, withered by hot winds, frozen by blizzards, eaten out by the grasshoppers, exploited by capitalists, and cozened by politicians,"[26] by turning to radical policies and movements in the 1890's were at least able to impress upon politicians and parties of the period the need to respect the farmers' aspirations if they were to be invested with political power. The first two decades of the Twentieth Century would see the agrarian-based reform movement occupy an important position in the strategy of the state's political leaders, until in the aftermath of the First World War a more conservative orientation came to dominate the Republican party and the politics of South Dakota.

Republican Ascendancy: Stalwarts versus Progressives. The Fusion party label was used once again, in the 1900 election, but the Republican ticket was uniformly successful. Charles N. Herreid of Leola, a conservative, had won the Republican nomination for governor and in November defeated Burre H. Lien of Sioux Falls, a Pettigrew man, 53,803 to 40,091, carrying the entire Republican state office slate with him. The Republicans re-elected Congressman Burke and sent Eben W. Martin of Deadwood to join him. The Republicans, with an eye to Senator Pettigrew's term ending March 4, 1901, concentrated much effort on the legislative races,[27] where they earned majorities of 39-6 in the Senate and 79-8 in the House. The legislature subsequently elected Congressman Gamble to replace Pettigrew.[28] The state's electoral votes went to Republican William McKinley.

In spite of the fact that the Fusion candidates won more than 40 percent of the vote in 1900, the Populist-Democratic alliance was at the end of its rope.

"The election [of 1900] marked the end of the Populist Party in South Dakota. The Populist administration had failed to distinguish itself with any noteworthy achievements. Frustrated in its efforts to control the railroad corporations, it remained content for the most part to play politics. The initiative and referendum were the only reform measures to which it could rightly claim credit. The party lacked cohesion from the outset. Pettigrew, with the support of Lee, wished to fashion it into a free-silver party. The reformists among the Populists, on the other hand, had little interest in the monetary issue, and became more and more impatient as they watched the party organization falling under the shadow of the Democratic party.

"As the Fusion movement disintegrated, most of the Populists and Silver Republicans returned to the Republican fold. Henry L. Loucks and Hugh Campbell led the way during the 1898 campaign, and others followed. Doctrinaire Populists, including former Congressman Freeman Knowles, Father Robert W. Haire, popular Aberdeen priest who also headed the Knights of Labor, and William E. Kidd, who succeeded Loucks as editor of the *Dakota Ruralist*, turned to the newly formed Socialist party. Such leaders as Lee, [William] La Follette [of Chamberlain], and Pettigrew had become too involved in the political struggle to turn back to their former party allegiance and identified themselves with the Democratic party for the future." [29]

The Stalwarts increased their power in the election of 1902, when Herreid won 64.7 percent of the vote to defeat his Democratic opponent, John W. Martin. The state administrative posts, the Congressional delegation, and the legislature remained in Republican hands.

In 1904 the Republican gubernatorial candidate, Stalwart Samuel H. Elrod of Clark, Congressmen Burke and Martin, and the GOP administrative slate were easily victorious; the Republican control of the 1905 legislature was even stronger than it had been two years before. The state enthusiastically supported President Theodore Roosevelt, giving him 77 percent of the two-party vote.

Now, however, a Progressive movement, owing much to the Populist ferment of the 1890's, began to seek power within the Republican party.[30] Though unable to prevent Elrod's nomination in 1904, the Progressives had been busily laying the foundation for victory in the future.[31] The hub of the Progressive wheel was Coe I. Crawford of Huron, former attorney general and railroad attorney who had broken his latter connections to gather a reform movement protesting against abuses in state government. Taking advantage of Chautauqua appearances by Senator Robert La Follette of Wisconsin in 1905, the popularity of President Roosevelt, and public reaction against Stalwart efforts to halt liberalization of party nominating processes, the Crawford forces gained control of the Republican Convention in 1906.[32] Crawford won the gubernatorial nomination over Governor Elrod, 893 to 476, and the Progressives named most of the state candidates and replaced Congressmen Burke and Martin with Philo Hall of Brookings and William H. Parker of Deadwood. This Progressive Republican ticket rolled up percentage margins as impressive as the Stalwart victories of 1900, 1902, and 1904, as roughly two of every three voters chose the Republican candidates up and down the state ticket. The Progressive movement was adding important converts to the Republican cause; a businessman from Redfield named Peter Norbeck wrote Crawford of his approval of the Progressive reforms and became a member of the Progressive inner circle.[33]

In 1908, with the establishment of a primary election system, Governor Crawford challenged Senator Kittredge, the Stalwart leader, and narrowly defeated him 35,151 to 33,086.[34] Sharing Crawford's triumph was Robert Vessey of Wessington Springs, who defeated John L. Browne for the gubernatorial nomination.[35] But the Stalwarts were able to recapture the two at-large Congressional seats as former Congressmen Burke and Martin ousted Congressman Hall and defeated a fourth candidate, Wilbur S. Glass. Republican nomination was again tantamount to election. Vessey defeated ex-Governor Lee, running on the Democratic ticket, receiving 55 percent of the vote; most lesser state GOP candidates received upwards of 70 percent. Crawford's election to the Senate by the 1909 legislature was virtually automatic. Republican control of the legislature was not seriously challenged, and among the legislators winning their first term was Peter Norbeck.

As in previous years, the principal political struggles of 1910 took place in the Republican primary, and in general the Progressives were able to hold their own. The gubernatorial race developed into a three-way struggle, with former Governor Elrod and a colorful and controversial Sioux Falls Irishman, George W. Egan, challenging Vessey's second term hopes. Vessey won renomination by attracting 39 percent of the vote, with Egan and Elrod trailing in that order. Thomas Thorson and John F. Schrader unsuccessfully challenged the re-nomination of Congressmen Burke and Martin; in the at-large election, Burke and Martin received 28 and 27 percent of the vote respectively, their opponents 23 and 22 percent. Frank Byrne of Faulk county won the GOP nomination for lieutenant governor, and Royal Johnson of Aberdeen for attorney general. In November, the Republican ticket was again uniformly successful, most of the GOP candidates receiving over 60 percent of the vote.

A number of factors conditioned the state's political situation between the 1910 and 1912 elections. As a result of the 1910 census, South Dakota's representation in Washington was increased by one Congressman. Accordingly, the legislature for the first time laid out Congressional districts. The West River area was made a single district. The two remaining districts were formed with the Missouri River as their western boundary and the northern boundary of Moody, Lake, Miner, Sanborn, Jerauld, and Buffalo counties as their common border. Aberdeen, Huron, Watertown, Brookings, and Pierre thus became the principal cities of the northeastern (second) district, Sioux Falls, Mitchell, and Yankton of the southeastern (first) district and Rapid City, Deadwood, Lead, and Hot Springs of the western (third) district. Given the general Republican predominance, each of the districts appeared to be safe for the GOP. The populations of the districts were substantially equal.

Both LaFollette's burgeoning national Progressive movement and

Theodore Roosevelt's drive to return to the White House had important repercussions among South Dakota Republicans. Norbeck became president of the South Dakota branch of the National Republican Progressive League, a LaFollette vehicle.[36] Senator Crawford, not entranced by the thought of LaFollette in the White House but impressed by the obvious popularity of his Senate colleague from Wisconsin in South Dakota, threw his weight behind LaFollette and found himself "at the forefront of Progressive sentiment in the state" for the first time since his election to the Senate three years before.[37] Even so, R. O. Richards, an old side-kick, nearly gained control of the LaFollette movement.[38]

Ultimately, the South Dakota Progressives sent a delegation to the 1912 National Republican Convention pledged to LaFollette or, if the Wisconsin Senator withdrew, to Roosevelt. The Stalwarts saw a chance to drive a wedge between the Progressive factions and loudly championed the re-election of President Taft. But the 1912 GOP primary was of little comfort for the Old Guard; Roosevelt received 38,106 votes, LaFollette 19,960, and Taft 10,944. In a very close race, Thomas Sterling of Vermillion, dean of the law school at the University of South Dakota, defeated the veteran Stalwart Senator Gamble, 25,896 to 25,161, with Richards running a poor third with 16,983 votes. In the Congressional primaries, Charles Hall Dillon of Yankton won the First District nomination, while Congressmen Burke and Martin carried the day in the Second and Third Districts. For Governor, Lieutenant-Governor Byrne defeated the ambitious Egan, 38,660 to 29,481.

In the 1912 general election the Democrats achieved their best showing in South Dakota up to that time, though they won no statewide victories. Roosevelt won the state's five Presidential electors by a comparatively close margin of only ten thousand votes. Byrne defeated Democrat Edwin S. Johnson by less than four thousand votes, 57,160 to 53,850. And the Democrats managed to win 25 of 148 legislative seats, topping their previous high of 22 seats won in the 1890 election.

The election of 1912 can be said to mark the major divide in Republican progressivism in the state.[39] Though it was not apparent at the time, Crawford's days as a major force in state politics were numbered. The veteran Congressmen, Burke and Martin, had scored their last victories. And Norbeck's star was steadily rising higher in the state's political firmament.

1914 is chiefly notable in South Dakota's politics because it marked the end of Crawford's political career and because Norbeck for the first time placed his name on a statewide ballot. Crawford was challenged in the Republican primary by the veteran Stalwart Congressman Burke. Despite Burke's long record as a vote getter in South Dakota, most observers expected that Crawford would win the nomination handily.⁴⁰ But Burke won by a relatively easy margin, 25,201 to 19,992. Meanwhile Norbeck, reluctantly contesting for the post of lieutenant governor, decisively defeated T. S. Everett, 24,501 to 16,443, running considerably ahead of Governor Byrne.⁴¹ Byrne himself was re-nominated although he failed to receive a majority of the votes in the three-man gubernatorial primary. With Burke running for Crawford's Senate seat and the second Stalwart Congressman, Martin, not contending for the Republican nomination, the state's Congressional delegation underwent extensive changes as the result of the 1914 election. In November, two Republicans were elected to the U. S. House of Representatives, the incumbent First District Congressman, Dillon, and, from the Second District, former Attorney General Royal C. Johnson. A Democrat, Harry L. Gandy of Rapid City, edged out Republican William G. Rice by a vote of 12,364 to 10,732 in the West River district. At the state level, Byrne and Norbeck led a general Republican victory. The Senate campaign resulted in the second big surprise of the year, as Johnson, the Democrat, defeated Congressman Burke by about 4,000 votes. Thus, in two short years, South Dakota had witnessed a complete turnover among its U. S. Senators and Representatives.

Republican Ascendancy: The Norbeck Era. The election of 1916 brought to office the man described as "perhaps the greatest and undoubtedly the most liberal Governor and Senator of the state of South Dakota." ⁴² With Governor Byrne completing the second of his two terms and with so many of the other Republican political leaders removed from the scene aş a result of the 1914 election, Norbeck found himself at the head of a progressive and united Republican state organization.

"In almost every way by 1916 Norbeck was prepared for a more important political position. He knew practical politics, an absolute necessity for a successful administrator under the American democratic system; he was an experienced legislator; and he had at least some understanding of the major forces which were influencing American life. He did not have long to wait." ⁴³

Norbeck's nomination was only mildly contested by Egan and Richards who in the primary election of 1916 received fewer than 22,000 votes together while Norbeck was polling 32,000. Otherwise, the primary was perhaps most notable for the fact that Governor Cummins of Iowa drew three times as many votes on the Republican Presidential primary ballot as did President Woodrow Wilson on the Democratic ballot. In November, Norbeck defeated Rinehart, 72,789 to 50,545, carrying the remainder of the Republican slate with him. The Republican ticket was much stronger at the state level than it proved to be at the national level, for the Republican Presidential electors outpolled their Democratic opponents by less than 5,000 votes. The three Congressmen were re-elected with comparative ease. A number of constitutional amendments and initiated and referred laws were on the ballot. The voters of the state approved constitutional amendments to allow the state to construct and maintain irrigation systems, to embark on a rural credits system based on real estate security, and to allow the state to supply coal. By one vote, 47,926 to 47,925, the voters rejected an initiated law that would have created a state banking board. The subject of many of these measures is a tipoff to the strategy employed by Norbeck in response to the radical proposals being made in the upper middle west by the Nonpartisan League, a strategy to be followed again by Norbeck in the 1918 election.

The inconsistency of much of the Norbeck program was and has remained apparent to many observers.

"Oddly enough, he was bitterly attacking the Leaguers as Socialist agitators for proposing much the same things as he recommended, but he stoutly insisted that he was not a Socialist and that his program did not entail Socialism; it was just sensible cooperation. While he was unwilling to go quite as far as the League, he was quite ready to undertake 'practical' measures of state ownership. To the question of how to beat the Nonpartisan League Peter Norbeck had a ready answer: 'When the water gets too high, let a little of it over the dam'." [44]

In Morlan's opinion, Norbeck was certainly not an extreme liberal, "but he was a believer in the use of governmental powers to alleviate social and economic distress and was a sufficiently astute politician to listen carefully to farmer demands." [45]

The key primary fights in 1918 involved the Congressional delegation in Washington. Former Governor Byrne challenged Senator Sterling's bid for a second term but was unsuccessful, trailing the Vermillion lawyer by 4,000 votes. Charles A. Christopherson of Sioux Falls was successful in his attempt to unseat the incumbent Congressman, as he defeated Dillon, 5,572 to 5,317. In the general election,

Norbeck found himself confronting the perils of radicalism and pacifism, both represented by the Nonpartisan League which had enjoyed such success in North Dakota.[46] Reminiscent of the state's political situation in the early 1890's, the Nonpartisan League ran in 1918 under the "Independent" banner, nominating for Governor against Norbeck a prominent and highly respected Letcher stockman, Mark P. "Roy" Bates.[47] Norbeck acquitted himself capably in the election, attracting 51,175 votes against 25,118 for Bates and 17,858 for the Democratic candidate. Senator Sterling and Congressmen Johnson and Gandy were re-elected and Christopherson joined the delegation. The Republican hold on the legislature was not seriously challenged, with the Republicans winning 43 out of 45 Senate seats and 90 out of 103 House seats.

Norbeck moved on to the Senate in 1920. He defeated Dick Haney for the Republican nomination while his lieutenant governor, William H. McMaster of Yankton, was defeating the veteran gadfly, R. O. Richards, by 17,000 votes for the gubernatorial nomination. Norbeck's Senate victory in November was comparatively easy as he alone gathered more votes than did the combination of his enemies, Tom Ayres of the Nonpartisan League, U. S. G. Cherry of the Democratic party, and Independents Richards and L. J. Manbeck. McMaster defeated Bates and Democrat W. W. Howes by a margin even larger than Norbeck's. Republican Congressmen Christopherson and Johnson won impressive victories and were joined by a third Republican, William Williamson of Oacoma, who defeated the three-term Democrat Gandy by 3,000 votes.[48]

The Republicans presented the same major candidates to the voters in 1922 as two years before, and with as much success. The Nonpartisan League and the Democratic parties each had their own tickets, with results similar to those of thirty years before, prior to the Populist-Democrat fusion of 1896. Had they combined their votes, the NPL-Democratic bloc would have elected two congressman and a Governor. Running for his second term, Governor McMaster won 78,984 votes compared to 50,409 for Democrat Louis N. Crill and 46,033 for the NPL candidate, Alice Lorraine Daly. Congressman Christopherson received 50 percent and Congressman Williamson 67 percent of the vote, each against two opponents. Republican control of the legislature and the state administrative officers was maintained easily.

In 1922 the voters were confronted, as had become usual, with a spate of constitutional amendments and initiated laws. Under the

administration of McMaster, many of the radical measures approved
during the Norbeck administration were being put into effect, such
as the rural credits program, the coal mine, and the hail insurance
program. [49] When the prevailing retail price of gasoline reached 26.6
cents per gallon in the summer of 1923, McMaster even ordered the
supply stations of the Highway Department to sell fuel to the public
at 16 cents. [50] For one reason or another, many of the voters seemed
to be tiring of the progressive innovations; the voters decisively
rejected a plan for hydro-electric development of the Missouri with
a dam at Mobridge, 106,409 to 55,563, and a plan for state-owned
banks, 122,807 to 33,032. [51]

Though the voters never accepted the Nonpartisan League candidates in sufficient numbers to give that organization a political
foothold, it would be wrong to conclude that the state in the period
1916-1924 was anti-progressive. Virtually without exception, the
major political leaders were Progressive Republicans, and it was
under the dispensation of these leaders that a number of surprisingly
radical ventures were undertaken. In short, whatever the motives
of the individual leaders, they were known then as Progressives and
still deserve the title today. As such, they were part of the Progressive wing of the national Republican party which seldom was
in command but always in contention from the days of Theodore
Roosevelt until those of Franklin Roosevelt. Since the New Deal,
the Republicans of South Dakota have been if anything more conservative than the national party leadership, perhaps a function of
the state's relatively static post-1930 economic situation. [52]

With no serious primary challenges for state office, the primaries
of 1924 were fairly tame. Senator Hiram Johnson of California
slightly outpolled President Calvin Coolidge in the G.O.P. Presidential preference primary, 40,935 to 39,791. No one challenged
Lieutenant Governor Carl Gunderson's bid for the G.O.P. gubernatorial nomination, and he led the ticket handily in November.
Gunderson received 109,894 votes; Democrat W. J. Bulow of Beres-
ford had 46,663, Farmer-Labor [53] candidate A. L. Putnam had 27,027,
and the perennial candidate, R. O. Richards, ran as an "Independent"
and attracted 20,359 votes. McMaster challenged two-term Senator
Sterling and was successful, 45,213 to 32,292. [54] Governor McMaster
in November had little trouble defeating an assortment of candidates
for Sterling's Senate seat who had "gone to the well" many times
before. The vote is shown on the next page.

William McMaster, Rep.	90,006	Mark P. Bates, Ind.	8,442
U.S.G. Cherry, Dem.	63,728	C. H. Dillon, Ind.	3,835
Tom Ayres, F. L.	20,952	H. L. Loucks, Ind.	1,378
George W. Egan, Ind.	14,484	Don Livingston, Ind.	1,138

1926 witnessed the election of the first Governor in South Dakota running on the Democratic ticket. The primary election gave few hints of such an unusual occurrence. Governor Gunderson turned aside the bid of Secretary of State C. E. Coyne, 48,782 to 30,116, while in the Democratic primary Bulow attracted only 5,775 and his irrepressible opponent, Richards, only 2,579. That there were in these statistics material for a Democratic general election victory must have seemed dubious. But Gunderson became involved in factional quarreling as well as a scandal in the administration of the rural credits system and in November trailed Bulow by thirteen thousand votes, and this in spite of the fact that two minor opponents were draining off more than 22,000 votes. Congressman Williamson narrowly beat off the challenge of Democrat Arthur W. Watwood, but otherwise there were few worries for the Republican ticket. The Governor-elect would greet only 37 Democrats among the 148 legislators in the coming session.

Conservative Republicans saw fit to challenge Senator Norbeck in his second-term bid in 1926. Attacking Norbeck for failure to support the Coolidge program,[55] they supported George J. Danforth, but Norbeck earned over two-thirds of the primary ballots and went serenely on to win over Democrat C. J. Gunderson and Farmer-Labor candidate Howard Platt in November, attracting 60 percent of the total vote.

Comparatively little of note happened in the 1928 primaries in South Dakota. The young West River publisher, Francis Case, challenged Congressman Williamson's re-nomination, but failed by more than 3,000 votes. The election of delegates to the Republican National Convention was chiefly notable for the presence on the Republican slate of former Governor Samuel Elrod and A. O. Ringsrud of Elk Point, who had been involved in South Dakota politics in the 1890's. In November, Herbert Hoover easily carried the state over the Democrat Al Smith. Governor Bulow defeated his Republican challenger, Buell F. Jones, winning 53 percent of the votes. The voters gave Bulow a supporting administrative cast entirely made up of Republicans, and compounded their villainy by electing 116 Republicans and only 32 Democrats to the legislature.

The Republican primary election of 1930 witnessed three key races. Senator McMaster was able to defeat Danforth's second bid for a Senate seat. Tom Ayres, formerly a Farmer-Labor candidate, unsuccessfully challenged Royal Johnson for the Republican party's nomination in the Second Congressional District. Five candidates were involved in the Republican gubernatorial primary, finishing in this order:

Gladys Pyle	33,153	Carl Trygstad	21,224
Carl Gunderson	31,543	Warren E. Green	8,701
Brooke Howell	22,549		

Since no candidate received the 35 percent of the primary vote required for nomination, the decision went to the state convention, where with the support of the Howell faction, Green was eventually nominated. In November, Green continued victorious, defeating his Democratic opponent, D. A. McCullough, by a vote of 107,643 to 93,954. Governor Bulow waged a vigorous campaign and was able to unseat the Republican Senator McMaster by a vote of 106,317 to 99,595. The Republican Party again won the administrative elections and held a 110-38 margin in the subsequent session of the legislature.

The New Deal Years: 1932-1936. In the 1932 Republican Senatorial primary Peter Norbeck easily withstood the challenge of H. F. Brownell. In the Congressional races, change was imperative since the reapportionment of Congressional seats following the 1930 census resulted in the loss of one of South Dakota's three seats. Royal Johnson did not run for the new First District seat which comprised the entire East River area; Congressman Christopherson defeated Harold King for the Republican nomination, 57,918 to 31,829. In the gubernatorial primaries, Governor Green defeated former Governor Carl Gunderson and Tom Ayres for the Republican nomination and Tom Berry of Belvidere defeated L. M. Corey for the Democratic nomination. In November, Senator Norbeck was the only Republican candidate to successfully withstand the Democratic tide that swept over South Dakota as well as the rest of the nation.[56] He defeated the perennial Democratic nominee, U. S. G. Cherry, by 26,000 votes, while Franklin D. Roosevelt was victorious over President Hoover by over 83,000 votes and Berry defeated Governor Green by 37,000 votes. Democrats won both Congressional seats, Fred Hildebrandt of Watertown defeating Congressman Christopherson and T. B. Werner of Rapid City defeating Congressman Williamson. For the first time in history, the Democratic party controlled all of the state-wide administrative elections and also earned a wide majority in the legislature with 99 of the 148 seats.

Despite the general Democratic victory of 1932, not all of the former Republican office holders were content to accept retirement gracefully. In the 1934 primaries former Congressman Christopherson won nomination for one Congressional seat, but Williamson failed to win the requisite 35 percent of the primary vote and the subsequent party convention awarded the Second District nomination to Francis Case. W. C. Allen was the Republican choice for Governor. But the crucial election in 1934 was the general election. Here the Democratic candidates firmly held onto their gains of two years before. Governor Berry and Congressmen Hildebrandt and Werner repeated their 1932 victories, and the Democrats again controlled all of the state administrative offices. The Republicans were able to improve their standing in the legislature by gaining five seats over their previous showing, but this still left the Democratic party in substantial control of the legislature as well as of the executive branch of state government.

As a result of the 1936 primaries, the Republican party presented a new cast of candidates for the inspection of the voters. Chan Gurney of Yankton won the Senatorial nomination over former Congressman Christopherson, and Case defeated former Congressman Williamson and four other candidates for the Second Congressional District nomination. In the Presidential primary, an uncommitted slate headed by former Governor Green narrowly defeated a slate pledged to the candidacy of Senator Borah of Idaho, 44,518 to 44,261. [57]

The 1936 general election resulted in some significant victories for both parties. President Roosevelt for the second time received South Dakota's votes, and Senator Bulow was able to defeat his Republican challenger Gurney. Congressman Hildebrandt narrowly held onto his seat over Karl Mundt, 110,829 to 108,259. Against this continuing Democratic strength, the Republicans were able to win two significant victories, those of Leslie Jensen of Hot Springs over Governor Berry and Francis Case over Congressman Werner. The administrative positions were split between the two parties, and in the legislature the Republicans were able to win 88 of the 148 seats. The Democrats, however, held a slight majority of 23-22 in the Senate.

Certainly an important event of 1936 was the death in December of Peter Norbeck, who had been suffering for several years from cancerous growths in his mouth and on his tongue. His career has been summed up as follows: "[Norbeck's] death left a wide gap in the ranks of Republican progressivism. For almost thirty years he had carried the banner of liberalism . . . through peace and war, depression and prosperity, his progressivism represented that of a majority of South Dakota Republicans. . . . He knew the people of his state as no other man had ever known them, and he sensed their desires." [58]

Coming in the midst of the New Deal, Norbeck's death emphasized the change in leadership and direction of the Republican party in South Dakota. The new leadership was to be established in the elections of 1938 and 1940.

New Republican Domination: 1938-1954. The key race in the Republican primary of 1938 was the victory of Chan Gurney of Yankton over Governor Jensen for the right to fill Norbeck's Senate seat. Meanwhile, Harlan Bushfield of Miller defeated Blaine Simmons for the Republican gubernatorial nomination. In the fall, Gurney turned back the challenge of former Governor Berry to win the Senatorial election, 146,813 to 133,064. Bushfield defeated Democrat Oscar Fosheim by a slightly wider margin and Karl Mundt, by defeating Democrat Emil Loriks, joined Case in the U. S. House of Representatives. The Republicans captured all of the state administrative offices, [59] and also achieved a 92-18 majority over the Democrats in the legislature. [60]

In 1940 there was only minor opposition to Governor Bushfield in the primary, and in November he defeated his Democratic opponent, Lewis Bicknell, 167,686 to 136,428. The state's presidential electors voted for Wendell Willkie and Congressmen Case and Mundt won re-election over Arthur Watwood and Oscar Fosheim respectively. The Republicans continued in firm control of the administrative offices and the legislature, where they held 96 of the 110 seats.

In 1942 Governor Bushfield entered the lists against the veteran Senator Bulow. Bushfield defeated Secretary of State Olive Ringsrud for the Republican nomination, but Senator Bulow was unable to withstand the challenge of former Governor Berry, who won the right to contest the Senate seat against Bushfield in November. The Republican gubernatorial primary witnessed another close race involving a number of candidates. When the votes had been counted, the four candidates finished as indicated on the next page.

| Joe H. Bottum | 23,714 | Leo A. Temmey | 20,107 |
| M. Q. Sharpe | 21,108 | Millard G. Scott | 17,272 |

Since no candidate received 35 percent of the primary vote, the decision again went to the state convention where Attorney General Sharpe won the nomination. In November the Republicans continued their domination up and down the ticket. Bushfield defeated Berry for the Senate seat, Congressmen Mundt and Case were re-elected, and Sharpe defeated Bicknell for the Governorship. Republicans again held the administrative positions and increased their legislative membership to 100 of 110.

In 1944, A. C. Miller of Kennebec challenged Senator Gurney for the Republican Senatorial nomination and came within 8,000 votes of success. A Dewey slate headed by former Congressman Christopherson defeated a Stassen slate headed by Joe Bottum, 33,497 to 22,135. In November, Gurney was re-elected to the Senate over Democrat George Bradshaw, Mundt and Case were re-elected to Congress, and Sharpe was re-elected Governor over Democrat Lynn Fellows. Dewey gained the state's electoral votes over Roosevelt and the administrative positions and the legislature remained under Republican control; in the latter the Republicans increased their membership to 107, leaving only three legislative seats to the Democrats in the 1945 session.

In 1946 Governor Sharpe decided to defy tradition by attempting a third term. His ambitions were quickly cooled however when Attorney General George T. Mickelson defeated the incumbent Governor in a three-way gubernatorial primary. Mickelson repeated the victory over Democrat Richard Haeder in November. The Republicans again controlled the two Congressional seats and the state administration; in the legislative struggle, the Democrats increased their seats by 33 percent, but the actual increase of one seat to a new total of four was not as impressive as the percentage increase.

1948 featured two Republican contests in the primary election, one involving the Senate seat vacated by the death of Senator Bushfield and the other involving the House seat vacated when Congressman Mundt moved into the Senate contest. In the Senatorial primary, Mundt easily defeated Otto B. Lindstad, 65,595 to 12,022. The Congressional primary involving Art B. Anderson of Sioux Falls, Harold O. Lovre of Watertown, William H. Pringle, and E. L. Stavig was inclusive and the decision was referred to the state convention where Lovre, who had achieved a plurality in the primary election, was nominated. The November, 1948, elections again saw a general Republican victory, although Democratic candidates up and down the ticket received a higher percentage than they had been receiving in recent elections. The Democrats increased the number of legislative seats from four in 1947 to 19 in 1949. Governor Mickelson defeated Democrat Harold Volz, Mundt defeated Democrat John A. Engel of Avon for the Senate, and Governor Thomas Dewey of New York received the state's Presidential votes over Harry Truman.

1950 witnessed three key primaries on the Republican ticket. Congressman Case successfully challenged Senator Gurney in the latter's bid for a third term, 59,314 to 42,823. To replace Case in the House, Republican E. Y. Berry of McLaughlin narrowly defeated Joe Bottum of Rapid City, 13,540 to 12,218. Three prominent candidates entered the Republican gubernatorial primary: Attorney General Sigurd Anderson of Webster, war hero and state legislator Joe Foss of Sioux Falls, and Boyd Leedom. Anderson outdistanced Foss in a close race, 35,609 to 33,257, with Leedom getting 20,059 votes. In November, the Republicans were again successful. Case defeated Democrat Engel for the Senate seat held by Gurney, Lovre defeated Merton Tice of Mitchell and Berry defeated Sam Bober for the Congressional seats, and Anderson defeated Democrat Joe Robbie for the Governor's chair.

The 1952 primaries saw fights in both parties over the presidential ticket. For the Republicans, a Taft slate was given a slight majority over an Eisenhower slate headed by former Governor Mickelson, 64,695 to 63,879. On the Democratic side a Kefauver slate defeated an opposing slate headed by Ed Downs, 22,812 to 11,741. In November, Eisenhower and Governor Anderson led the Republican ticket to one of its greatest victories in South Dakota history. Anderson received the highest vote ever earned by any gubernatorial candidate in the state, and Eisenhower buried Adlai Stevenson's bid, 203,857 to 90,426. Congressmen Lovre and Berry were duly re-elected, and the Republicans easily held the administrative positions and attained their highest percentage of seats held in the legislature, 108 of 110.

That Republican strength had hit a peak in 1952 was very evident in the 1954 elections, even though the Republicans once again won all of the major races. Joe Foss won the Republican gubernatorial primary over Rex Terry and Harold Lund, and then defeated Democrat E. C. Martin in the general election. Senator Mundt won his first bid for Senate re-election over Democrat Kenneth Holum and

Congressmen Berry and Lovre were re-elected again. Again the Republicans controlled the administrative positions, but their legislative margin was reduced by 22 seats as a result of the 1954 elections.

Competitive Politics in the Contemporary Period: 1956-1964. In 1956 there were no primary elections of note. In the fall, President Eisenhower easily defeated Stevenson once again, and Governor Foss won re-election over Democrat Ralph Herseth of Houghton with comparative ease, 158,819 to 133,198. But Senator Case's victory over Holum was quite close, 147,621 to 143,001. Congressman Berry was re-elected over Democrat Tom Eastman, but Democrat George McGovern of Mitchell, after several years of arduous preparation as a Democratic worker, ousted four-term Congressman Lovre by a vote of 116,516 to 105,835. The Republican party again controlled the administrative positions, but their edge in the legislature was further reduced by 20 more seats, the party winning only 66 of the 110 seats. The Republican majority was severely challenged in the Senate, where the Democrats were able to win 17 of the 35 seats.

The only significant primary election of 1958 involved the Republican nomination for Governor, where Foss was retiring after two consecutive terms to challenge McGovern for the First Congressional District seat. Attorney General Phil Saunders of Milbank defeated Lieutenant Governor Roy Houck and Charles Lacey for the Republican gubernatorial nomination. In the fall of 1958, the Democrats extended their good fortune of 1956; Congressman McGovern was re-elected over the formidable challenge of Governor Foss and Ralph Herseth defeated Saunders by seven thousand votes. The Democrats also won most of the administrative positions and although they fell six short of a majority of the total legislative seats, the Democrats were able to control the 1959 State Senate. Congressman Berry won the only major Republican victory in the fall by defeating Democrat J. T. McCullen.

In 1960 Congressman McGovern went out after bigger game when he decided to challenge the re-election of Senator Mundt. His decision to run for the Senate left a vacancy in the First Congressional District, and as a result both parties witnessed vigorous contests for the Congressional nomination. On the Republican side, Ben Reifel of Aberdeen outdistanced Dan Stuelpnagel of Yankton and Ray Dana of Sioux Falls by a surprisingly wide margin, winning 54 percent of the votes. On the Democratic side, Ray Fitzgerald defeated Robert Chamberlin, 16,409 to 12,175. In November, the Republicans re-established their control over the major positions. Presidential candidate Richard Nixon led the GOP ticket in his state victory over John F. Kennedy. Senator Mundt withstood the formidable challenge of Congressman McGovern, 160,181 to 145,261, and, by a much closer margin, Republican Archie M. Gubbrud of Alcester defeated Governor Herseth in the latter's bid for re-election, 154,530 to 150,095. Reifel and Berry were victorious over their Democratic Congressional opponents, Ray Fitzgerald and W. H. Raff of Rapid City, respectively. The Republicans gained control once again of all the administrative positions and returned an 80-30 majority in the legislature.

The death of Senator Case in the spring of 1962 had a profound impact on South Dakota politics. Prior to Case's death, McGovern had left his position in the White House as director of the Food for Peace Program and secured the Democratic Senate nomination.[61] The fight for the Republican Senate nomination was resolved in a meeting of the state central committee in Pierre and was one of the most interesting of such power struggles in the state's history. After twenty ballots, Joe Bottum of Rapid City finally achieved a majority of committee votes over former Governor Anderson, former Speaker of the House Nils Boe of Sioux Falls, former Governor Joe Foss of Sioux Falls, Attorney General A. C. Miller, and Congressman Reifel.[62] In November, Gubbrud repeated his victory over Herseth, this time by a somewhat wider margin, and Berry and Reifel were re-elected to Congress. But McGovern won a very close and crucial victory over Bottum for Case's seat in the United States Senate, 127,458 to 126,861. The Republicans maintained control of the administrative positions and the legislature.

In 1964 Nils Boe defeated former Governor Sigurd Anderson in a hard fought campaign for the Republican gubernatorial nomination to succeed the retiring Governor Gubbrud, and an uncommitted slate of delegates defeated a Goldwater slate to the Republican National Convention. In the Democratic gubernatorial primary, John Lindley of Chamberlain defeated Merton Tice of Mitchell. In November, while President Johnson won a decisive victory over Barry Goldwater despite a *South Dakota Poll* assessment giving the Arizonan a slight edge, the Republicans were able, by close margins, to hold the major offices. Boe defeated Lindley, 150,151 to 140,419, and Congressmen Berry and Reifel won over George May of Aberdeen and Byron Brown of Custer. The closest race involved the lieutenant-governor position, where Republican Lem Overpeck of Belle Fourche edged

Robert Chamberlin, 141,212 to 140,882. Both houses of the legislature remained in GOP hands, the Senate by 19-16 and the House by 45-30.

In 1966 Senator Mundt defeated Democrat Donn Wright and thus became the first South Dakotan to win four U. S. Senate elections. Governor Nils Boe was re-elected to his second term in spite of the vigorous opposition of Robert Chamberlin, and the state administration and the legislature remained substantially under Republican control.

Summary. In terms of length of service in major offices, which is a simple index of political success, Karl Mundt has served longer than any other South Dakotan (see Table 5). Mundt is closely followed by his colleague of so many years, Francis Case, and then by Peter Norbeck and Royal Johnson. Because his service included both state executive and national legislative experience, the former involving direct leadership responsibilities and the latter a more generalized, non-specific role, it seems reasonable to conclude that it is Norbeck's career, more than any other individual career, that is the most impressive in terms of the use of political power.

Seldom are small state politicians in a position to gain sufficient stature to earn national repute and influence. Of her neighboring states, only Nebraska, Minnesota, [63] and Wisconsin have produced a notably more impressive list of political personalities, and all are older and much more populous states. In the Populist and Progressive eras, South Dakotans contributed importantly to re-orientations of state and national policy. These leaders, in speaking to their own South Dakota constituents, often found a receptive audience for the same doctrine far beyond the state. Then, South Dakota was in the van of national progress, in terms of economic and population growth as well as political ideas. Since the New Deal, the state has been something of an economic and political backwater; seldom do the ideas that attract votes in South Dakota attract much attention elsewhere in the nation. [64] Where the differences are so great between an area served by a representative and the arena in which he serves, a political leader must sell much of his national influence capital in order to buy the continuance of his national influence potential, that is, his seat in the Congress of the United States. The national leaders of the Republican and Democratic parties, for the most part, have since World War II adopted a positive and optimistic attitude about the potentialities of all kinds of governmental

TABLE 5

PUBLIC OFFICIALS RANKED IN ORDER OF LENGTH OF SERVICE[a]

Name	Years in Major Office[b]	Offices held	Years of defeat
Karl Mundt	28	House. Senate.	1936.
Francis Case	26	House. Senate.	1928[c]. 1934.
Royal Johnson	22	Attorney General. House.	None.
Peter Norbeck	22	Lt. Gov. Governor. Senate[d].	None.
E. Y. Berry	16	House.	None.
William Bulow	16	Governor. Senate.	1924. 1942[c].
Robert Gamble	16	House. Senate.	1896. 1912[c].
Charles Burke	14.	House.	1906[e]. 1914.
C. A. Christopherson	14	House.	1916[c]. 1932. 1936[c].
William McMaster	14	Lt. Gov. Governor. Senate.	1930.
Coe I. Crawford	12	Attorney General. Governor. Senate.	1896. 1914[c].
Chandler Gurney	12	Senate.	1936. 1950[c].
William Williamson	12	House.	1932. 1934[c]. 1936[c].
Richard Pettigrew	12	Senate.	1901[f].
Harlan Bushfield	10	Governor. Senate[d].	None.
James Kyle	10	Senate[d].	None.
Eben Martin	10[g]	House.	1906[e].

[a] As of January 1, 1967. Only those with ten years or more in major public office are included.
[b] "Major office" includes U. S. Senate or House of Representatives, governor, lieutenant governor, and attorney general.
[c] Defeated in a primary election.
[d] Died while in office.
[e] Rejected for nomination in party convention after or in lieu of primary election.
[f] Rejected by legislature in bid for re-election to U. S. Senate.
[g] Data in South Dakota Legislative Manuals indicating that Martin entered the Congress in 1899 is incorrect. See A Biographical Directory of the American Congress, 1774-1961, (Washington: Government Printing Office, 1961), at pp. 271, 277, and 1268.

actions; in South Dakota, voters and candidates alike, for the most part, have been marching to a different drummer.

For South Dakota, the trouble with the political situation since 1932 has been that the state's election results have seldom conformed with the national; its Republicanism has rarely presented it with the opportunity for Congressional leadership. [65] The Southern conservative Democratic backwater has been in recent Congressional history much more potent that the Midwestern conservative Republican backwater.

History teaches different people different things. This sketch of South Dakota's political heritage does suggest a number of obvious but no less useful conclusions.

First, the state has been predominantly Republican over the years.

Only for eight years, in 1897-1899, 1933-37, and 1959-61, have the Republicans failed to control the bulk of major political offices at the disposal of the voters of the state. To put it another way, the Republicans have been in political control of South Dakota in 70 of the state's 78 years, or 90 percent of the time in the period 1889-1967.

Secondly, anti-Republicanism has usually been based on agrarian discontent, as the voting records of the Populist, Progressive, New Deal, and "modern" eras abundantly and consistently attest. Conversely, the Republican party has always found its greatest electoral strength in the cities and towns of the state.

Thirdly, both major parties are non-ideological and in this sense are typical of the American political tradition. Ideological struggles are as likely to occur within the parties as between them. Thus, basic policy reorientations in the state can occur with no change in party control, as evidenced by Crawford's election in 1906 and Mickelson's forty years later; conversely, change in party control does not necessarily result in any change of policy, as evidenced by Bulow's election in 1926 and Gubbrud's in 1960, neither administration being characterized by vigorous attempts to vitalize the role of state government and in this sense continuing rather than reversing the policies of the preceding administrations of the opposing party.

Finally, political careers in South Dakota are not notably long. In terms of years of public service, no South Dakotan can match the political longevity of such figures as Carl Hayden of Arizona, who has served in the U. S. Congress ever since his state entered the Union in 1912, or George Norris of Nebraska, who served in Congress from 1903 to 1943. No Governor, lieutenant governor, or attorney general of South Dakota has served longer than four years, no U. S. Senator longer than 18 years, no Congressman longer than 14 years. In sum, no South Dakotan has served longer than 28 years in major political office.

To discuss the development of South Dakota politics in terms of a Norbeck era or a Mundt era—to name the principal political patriarchs of the state—is to mute the testimony of numerous burgeoning careers nipped in the bud by a single but final defeat. It should not be forgotten that Lee, Crawford, Bulow, Mundt, and McGovern all suffered defeat, and that many others decided after a brief service to leave the heartless struggle to stronger men. None of these men could know how long they would be able to keep the support of the people, and this conditioned their responses to the issues of their terms. Some few have known the responsibilities of power until their final breath, but more have suffered years and even decades of frustrated removal from the gaming table of politics. As long as people govern themselves by the process of casting and counting discreet votes, politics will remain a hazardous vocation.

What John J. Ingalls said of Kansas is, according to one authority, applicable to the entire Plains area and thus to the politics of South Dakota. "There has been neither peace, tranquility, nor repose. The farmer can never foretell his harvest, nor the merchant his gains, nor the *politician his supremacy*. Something startling has always happened, or has been constantly anticipated." [66]

The prairie's radicalism, conditioned as it was by social isolation and primitive physical conditions, might be considered rational to the extent that it used its votes to oust from political office the enemies it perceived; and yet there was at the same time present a certain irrationality in the sense that too often the radical movements did not find the responsible leaders nor discern the proper policies that might have enabled their individualistic, agrarian elements to maintain control over the government. South Dakota agrarian radicalism only rarely achieved temporary success and never anything like a tenured incumbency which might have reshaped the state's history. It remains to wonder why the Nonpartisan League and Farmer-Labor movements did not become for South Dakota, as they did for North Dakota and Minnesota, the vehicles of a permanent and institutionalized radicalism. If the reason for their failure was largely the acumen of Peter Norbeck, then he is perhaps an even more significant figure in American political history than we have imagined.

IV

PARTY POLITICS: AGENCIES OF PARTICIPATION

As eminent a political scientist as Professor V. O. Key was hard put to enunciate a simple and unqualified definition of a political party. After discussing the party-in-the-electorate, the professional political group, the party-in-the-legislature, and the party-in-the-government, he finally concluded that the term "party" applies to several types of groups.[1] These groups occupy different geographical locations, are active at various times, and only occasionally function as a monolithic organization.

As is well known, parties do not regularly divide on issues. On some issues most members of both parties will vote "yes," while on other issues both sides will vote "no." Comparatively rare are the occasions when the overwhelming majority of one party is opposed by the great majority of the other party. Thus Edmund Burke's classic definition of party as "a body of men united, for promoting by their joint endeavours the national interest, upon some particular principle in which they are all agreed"[2] has little reference to modern American political parties. An organization possessing the qualification of cohesion on a particular policy question, as per the Burke conception, would be quickly identified as a "pressure group" by a reasonably observant student in a freshman college course in American government. In spite of this, on some occasions it is possible to find significant divisions on a party basis, as will be discussed below in this chapter. The important point here is that party membership as such does not commit the citizen or the public official to a particular course of action or even necessarily give much indication of his attitude on a given issue.

What distinguishes a political party is its persistent urge to elect its members to office. The goal for the party is not the resolution of the political issues currently at stake, but rather the acquisition of the statutory and moral authority to resolve such disputes through the power of public office. In one scholar's words: "A political party is an organization whose members are sufficiently homogeneous to band together for the overt purpose of winning elections which entitles them to exercise governmental power, in order to enjoy the influence, perquisites, and advantages of authority."[3]

The problem of defining "party" can be illustrated by a cursory glance at some South Dakota political statistics. In 1964, 369,782 citizens of the state were registered with one party or the other, the Republicans enjoying a 3-2 edge over the Democrats. In the primary elections of that year, 94,144 Republicans and 41,122 Democrats expressed a choice between rival candidates of their respective parties for the gubernatorial nominations. In the general election that followed in November, 150,151 South Dakotans voted for Nils Boe, the GOP's candidate for Governor, while 140,419 voted for John F. Lindley, his Democratic opponent. On the same day, almost at the same instants in time, 130,108 South Dakotans marked their ballot for the Republican Presidential candidate, Senator Barry Goldwater, and 163,010 voted for President Johnson. Furthermore, according to one estimate, about 14,000 South Dakotans contributed money to the state Republican party in 1964 and about five thousand gave financial support to the Democrats. The voters elected over six hundred of their fellow citizens to public office at the state and county levels. Both parties alike elected nearly four thousand residents of the state to national, state, county, or precinct office in the party. The question arises, which of these groups actually constitutes the real political party: registrants, voters, contributors, elected public officials, or elected party officials? The answer will depend on a number of factors. No answer will be attempted here; our purpose is simply to suggest that the political party which exists in the mind of many citizens is in reality very difficult to locate or define precisely. This chapter may be considered as an extended definition of a political party in that it is concerned with locating party leadership, assessing the functions performed by the party, and studying its multitudinous relationships with policy questions, pressure groups, and national party elements.

Political Parties in South Dakota. Basically, but not entirely, the party struggle in South Dakota politics has involved the Republicans and the Democrats. The GOP has presented a ticket in every general election since statehood, but there was no Democratic ticket in 1896, 1898, or 1900 when that party fused its efforts with the Populist movement.[4] A number of other minor parties have become involved in South Dakota politics, but have never won a major election and have only rarely wielded a significant amount of influence on the state.[5] The "Independent" party of 1890, 1892, and 1894 was agrarian-based and ultimately became the "People's" or

"Populist" party of 1896 and the "Fusion" party of 1898 and 1900. In these six elections this shifting alliance never finished worse than second, so that for the period 1890-1900 it constituted the major competition for the Republican party.

Tripartisan politics returned to South Dakota in the Norbeck period. The "Independent" party captured more than twenty-five percent of the vote in 1918, finishing behind the Republican slate but ahead of the Democratic ticket. This faction had become the Nonpartisan League on the ballot by 1920, and it again polled in excess of one-fourth of the vote in that year, as it did once again in 1922. A split in the agrarian ranks in 1924 returned the Democratic party to major party status, where it has remained ever since. In 1924 and 1926, there were both "Farmer-Labor" and "Independent" tickets receiving from between five to fifteen percent of the vote.

Several other minor parties have appeared on the state ballot, including the Prohibition, Socialist, Progressive, Scales of Justice, Good Government, and Liberty tickets. No party other than the Republican and Democratic has been listed on state ballots since the 1934 election, however.

By statute, a political party in South Dakota is defined as a "party whose candidate for Governor at the last preceding general election received at least ten percent of the total votes cast for Governor."[6] Thus, once established and recognized, a party maintains its status by continuing to poll at least one of every ten gubernatorial votes in the biennial general elections. A new political party may participate in the general election by filing a petition signed by at least ten percent of the number of votes cast for Governor in the last preceding general election.[7]

The political party is a permanent organization, as long as it polls a substantial number of votes. Membership is established by the voter on registration. In turn, party leadership is determined by primary elections in which registered party members participate. Voters choose delegates to the state and county conventions of their party and members of the state and county committees of their party every two years.[8] National convention delegates are chosen in Presidential election years.[9] The national delegate slates are grouped on petitions indicating their collective preference choice for President, if they have a preference.[10]

After their election, the county committees choose a county chairman, a vice-chairman, and a secretary-treasurer.[11] The state convention elects the state chairman and vice-chairman.[12]

South Dakota law thus supports the principle of popular control of both political parties and public office. In the primary election, party members choose their party nominees for the November contests and also vote for party officials at the precinct and state levels who will in turn elect other state and local party officials. In the general election, officials are chosen for county government posts and for executive, legislative, and judicial positions in the state government.

Although the law provides for popular control of political parties, the question remains whether many voters seriously inquire into party affairs. The choice of the major party positions, the state chairmanship and membership on the national committee, falls to the state convention, so that the general membership of the party is unaware of the candidates involved or, for that matter, of the duties they are expected to perform.[13] At the local level, where the county chairmen and members of the state convention and state central committee are chosen, the parties consider themselves fortunate if they can fill all the positions on the ballot with the names of willing and well-known people. And how many of these have the experience, interest, and economic independence to provide vigorous leadership? Frequently, there is no opposition to candidates for these party offices, and therefore little interest. Most primary election voters are more interested in their party's choice for President or for Congressman than in selecting their party's precinct committeeman.[14]

Party leadership is in a sense self-perpetuating, with local influentials serving duty tours on committees or as chairmen and then encouraging their friends to run, thus removing themselves from responsibility while keeping some power over party actions. County chairmanships may involve some honor and even a little power, but they are also a nuisance at best and a serious threat to one's social and economic equanimity at worst. The chairman is expected to "run" the party in the county even though he may have difficulty locating its working members a week after the central committee meeting at which he was elected. He is expected to collect money to meet the county's financial goals as set by the state organization. He is expected to find jobs for the surprisingly large number of people who believe the party—or at least the people—owe them a living. He is expected to turn out a strong vote for President, Governor, Senator, and so on down to the county officers. In short, at the county level, he is responsible for a wide range of functions and is more likely to hear about his alleged shortcomings than about his accomplishments. He is likely to be tolerated at best by his presumed followers in the county party, and if he dares offend anyone he may suffer the indignity of being dumped suddenly and unceremoniously in favor of a brash youth fresh out of law school who is looking for the quickest avenue to political attention and preferment. He should not expect a gold watch and a few kind words at the end of his service, although he will probably get a sympathetic pat on the back from the Congressman next time through Central City.

Where the generality of voters is apathetic, it is likely that small groups will be able to control local party decisions. Most party members seem to be politically minded about one month in twenty-four, somewhat like the one-day-a-week Christians, and could care less about the problems that face the local party officials between elections.

In short, the people can control their party organization if they want to, but because of the difficulty of finding party officials to do the jobs that are to be done and the lack of authority exercised by these officials, in most counties the leaders feel satisfied if they can find enough citizens to fill the positions of party responsibility. This is true at higher levels of party control as well. The principle of popular control has taken away so much of the flexible, discretionary power of party leaders in South Dakota that they can seldom make important decisions, and many of the same leaders would shrink from making such crucial decisions if they had the opportunity. No power, no interest; no interest, no power. Thus have the policy-makers and voters of South Dakota emasculated the role of political party leaders.

The Election System. Political parties nominate their candidates for the major partisan offices by means of a primary election in which only duly registered party members may vote. [15] In addition to determining party candidates for Presidential electors, United States Senator, Representative, Governor, and state legislature, the party primary election also chooses the nominees for the partisan county officer positions (county commissioners, sheriff, auditor, treasurer, register of deeds, clerk of courts, and state's attorney; educational and judicial positions are filled on a non-partisan basis). [16] It is worth noting that South Dakota has experimented frequently with her election laws and was in the forefront of movements around and after the turn of the century to popularize the selection of party candidates. [17]

If a primary candidate's total party vote equals or exceeds thirty-five percent, he is declared nominated. If his plurality is less than thirty-five percent, however, the decision is referred to the state convention. This eventuality has occurred four times since the adoption of the 1929 primary election law. In 1930 the Republican convention nominated Warren Green for Governor after he had finished behind Gladys Pyle, former Governor Carl Gunderson, Brooke Howell, and Carl O. Trygstad in the GOP primary. Four years later, the Republican convention nominated Francis Case for the Second Congressional District seat after he had finished third in a field that included former Congressman Williamson, Dan McCutcheon, and Earl N. Hammerquist. In the 1942 Republican primary, less than seven thousand votes separated four gubernatorial candidates, Joe Bottum, M. Q. Sharpe, Attorney General Leo A. Temmey, and Millard G. Scott. In the convention, Sharpe won the nomination. Finally, in 1948, the Republicans again failed to give any candidate the requisite percentage in the race for the First Congressional District nomination between Harold O. Lovre, William H. Pringle, Art B. Anderson, and E. L. Stavig; Lovre was subsequently chosen by the convention. In three of these four cases, it is pertinent to note, the candidate finally chosen by the state convention had not been the leading vote-getter in the primary election. And, in each of these four cases, the nominee chosen by the GOP convention was ultimately elected in November. [18]

Another way to be placed on the general election ballot is by submitting a petition containing signatures numbering between two and five percent of the number of votes cast in the previous gubernatorial election in the district or political subdivision involved. [19] Despite the fact that this independent candidate provision has been on the books for more than forty years, it has not been utilized for a statewide candidate since 1932.

We have seen that the state party convention sometimes makes major nominations where no candidate has received the necessary thirty-five percent of the votes cast in the primary election. The state convention regularly determines who shall be the candidates of the party for lieutenant governor, attorney general, secretary of state, state auditor, state treasurer, commissioner of school and public lands, and public utilities commissioner. In Presidential election years, the convention also chooses the national committeeman and committeewoman for their party. [20]

Formerly, the state's election laws provided that these lesser nominations for state constitutional offices be filled in the primary election. From 1908 until 1924, there was competition for many of the positions on one or more of the various party tickets being offered to the voter. In more recent years, with the convention choosing the candidates, the Republican nominations in particular have been a chief means of distributing patronage among the party faithful. Many of the nominees are not well known, and only rarely has there been much variation in the votes received in the subsequent general election by candidates of the same party for these offices.

In rare instances another party agency, the state central committee, may make an important nomination. This occurs when a nomination is left vacant by the death or resignation of the nominee, as happened in 1962 when Senator Case died after the primary election at which he had been nominated for his third term. After a day-long struggle among supporters of Joe Bottum, Sigurd Anderson, Nils Boe, Ben Reifel, A. C. Miller, and Joe Foss, the decision finally went to Bottum. [21]

For the most part, the party hierarchy, as such, does not play a crucial role in nominations for major office at the national, state, or local level. The convention has some power over the lesser state administrative nominations, though such choices are made with considerable informality and there are no "liberal" or "conservative" or "rural" slates as there had been early in the present century. If "deals" are made, as they are widely thought to have been made to secure Vessey's nomination for governor in 1908 [22] and Boe's in 1964, for example, the deals are made by politicians speaking and working as individuals rather than as official party leaders. South Dakota seems to have marked preference for party officials who know their place and are content to play a limited role in determining policy and choosing candidates. [23]

In addition to the biennial general elections, [24] state law provides for special elections to fill legislative and Congressional vacancies. [25] Registration and voting laws are not stringent and contribute to the fact that South Dakota has one of the highest voting turnout percentages among the states.

Parties and Issues. Before plunging into a discussion of parties and issues, our terms of reference ought to be defined as precisely as possible. Use will be made of the terms "liberal" and "conservative." Indefinite as these terms are in common American parlance, they can be employed meaningfully if the user has a clear idea of just what he is talking about. By liberal this discussion will mean a person who tends to favor change, who tends to favor increased government spending, who tends to favor an expanded role for government, particularly at the national level—in short, a person who is optimistic about the benefits to be derived from positive and dynamic government action. Conversely, by conservative this discussion will mean a person who tends to oppose change for change's sake, a person opposed to more government spending, a person who wishes to restrict or limit the role of government—in brief, a person who is pessimistic about the benefits to be derived from governmental activity.

The phrases used in the 1962 party platforms can be used to illustrate in general terms the ideological differences that distinguish Republicans and Democrats in South Dakota. The Republican platform refers to its "demonstration of honest, clean, wholesome, decent government based on sound fiscal policies." References are made to liquidating debts on a "pay-as-you-go-basis" and to the strength and wisdom of "the foremost Architect of the universe." The Democratic platform on the other hand is concerned with change, the "vested interests of a privileged few," the "challenges" that face the nation, and the "vigorous and forward looking administration in Washington." There is concern about helping South Dakota "move forward with the nation and the world." [26]

As mentioned in Chapter III, there are ideological struggles in both Republican and Democratic parties in South Dakota. The parties thus are not consistently of one particular ideology or the other. There is and always has been a mixture of liberalism and conservatism on both sides of the political fence in the state. Basically, however, both of the state's political parties are conservative when compared with the larger, growing, and more urban states to the East and West. The voters of the state have the same conservative characteristics, and inevitably so do the state's political leaders. A notable exception to this generalization is Senator McGovern, who is unusually liberal for a major South Dakota political figure of either party. In this respect, McGovern may be similar to the leaders of the Progressive era in the sense that he is optimistic about expanding the role of government and that he makes a conscious effort to persuade voters to his way of thinking.

McGovern's action in building a Democratic party machine from virtually nothing and then running successfully for major office in 1956, 1958, and 1962, and strongly against the powerful Senator Mundt in 1960, constitute a remarkable performance paralleled in South Dakota politics only by Crawford and Norbeck. McGovern's entrance into politics was different from that of his two successful Democratic antecedents, Bulow and Berry. Bulow became a major candidate by a stroke of fortune,[27] and Berry owed his election largely to the national popularity of the New Deal. McGovern built a party corps almost single-handed. None of these three Democrats were creatures of a party organization.

McGovern is the most notable of South Dakota's modern liberals. More than any other figure, he is responsible for the existence of both a partisan and an ideological choice in contemporary South Dakota politics. Neither choice was available from 1938 until 1956. His presence on the political scene probably contributes to a moderation of the ideological position of the still-dominant Republican party.

The point that political parties in South Dakota, in keeping with the American tradition, are non-ideological would seem to indicate that the party is not a notably consistent vehicle by which the course of governmental policy might be changed. The point was made in Chapter III and needs to be reiterated that a change in party control does not necessarily mean a change in policy orientation; and, conversely that re-direction of policy can occur even though party control does not change.

There is of course a basic question of determining whether there is such a thing as a party policy in the first place. The only concrete evidence one can find as to party policy is contained in the party's platform, on which (presumably) the party's candidates run for office. While platforms are better evidence of a party position than are statements of individual politicians, they are not as conclusive as the votes of legislatures and the orders of Governors.

Early party platforms frequently stated definite positions and were more specific than are the more contemporary party platforms. This was perhaps a function of the keen competition that existed between the Republican and Populist parties throughout the 1890's and between the Stalwart and Progressive factions of the Republican party in the first two decades of the present century. Much of the state's political hsitory reveals a comparatively low degree of political competition, one result of which has been more generalized platform pro-

visions. As one observer has pointed out, "few measures submitted
to roll call votes in the South Dakota Legislature produced definite
party-line splits, suggesting that where opposition to a bill does exist
it is often generated from non-party motives. Issues that do produce
party-line votes are frequently identifiable with national Republican
and Democratic positions."[28]

Since the Norbeck era there has been a tendency for party stands
to be muted. Political parties as such have tended to moderate
extreme elements in the state as part of their attempt to generalize
their own appeal to a minimum number of prospective voters. The
party platforms have drawn lines that are at best blurred, indistinct,
and hazy, so that it has often been difficult to find consistent lines of
ideological demarcation between political parties. As on the national
scene, South Dakota has produced liberal Republicans (such as Norbeck and Foss) and conservative Democrats (such as Bulow and
Herseth),[29] but for the most part it seems safe to say that most Republicans are more conservative than most Democrats.

If policy questions are not processed in any detail in party deliberations, one may ask where it is that such discussion takes place. The
answer, in simple terms, seems to be that political discussions and the
responsibility for enunciating them clearly and publicly are largely left
to the formal governmental officials, especially in the legislative session.
Given the capital city's relative geographical isolation and the brevity
of the legislative sessions, it is easy to conclude that the policy-making process is poorly suited to a public, coherent, and considered statement and resolution of political issues. The difficulties are increased by
the state's lack of a politically sophisticated metropolitan newspaper.

One illustration of the tendency of political party leaders to avoid
recommending policy in public was the situation in 1964 when a number of controversal issues, including Indian jurisdiction, property class-
ification, and voter registration, were referred to the general voters of
the state in the November election. The Republican party, which as
the majority party in the legislature was responsible for the original
bills, tried diligently throughout the remainder of the year to divorce
itself from responsibility in the matters. It is possible that a more
competitive situation between the two parties over a number of years
might tend to make the position of party officials more visible to the
public, but as it now stands, the majority party seems to prefer to
avoid taking a definite public stand on the controversial issues of the
day.

Parties and Pressure Groups: There has been no systematic study
of the interrelationships of political party organizations and pressure
groups in South Dakota. This fact lends credence to the presumption
that connections between groups and parties in the state are informal
and unsophisticated. It is difficult to link groups with one or the other
party exclusively; groups typically seek support in both parties, and
conversely both parties seek support in every group.

In general, however, one can state that the GOP in South Dakota
receives support from groups that traditionally favor conservative
policies, such as the Farm Bureau, the Chamber of Commerce, and
many professional organizations. The pro-Republican group should
also probably include the vast Homestake Mining interest, the railroads, and the stock growers organization. The Democratic party
is supported by the National Farmers Union, the National Farmers
Organization, labor groups, and rural electrification interests.

The general linkages are supported by what little survey data exist
on South Dakota's political disposition.[30] But group membership is
not an absolute criterion of individual behavior. In fact, it might be
hypothesized that South Dakota's low population density encourages
individual as opposed to group action, suggesting that group affiliation
may be even less determinate of individual behavior than in the
nation as a whole.

In a discussion of pressure groups, one should consider the types of
issues on which groups state definite positions. Many groups have
a general orientation independent of their special interest that determines basic group attitudes about governmental principles and
policies. For example, business groups tend to favor restrictions on
the scope and size of government, while labor groups tend to favor
expansion. Thus the general orientation of the National Association
of Manufacturers will condition its responses to a wide range of governmental policies that are not particularly crucial to American small
manufacturers, issues such as Medicare, foreign aid, federal aid to
education, legislative reapportionment, and farm price supports. The
same things would be true of the Farmers Union, for example, sub-
stituting in the previous list business regulation for farm supports.

In addition to these general group orientations, groups are closely
affected by certain policies in their specific area of operation or interest. Farmers are vitally interested in agricultural price supports,
minority groups in civil rights legislation, professional groups in licensing, labor groups in public welfare and labor legislation, and so forth.

While we have no systematic study in this area, a number of studies have discussed several points on which groups have attempted to influence the policy decisions of South Dakota officials. Railroad regulation was of particular concern in the first two decades of statehood.[31] Mining interests have long been important in South Dakota and have affected national as well as state policies.[32] A number of recent monographs have discussed the role of pressure groups in recent legislative sessions and elections, including the role of the League of Women Voters in revision of the registration laws and the role of several groups in Indian jurisdiction legislation,[33] the role of farm groups in U. S. sugar[34] and beef imports,[35] and the roles of the Municipal League and the electric cooperatives in utilities regulation.[36] The daily press frequently carries the pronouncements of conservative groups such as the stockgrower's association and of liberal groups such as organized labor. But for the present, our conclusions must be limited by the paucity of data with which we might more confidently discuss the role of pressure groups in affecting party and policy in South Dakota. Given what has already been said about the comparative insignificance of modern South Dakota political parties in originating or implementing governmental decisions, however, one would expect to find that the major avenues of communication between groups and policy-making in South Dakota connect those groups directly with individual public officials rather than with political party officials as such.

Parties and National Candidates and Committees. South Dakota's comparatively low population does not encourage its hopes to cut much of a swath on the national political scene.[37] The size of her delegations to national nominating conventions is so small as to be nearly invisible to the national king-makers in their convention political strategy. The few South Dakotans who have played an important national political role have relied on their own rather than on the state's resources.

The state held its first presidential primary in 1912, when Theodore Roosevelt won a clear-cut victory over Senator LaFollette of Wisconsin and the incumbent President, William Howard Taft (see Table 6).[38] Invariably the largest turnout in these presidential primaries has occurred on the Republican ballot. The GOP primary also is almost always the more exciting, due to two factors: first, Democratic Presidents were running for re-nomination in six of the 14 primaries, compared to only three such circumstances for the GOP; and second, South Da-

TABLE 6

PRESIDENTIAL PRIMARIES IN SOUTH DAKOTA

Year	Republican Party		Democratic Party	
1912	Theodore Roosevelt	38,106	No Election	
	Robert LaFollette	19,960		
	William H. Taft	10,944		
1916b/	Cummins a/		Woodrow Wilson a/	
1920	Leonard Wood	31,265	James W. Gerard	4706
	Frank Lowden	26,981	James O. Monroe	1906
	Hiram Johnson	26,301		
	Miles Poindexter	1,144		
1924	Hiram Johnson	40,935	No Election	
	Calvin Coolidge	39,791		
1928	No Election		No Election	
1932	Royal Johnson slate	64,464	W. J. Bulow slate a/	
	Alan Bogue slate	35,133		
1936	Warren Green slate	44,518	Tom Berry (Roosevelt) slate a/	
	Peter Norbeck (Borah) slate	44,261		
1940	No Election		No Election	
1944	Christopherson (Dewey) slate	33,497	Hildebrandt (Roosevelt) slate	7414
	Bottum (Stassen) slate	22,135	Powell (Roosevelt) slate	6727
1948	Hitchcock slate a/		Fellows (Truman) slate	11193
			Hildebrandt (uncom-	
			mitted) slate	8016
1952	Robert Taft	64,695	Estes Kefauver	22812
	Mickelson (Eisenhower)		Ed Downs (uncommitted) slate	11741
	slate	63,879		
1956	Joe Foss slate a/		Estes Kefauver a/	
1960	James Lloyd slate a/		Hubert Humphrey a/	
1964	Archie Gubbrud	57,653	Lyndon Johnson a/	
	Barry Goldwater	27,076		

a/ Unopposed
b/ In 1916, the Socialist party in South Dakota nominated a presidential candidate.

kota Republicans have rather consistently opposed the orientation of their national party leadership, being more progressive from 1912 to 1936 and less progressive from 1940 to the present.

Three Republican Presidential primaries were agonizingly close, with the winning candidate or slate receiving less than 51 percent of the vote in a two-way race. In 1924, Senator Hiram Johnson of California, running as an Independent-Republican, attracted 40,935 votes to 39,791 for President Calvin Coolidge. In 1936, a slate headed by ex-Governor Warren Green and sympathetic to Governor Alfred Landon of Kansas defeated the Norbeck slate pledged to Senator William Borah of Idaho, 44,518 to 44,261. And in 1952, Senator Robert Taft of Ohio narrowly defeated an Eisenhower slate headed by former Governor George Mickelson, 64,695 to 63,879.[39]

The four-way Republican primary of 1920 involved three major contenders for the wide-open GOP nomination, General Leonard Wood, ex-Governor Frank Lowden of Illinois, and Senator Johnson. Wood was supported by Governor Norbeck, who in the same election was making his first bid for the U. S. Senate, and the famed general won by a margin of less than five thousand votes over his two major opponents.[40] There was competition in the Republican Presidential primaries of 1932, 1944 and 1964, but the results were not close.

On the Democratic side, the closest Presidential primary occurred in 1944 when two slates pledged to President Franklin D. Roosevelt finished within seven hundred votes of one another. President Truman found tough going in the 1948 primary, but attracted 58 percent of the vote. Senator Estes Kefauver easily defeated an uncommitted slate by a 2-to-1 margin in 1952, and won unopposed four years later. Senator Hubert Humphrey of Minnesota, a native of South Dakota, was the only entrant in the 1960 Democratic primary, as was President Johnson in 1964.

The Republican party has given its voters a real choice in its South Dakota Presidential primary much more often than have the Democrats. In the 14 presidential years, 1912-1964, Republican voters have had a choice eight times, including two occasions (1924 and 1932) when an incumbent Republican President was challenged. Meanwhile, the Democrats of South Dakota were given a meaningful choice twice, in 1948 and 1952. Both parties put up only one non-incumbent slate on three occasions, while the Democrats on four occasions and the Republicans on two occasions failed to have any Presidential primary at all. The Democrats four times and the Republicans once ran the incumbent President unopposed.

The actions of South Dakota delegations to national nominating conventions have not been subject to rigid, scholarly study, but we do have three recent extended if subjective treatments.[41]

In the 1948 Republican National Convention, the South Dakota delegation split eight for Stassen and three for Dewey on the first ballot, seven for Dewey and four for Stassen on the second ballot, and went unanimously for Dewey on the third ballot.[42]

The South Dakota Republican delegation of 1952, which Senator Taft had won by only 816 votes in the primary election, voted solidly for the Ohioan's interests throughout the early parliamentary maneuvering that was to have such a crucial effect on the national convention's final choice for President. By the time the clerk called for South Dakota's votes on the first balloting, it was apparent that Eisenhower had won the nomination. Even so, the South Dakota delegation gave half its 14 votes to Taft, "attesting to the 'bitter end' attitude of some delegates." [43]

In the Democratic convention of 1952, the South Dakota delegation remained true to its commitment to Senator Kefauver until the conclusive third ballot, when, after first recording their Kefauver preference, they joined with the convention in making Adlai Stevenson's nomination unanimous. [44]

The 1960 Republican delegation headed by former Governor Joe Foss was, like most uncommitted South Dakota delegations, representative of the major shades of party opinion in the state. On the only ballot taken, the state voted unanimously for Vice President Richard Nixon, although earlier in the week as many as six South Dakotans had said they would vote for Senator Barry Goldwater of Arizona if he would allow his name to come before the convention. [45] After Nixon's nomination for President, the South Dakota delegation was split as to whom to support for vice-president. The most obvious possibilities were Ambassador Henry Cabot Lodge, Secretary of the Interior Fred Seaton, Congressmen Walter Judd and Charles Halleck, and Senators Thruston Morton and Goldwater. According to Jones, "the overwhelming majority of the delegates were opposed to Lodge as the vice presidential candidate but were unwilling to commit themselves to any other candidate. The decision, as with the Presidential nomination, was *to await developments*." [46]

Jones's comments on the delegation's reactions to the "developments" which resulted in Lodge's nomination are worth quotation: "Nixon's choice of Lodge was announced early Thursday morning. By Thursday afternoon the [South Dakota] delegates seemed resigned to the fact that Lodge would be the candidate . . . Those delegates who were present (at a breakfast meeting) accepted the reasoning grudgingly. After the meeting several delegates expressed disgust because of the insignificant role that they were playing and suggested that they might return home before the final session of the convention. That evening, South Dakota gave her fourteen votes to Ambassador Lodge." [47]

The 1964 Republican delegation, uncommitted but containing strong

Goldwater support despite the fact that it had defeated a Goldwater slate in the primary, went to San Francisco with nine Goldwater and five Scranton supporters. Both pressures from home and the clumsy machinations of the various and largely uncoordinated anti-Goldwater forces at the convention had considerable impact on the South Dakota delegates. When the first ballot was called, Goldwater obviously had the nomination sewed up and the chief excitement for the delegation was whether or not its votes would be the ones to put the Arizonan over the top. As it turned out, this honor went to the South Carolina delegation. Even though Goldwater's nomination was thus assured when South Dakota announced its vote, there was still a voting split, with 12 votes going to Goldwater and two to Scranton.[48]

These studies add up to these conclusions: that South Dakota delegations do not participate crucially, are not very well informed or experienced in the national political arena, seldom actively attempt to widen their contacts or broaden their impact, and seem principally concerned with avoiding conclusive commitments with respect to either the national or the state balance of political power. Perhaps one reason for these results is the recent practice of excluding South Dakota Congressmen or Senators from the delegation itself.[49]

Local Politics. Politics co-exist with humanity. Political events occur in homes, garden clubs, and church socials, as well as in Washington, the state capitols, the court houses, the city halls, precinct polling booths and in the deliberations of local chapters of such special interest groups as the National Farmers Union, the American Medical Association, the Izaak Walton League, and the Chamber of Commerce. There are many and sometimes vital connections between politics at the humblest and the grandest levels.

The present study pursues its investigation of politics in South Dakota toward the humbler depths only to the point where findings relevant to its purposes are confident and useful enough to warrant the research effort. This point, akin to the "diminishing returns" concept in economics, is located somewhere in the hazy area wherein is drawn the tenuous boundary between traditional political science and that aspect of political science which makes use of the crafts of the sociologist and psychologist. The latter approaches can, by describing how and deducing why man behaves as he does, reveal much that is of use to persons concerned with making government a more responsive servant of man. Here, however, we will limit ourselves to more objective and less controversial data and will seek merely to correlate local politics in general terms with the state and national politics with which our study is otherwise mainly concerned.

County government and politics in South Dakota are largely conducted on a partisan basis. The board of county commissioners, which is composed of either three or five members, the states attorney, the sheriff, and the essentially administrative offices of auditor, clerk of the court, coroner, register of deeds, and treasurer are all elected on a partisan ballot. Educational and judicial officers are elected on a non-partisan basis. Competition for these offices is by no means universally keen. One study has shown that only 42.4 percent of county officer elections involve more than one candidate.[50] The degree of competitiveness varies from office to office. More than half of the elections for sheriff, commissioner, and register of deeds are contested, as are 47 percent of the elections for auditor and treasurer. The office of clerk of the court is contested only 35.7 percent of the time, of states attorney 25 percent of the time, of coroner 19.5 percent of the time, and of superintendent of schools (which is non-partisan) 14.8 percent of the time.

Variation in party affiliation of county officers has been analyzed in three ways. Party affiliation varies greatly from county to county and correlates generally with voting patterns discussed elsewhere in this study. Campbell county elected Republicans on every occasion in the period 1940 through 1960 and Charles Mix, at the other end of the political spectrum, elected Democrats to county office 82.8 percent of the time in the same period. Party affiliation varies to a lesser extent from year to year, the range being between a high Republican victory index of 84.9 percent recorded in 1944 to a low Republican victory index of 52.4 in 1958. The party affiliation variation is much less pronounced from one office to the next. Here the office of states attorney shows the highest percentage of Republican victors, 81.5, while 70.8 percent of the county commissioners are Republicans.

Some of the county offices, notably those of state's attorney, superintendent of schools, and coroner, require a considerable degree of professional training, and it is significant that these offices have the lowest amount of competition. The other partisan county offices are notably more competitive, and they are also more likely to be the primary objects of patronage allocation between the county political organizations and the potential candidates involved. Many of the county officers make careers out of the elective county positions, and their continuance in office would be made considerably more difficult than it already is were they to attract the criticism of their party's county chairman or committee.

Municipal government in South Dakota is conducted on a nonpartisan basis. Of the state's 306 municipalities, 165 operate under the town form, 128 under the aldermanic form, 11 under the commission form, and two (Vermillion and Yankton) under the manager form.[51] Many of the major municipal political controversies in the state have revolved around the questions of city manager government and of home rule.[52] While this study does not undertake to analyze politics in special district governments, school districts, interest group organizations, and other less formal associations, it should be kept in mind that politics and controversy are as characteristic here as at the state and national levels.

Local politics is not the pedestal of a political pyramid. Many officials involved in local politics give no thought to officials or issues at other levels of government and have no ambitions to move into those levels. Their concern with local governmental problems stems in many if not all cases from a desire to do their civic duty. For the most part, officials in other levels of government are content to leave local decisions in local hands. Thus there is not a great amount of interplay between local politics on one hand and state or national politics on the other. Some Governors, Congressmen, and legislators have had local political experience, but the ratio is not impressive.

Summary. Party organizations as such have seldom played a crucial role in South Dakota politics. In the early years, there were often factional fights for party control which meant that factions rather than parties made decisions. Later, in the more mature period when intraparty fighting was less prevalent, there was seldom much inclination on the part of party officials as such to exercise what power they had.

Party organizations have had little impact on candidate selection for major offices. They do not play a prominent role in patronage, although even in South Dakota there are a few jobs available to be filled. They do not control candidates. They have little to do with developing issues. They largely ignore and are largely ignored by national politics. They are not noted for strenuous or effective work in "getting out the vote." They are not particularly significant in state political life, outside of routine administration of party matters.

South Dakota seems to have a preference for keeping the political situation informal and inconclusive, as a means of preventing definite and conclusive governmental action. Party office, as well as public office, is used as often to prevent as to encourage governmental action.

V

ELECTORAL POLITICS:
VOTER VARIATIONS OVER TIME AND SPACE

The fact that political behavior varies considerably over space as well as over time had led scholars to inquire into variations in climate, terrain, land use, transportation routes, ethnic origins, religious affiliation, and time and density of settlement that might give some clues as to why behavioral inconsistencies exist. Two general methods of proceeding with such inquiries have been employed: the first making use of gross election data from the various political units, and the second making use of sampling techniques to survey the state of public opinion and partisan disposition.[1] The collection and analysis of South Dakota election data is now well enough advanced to permit confident interpretations to be made from them. Survey data for the state is much less in evidence, but some general conclusions will be made from the information that is available.

South Dakota can be divided into three broad geographical areas. The farming land in the east represents the western edge of the American corn belt. The Black Hills area at the western edge of the state has always been home to a significant part of the state's population, having received a great influx of settlers during the mining booms of the 1870's. Lying between the farmland and the Hills, and comprising the largest portion of the state's area, is a broad rangeland area where considerable wheat and cattle are produced. This rangeland has the lowest population density of the three regions, most of the population being concentrated in county seat towns. The only city in this area between the James River Valley and the Black Hills with a 1960 population of more than five thousand is Pierre, the state capital. Three other cities—Chamberlain, Mobridge, and Winner—have more than 2,500 inhabitants. The state's largest city, Sioux Falls, is located in the eastern area, as are eight other cities with populations of more than 5,000 (Aberdeen, Brookings, Huron, Madison, Mitchell, Vermillion, Watertown and Yankton); there are in addition four cities exceeding 2,500. The state's second largest city, Rapid City, lies at the eastern base of the Black Hills. Lead is the only other Hills city with a population over five thousand, but there are five more (Belle Fourche, Deadwood, Hot Springs, Spearfish, and Sturgis) with populations of more than 2,500.

Sixty percent of the state's 1960 population of 680,514 live in the counties comprising the eastern farm area, while sixteen percent live in the six counties in the Black Hills area. The balance of 24 percent are scattered among the remaining counties stretching from the James River Valley to the Hills.

The state's three largest counties, Minnehaha (Sioux Falls), Pennington (Rapid City), and Brown (Aberdeen), accounted for just under one-fourth of the total votes cast for President in 1960. Thus no single county can claim electoral dominance on the basis of numbers alone. The eastern third of South Dakota is the state's most heavily populated area, but as we will see the spread of party strength is not sufficiently concentrated to allow any section to control the results of either a primary or general election.

In order to show how party strength has varied over time, a set of maps has been prepared showing relative partisanship for each county in the gubernatorial elections of 1889 (Map A), 1902 (B), 1916 (C), 1932 (D), 1948 (E), and 1964 (F). In the state's first election, Republican strength is pronounced along the eastern border of the state and is generally greater in the entire East River area; the only West River area then extensively populated, the Black Hills, was much less Republican than the state as a whole, although each of the six counties then organized gave the Republican candidate a majority. The map on page 68 is quite similar, showing great, though shifting, Republican strength throughout the eastern half of the state and comparative Republican weakness west of the Missouri. By 1916 party strength seems to have become more evenly spread over the state, though three Russian-German counties (Campbell, Hutchinson, and McPherson) stand out as Republican strongholds and the West River area is still comparatively weak for the GOP. 1932 represents the first New Deal election and Map D shows the extent of Democratic success. By this time the Republican party seems to be gaining strength, relatively speaking, in the West River area. Western gains for the Republicans are more noticeable in the 1948 map. The 1964 map shows that the Black Hills area has now become one of the most important Republican strongholds. The GOP maintains its traditional strength in Sioux Falls, the Lincoln-Turner-Hutchinson corridor, the Campbell-McPherson enclave, and the Pierre area; conversely, Democratic strength is most apparent in the Chamberlain-Mitchell area, the

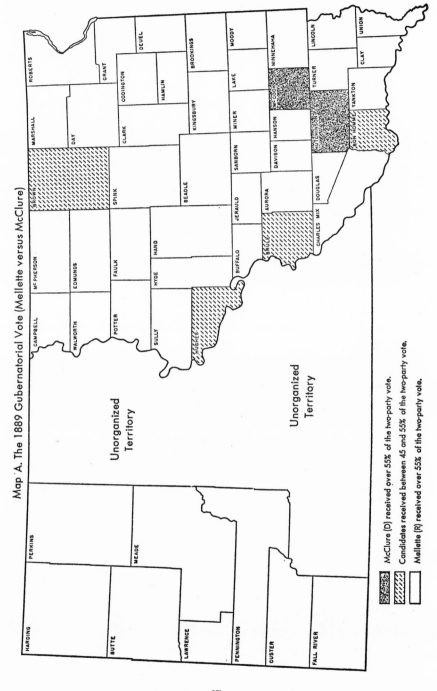

Map A. The 1889 Gubernatorial Vote (Mellette versus McClure)

McClure (D) received over 55% of the two-party vote.

Candidates received between 45 and 55% of the two-party vote.

Mellette (R) received over 55% of the two-party vote.

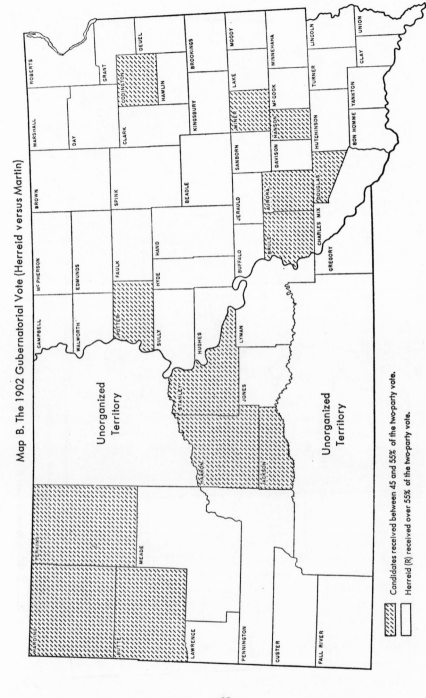

Map B. The 1902 Gubernatorial Vote (Herreid versus Martin)

Candidates received between 45 and 55% of the two-party vote.

Herreid (R) received over 55% of the two-party vote.

Map C. The 1916 Gubernatorial Vote (Norbeck versus Rinehart)

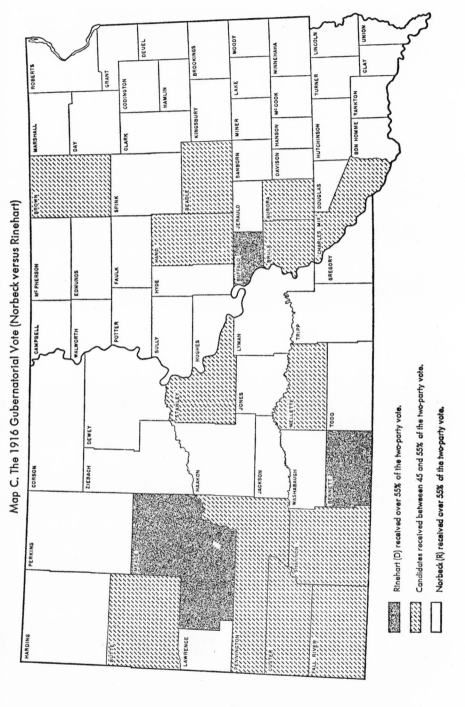

Rinehart (D) received over 55% of the two-party vote.

Candidates received between 45 and 55% of the two-party vote.

Norbeck (R) received over 55% of the two-party vote.

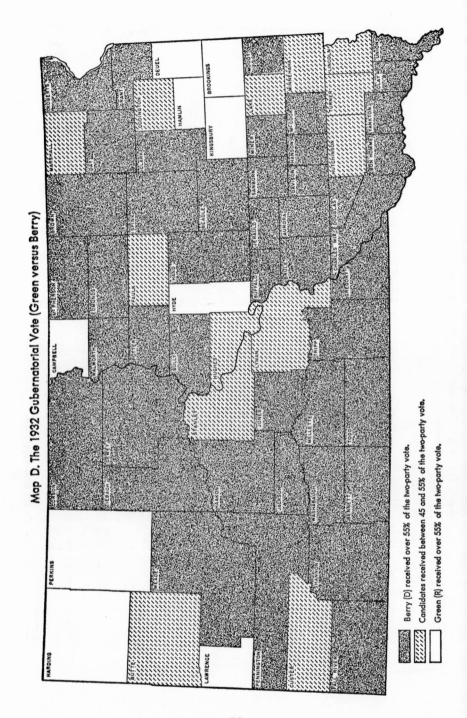

Map D. The 1932 Gubernatorial Vote (Green versus Berry)

Berry (D) received over 55% of the two-party vote.

Candidates received between 45 and 55% of the two-party vote.

Green (R) received over 55% of the two-party vote.

Map E. The 1948 Gubernatorial Vote (Mickelson versus Volz)

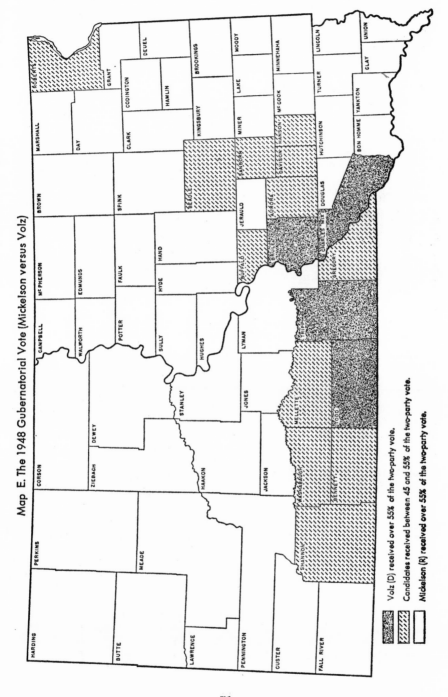

Volz (D) received over 55% of the two-party vote.

Candidates received between 45 and 55% of the two-party vote.

Mickelson (R) received over 55% of the two-party vote.

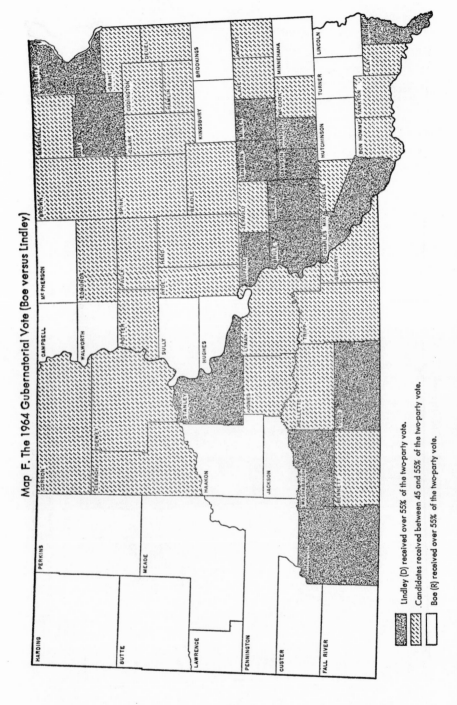

Map F. The 1964 Gubernatorial Vote (Boe versus Lindley)

Lindley (D) received over 55% of the two-party vote.

Candidates received between 45 and 55% of the two-party vote.

Boe (R) received over 55% of the two-party vote.

northeastern corner of the state, and some of the rangeland country, notably that juxtaposed to Indian reservations.

Maps G and H are attempts to display party strength in gubernatorial elections during two periods, 1926-1944 and 1946-1964.[2] For each county in each of the two periods, the Republican percentage of the two-party vote for Governor for each election was computed and then added, producing indices for each county allowing them to be placed in order of strength (Republican strength from top to bottom, Democratic strength from bottom to top).

The maps reveal a generally consistent pattern, but there are significant differences in relative partisan ranking for several counties (see Table 7). Seventeen of the state's 67 counties move more than ten places when the 1926-1944 and 1946-1964 rank orders are compared. Two of the moves are particularly noteworthy; Roberts county moved from thirty-third place in terms of comparative Republican strength on the early list to sixty-first place on the more recent list, while Shannon county's Republican decline was even more pronounced as it fell from twenty-fourth place to sixty-fifth. As a consequence of the more extreme Democrat-ward movements of these two counties, eleven of the remaining fifteen counties showing significant shifts in voting behavior moved in the Republican direction.

Maps G and H show essentially the same thing. There is notable and consistent Democratic strength in the south-central area of the state, in the upper James River valley, and in the northeastern corner. Republican strength is greatest in the east-central and far western sections and in the Russian-German Republican stronghold of Campbell and McPherson counties in the north central part of the state.

The most Democratic areas usually have a high percentage of Indians or Roman Catholics among their populations.[3] Lubell makes much of the Republican voting tradition of "Russian-German" areas,[4] of which Campbell, McPherson, Hutchinson, and Douglas counties are prominent examples in South Dakota. At the county level, there are no significant correlations between party strength on the one hand and raw population, population growth, urbanization or median family income on the other.[5]

County Trends in Presidential Elections. Analysis of the Presidential election returns in the period from 1928 through 1964 will allow the categorization of South Dakota counties in terms of the degree to which their partisan percentages vary from the statewide average. From such analysis, five categories of counties can be established.

The first category may be labeled the bellwether group. It consists

TABLE 7

COMPARISON OF PARTISAN RANK ORDERS OF SOUTH DAKOTA COUNTIES, BASED ON THE GUBERNATORIAL VOTE OF 1926-1944 AND 1946-1964

County[a/]	1926-1944 Republican Rank	1946-1964 Republican Rank	Rank Change
Campbell	1	1	--
McPherson	11	2	9
Turner	15	3	12
Hutchinson	10	4	·6
Butte	8	5	3
Harding	6	6	--
Lawrence	`2	7	5
Douglas	29½	8	21½
Kingsbury	5	9	4
Brookings	4	10	6
Hughes	21	11½	9½
Lake	13	11½	1½
Fall River	27½	13	14½
Potter	33	14	19
Perkins	12	15	3
Custer	14	16½	2½
Sully	20	16½	3½
Hamlin	9	18	9
Haakon	19	19	--
Pennington	18	20½	2½
Walworth	41	20½	19½
Deuel	3	22	19
Clark	17	23	6
Lincoln	7	24	17
Meade	16	25	9
Grant	25	26½	1½
Minnehaha	39	26½	12½
Clay	35	28	7
McCook	29½	29	½
Corson	28	30	2
Yankton	54	31	23
Hyde	22	32	10
Jackson	32	33	1
Dewey	31	34	3

TABLE 7—Continued

COMPARISON OF PARTISAN RANK ORDERS OF
SOUTH DAKOTA COUNTIES, BASED ON THE
GUBERNATORIAL VOTE OF 1926-1944 AND 1946-1964

County$\underline{a}$/	1926-1944 Republican Rank	1946-1964 Republican Rank	Rank Change
Jerauld	38	35	3
Lyman	26	36	10
Union	57	37	20
Mellette	56	38	18
Jones	23	39	16
Codington	42	40½	1½
Faulk	37	40½	3½
Hand	43	42	1
Moody	36	43	7
Ziebach	50	44	6
Bon Homme	53	45	8
Edmunds	45½	46	½
Washabaugh	61	47	14
Marshall	39	48	9
Tripp	60	49	11
Beadle	49	50½	1½
Stanley	44	50½	6½
Sanborn	48	52	4
Spink	51	53	2
Gregory	52	54	2
Bennett	45½	55½	10
Todd	59	55½	3½
Miner	55	57	2
Day	63	58	5
Hanson	58	59	1
Brown	62	60	2
Roberts	33	61	28
Buffalo	47	62	15
Davison	65	63	2
Aurora	64	64	--
Shannon	24	65	41
Charles Mix	66	66	--
Brule	67	67	--

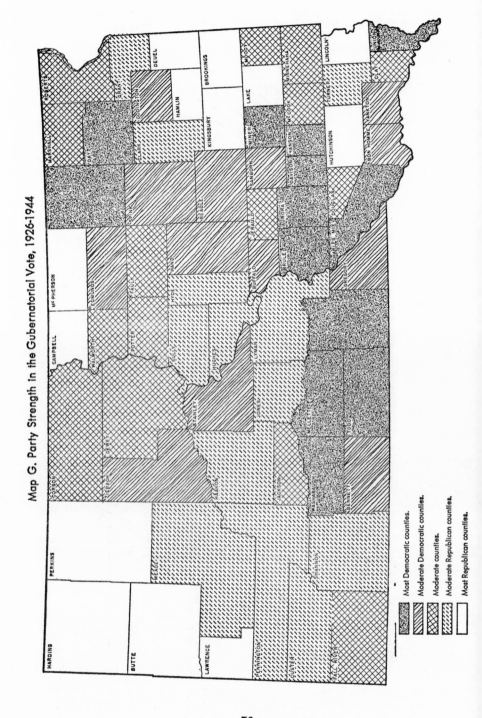

Map G. Party Strength in the Gubernatorial Vote, 1926-1944

Most Democratic counties.

Moderate Democratic counties.

Moderate counties.

Moderate Republican counties.

Most Republican counties.

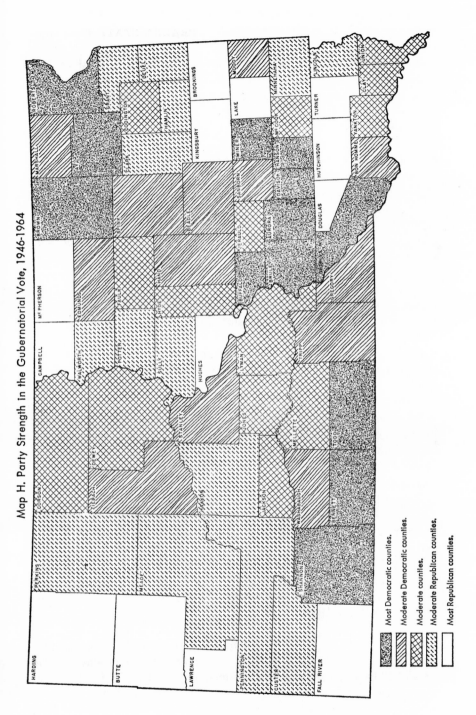

Map H. Party Strength in the Gubernatorial Vote, 1946-1964

Most Democratic counties.

Moderate Democratic counties.

Moderate counties.

Moderate Republican counties.

Most Republican counties.

of those counties where the percentage of the vote received by the Presidential candidate of a given party differed by five points or less from the statewide percentage in each of the ten elections involved. The counties are Clark, Hand, Grant, Jackson, Meade, and Walworth. In Grant county the percentage has never varied by more than three percentage points, which qualifies it as the state's most typical from the standpoint of the Presidential vote. A seventh county, Lyman, has not varied by more than one point from the state-wide average in the eight elections since 1932, but does not belong on the list because its deviation in 1928 amounted to six percentiles. There is no apparent characteristic common to these six counties, although none are particularly large in terms of population. They represent the major section of the state.

A second category, consisting of an additional 30 counties, includes those counties whose percentage never varied by more than ten points from the statewide norm. Half of the state's counties thus exhibit considerable conformity to statewide political behavior.

A third category encompasses the ten counties whose Republican percentage was aways above the statewide average, sometimes by more than ten percentiles; the list includes Brookings, Butte, Campbell, Haakon, Kingsbury, Lake, Lawrence, Lincoln, Sully, and Turner counties.

An opposing category consists of the ten counties whose Republican percentage was always below the statewide average, sometimes by more than ten percentiles; these are Aurora, Brown, Brule (always at least ten points below), Charles Mix, Davison, Day, Hanson, Marshall, Roberts and Todd.

The last category includes eleven counties whose voting behavior was irregular, sometimes above and sometimes below the statewide partisan average and sometimes by more than ten points. This list contains the names of three counties usually to be found in the strongly Republican category, Douglas, Hutchinson, and McPherson. As noted above, the 1932 election caused dramatic shifts in these counties, the Republican percentages falling as much as sixty points between 1924 and 1932.

The Precinct Vote. When one moves to the consideration of precinct voting returns, many additional meaningful conclusions become possible. Republican strength is much more apparent in the cities and towns than in the rural precincts.[6] As Table 8 shows, the city-town vote was more Republican than the rural vote in both the 1960

TABLE 8

RURAL, TOWN AND CITY VOTING PERCENTAGES, BY
SECTION, FOR PRESIDENT, 1960, AND SENATOR, 1962

Election	East River			West River·			State Total
	Rural	Town	City	Rural	Town	City	
1960 President							
Kennedy (Dem)	46.6	38.1	40.0	44.2	41.5	37.7	41.8
Nixon (Rep)	53.4	61.9	60.0	55.8	58.5	62.3	58.2
Total	100.0	100.0	100.0	100.0	100.0	100.0	100.0
1962 Senator							
McGovern (Dem)	56.0	47.2	48.6	49.5	49.3.	44.2	50.1
Bottum (Rep)	44.0	52.8	51.4	50.5	50.7	55.8	49.9
Total	100.0	100.0	100.0	100.0	100.0	100.0	100.0

Sources: 1960 data from Clem, Precinct Voting, op. cit., p. 231, and Clem, West River Voting Patterns, op. ·cit., p. 88. 1962 date from Clem, "Party Strength in Cities, Towns, and Open Country: An Investigation into South Dakota's '1962 Senatorial Election," South Dakota Municipalities, August, 1963, pp. 26-27.

presidential and 1962 senatorial elections. In the East River section, the town vote was slightly more Republican than the city vote, while west of the Missouri the city vote was considerably more Republican than the town vote.[7] Farm precincts are more variable in their voting behavior, both in terms of the percentages received by various candidates of the same party[8] and of the range of percentages received by party candidates over an extended period of time.[9] Further, the rural voting percentages vary to a greater extent from the county percentage than do the urban vote percentages.[10] As a result, with the more consistent urban vote, "changes in a county-wide partisan percentages are likely to be explained largely by fluctuations in the rural vote, which are commonly more drastic than city and town voting fluctuations."[11]

The relative Republican strength and Democratic weakness in cities and towns is further illustrated by the data in Table 9 showing the number of city, town, and rural precincts in various categories of partican victories in Presidential, Congressional, gubernatorial, and legislative elections in the period 1940-1960. Whereas 60 percent of the city precincts and 63 percent of the town precincts in the state are in the most Republican category, only 38 percent of the rural precincts qualify.

TABLE 9

PRECINCT TYPES AND PARTY STRENGTH

	Precentage of Republican Victories in Selected Major Elections, 1940-1960					
	80% & over	60-80%	40-60%	20-40%	Under 20%	All Precincts
City Precincts						
N	72	19	14	9	6	120
%	60.0	15.8	11.7	7.5	5.0	100.0
Town Precincts						
N	226	55	36	22	19	358
%	63.1	15.4	10.1	6.1	5.3	100.0
Rural Precincts						
N	489	296	227	159	122	1293
%	37.8	22.9	17.6	12.3	9.4	100.0
All Precincts						
N	788	370	276	190	147	1771
%	44.5	20.9	15.6	10.7	8.3	100.0

Sources: Data adapted from Clem, Precinct Voting, op. cit., tables 1-4, pp. 223, 226, 227, and 230, and Clem, West River Voting Patterns, op. cit., Tables 1-4, pp. 84, 85, 86, and 87.

Analysis of the precinct returns for the 1960 Presidential election allow one to categorize the cities in South Dakota in terms of their relative partisanship. In the accompanying continuum, the state's 25 cities have been placed in six categories.

The "most Republican" category includes the two cities where Nixon's percentage exceeded 70, while the "most Democratic" category includes the only two cities where Kennedy received a majority. The more moderate four categories are determined by the 65th, 60th, 55th, and 50th Republican percentiles. In a closer election, such as the 1962 Senatorial or 1964 gubernatorial races, more cities would show

Most Republican Cities				Most Democratic Cities	
Canton	Brookings	Vermillion	Yankton	Aberdeen	Sisseton
Spearfish	Belle Fourche	Lead	Mobridge	Chamberlain	Fort Pierre
	Deadwood	Pierre	Watertown	Mitchell	
	Winner	Redfield			
	Hot Springs	Madison			
		Milbank			
		Sioux Falls			
		Rapid City			
		Huron			
		Sturgis			

Democratic majorities. Still the above partisanship continuum is useful for showing the relative party support provided by each South Dakota city.

The returns from questionnaires concerning religion, ethnic origin, income, education, and length of residence in a sample of the most Republican and most Democratic precincts in the East River study resulted in a few generalized statements that bear repeating.

"The strongly Republican precincts were much more likely than the strongly Democratic to be Protestant in religion and to have a comparatively high level of both income and education. Little difference was apparent in the matter of racial background, although concentrations of Indian, French, and Bohemian groups were mentioned only for the strongly Democratic precincts. Length of residence seems to be equally prominent as a factor for both parties. . . .

"Length of residence thus appears to be the most important factor in the maintenance of a strong party loyalty of all the factors mentioned, and this holds true as much for one party as for the other." [1]

To revert again to the precinct studies, 102 of the state's precincts showed Republican majorities in every election in the period under study. Of these, 65 were east and 37 west of the Missouri. In the same period, 27 precincts showed Democratic majorities in every election. Of these, 26 were east and only one west of the Missouri.

The Presidential elections, 1940 through 1960, were investigated to determine from the two select lists discussed in the previous paragraph the most Republican and most Democratic precincts in the state. The Republican honors go to Rosenthal, a rural township lying just east of the town of Eureka in western McPherson county. Its Presidential returns for the twenty year period illustrate better than words its Republican disposition:

1940	Willkie (R)	100	99%	1952	Eisenhower (R)	70	100%
	Roosevelt (D)	1	1%		Stevenson (D)	0	0%
1944	Dewey (R)	71	100%	1956	Eisenhower (R)	55	92%
	Roosevelt (D)	0	0%		Stevenson (D)	5	8%
1948	Dewey (R)	51	100%	1960	Nixon (R)	62	98%
	Truman (D)	0	0%		Kennedy (D)	1	2%

On the Democratic side, the top most precinct is Richland, a rural township lying southwest of Kimball in south central Brule county. While not as extreme as Rosenthal in terms of Presidential partisanship, its Democratic sympathies are strong and persistent, as the figures on the top of the next page indicate.

1940	Willkie (R)	19	19%	1952	Eisenhower (R)	20	28%
	Roosevelt (D)	81	81%		Stevenson (D)	51	72%
1944	Dewey (R)	13	22%	1956	Eisenhower (R)	9	13%
	Roosevelt (D)	46	78%		Stevenson (D)	60	87%
1948	Dewey (R)	8	13%	1960	Nixon (R)	7	13%
	Truman (D)	52	87%		Kennedy (D)	49	87%

To a large extent, party strength from county to county and from precinct to precinct depends on such personal factors as racial origin, occupation, education, and so forth, and significant variations in the spread of these factors over the state usually affect the political disposition of a given area. But at the same time, it is probably true that local leadership has some impact on the party vote. The county party organizations have as one of their primary objectives the attainment of a maximum vote. In addition to the regular organization, most communities contain cell groups which work informally and more or less regularly for a particular candidate or faction. Such candidate-oriented groups are especially important in primary elections.

Issue Orientation and Personal Characteristics. While there are probably some Democrats who are more conservative than most Republicans, and some Republicans who are more liberal than most Democrats, it is evident from available survey data that most Democrats are more liberal than most Republicans. This corresponds with the general relationships among national samples of Democrats and Republicans.

Table 10 compares issue orientation with political disposition (as determined by usual voting habits). Three types of voters were identified, those who usually or always vote Republican, those whose voting habits are evenly mixed between Republican and Democratic candidates, and those who usually or always vote Democratic.

In terms of the definitions we have entered above (see Chapter IV), Democrats are consistently more liberal—that is, more willing to expand the role of government, particularly at the federal level—than are the Republicans. It is probable that all South Dakotans, Democrats and Republicans alike, are considerably less liberal and more conservative than their counterparts in the remainder of the United States, but we do not have precise comparable data with which to support this hypothesis.

A strong majority of Democrats in South Dakota would expand the government's role in the economy, while three-fourths of the Republicans would restrict or abolish such programs. More than half of the Democrats would expand or maintain the foreign aid program, while

TABLE 10

ISSUE ORIENTATION AND POLITICAL DISPOSITION

Issue	Usual Voting Habits Republican (figures	Mixed are percentages)	Democratic
Role of government in economy			
Expand programs	4	16	21
Maintain programs	21	47	68
Reduce or abolish programs	75	37	11
Foreign aid programs			
Expand programs	1	5	10
Maintain programs	11	23	42
Reduce or abolish programs	88	72	47
Voting rights of minority groups			
Strong stand by federal government	48	66	80
Leave problem to states	52	34	20

Source: Adapted from Neil M. Palmer and Alan L. Clem, "Public Opinion and Rural Electricity," (Vermillion: Opinion Survey Associates, 1964), mimeograph, pp. 116-117. The study presents the results of a 1964 survey of opinions held by a statewide sample of the adult population and is based on more than two thousand responses from all parts of the state. Inapposite replies such as "no opinion", "don't know", and "no response" are eliminated from these computations.

less than one of eight Republicans would. On civil rights, 80 per cent of the Democrats favor federal as opposed to state handling, while the Republicans are about evenly divided.

Turning to relationships between personal characteristics and political disposition (Table 11), one again finds South Dakota citizens generally conforming to national patterns. A substantially higher percentage of Republicans than of Democrats are involved in law, realty, insurance, banking, small business, medicine, and teaching. A substantially higher percentage of Democrats than of Republicans are involved in manual labor and government service.

As to education, Republicans on the whole have been exposed to more formal schooling. The percentage of persons with college and post-graduate experience is more than twice as high for Republicans as for Democrats.

Income differences appear to be less pronounced, but here again the Republicans rank somewhat higher overall, particularly in the "more than $15,000" category.

As to organizational membership, Republicans have a much higher percentage than Democrats in service clubs, Chambers of Commerce, and Masonic lodges, while Democrats have a much higher percentage

Table 11
PERSONAL CHARACTERISTICS AND POLITICAL DISPOSITION

Characteristics	Usual Voting Habits		
	Republican	Mixed	Democratic
	(figures are percentages)		
Occupation of head of household			
Law, realty, insurance, banking	12	6	5
Ranching, livestock growing	7	7	5
Farming, livestock feeding	22	28	24
Small business, merchant, etc.	14	11	8
Laborer, carpenter, etc.	14	14	20
Salesman, clerk, white-collar, etc.	5	8	3
Radio, television, journalism	1	1	3
Doctor, dentist, engineer	5	2	1
Teacher	5	5	2
Government service	7	9	14
Other	11	9	15
Organizational membership of anyone in household			
Rural Electric co-op	31	37	44
Grain co-op	17	20	21
Other co-op	2	4	8
Farmers Union	9	17	26
Cattle Feeders Association	0	1	1
Rotary, Lions, Kiwanis, etc.	16	10	6
Elks, Moose, Eagles, etc.	17	16	15
Knights of Columbus	3	5	13
Farm Bureau	4	3	2
Oil co-op	13	17	17
Dairy co-op	3	4	10
National Farmers Organization	3	4	5
National Grange	0	0	0
Stockgrowers Association	6	5	4
Chamber of Commerce	19	10	3
Masonic lodge	27	11	8

Characteristic	Usual Voting Habits		
	Republican	Mixed	Democratic
	(figures are percentages)		
Education			
No formal education	2	1	2
No higher than elementary	17	22	25
No higher than secondary	35	43	52
No higher than college (4 years)	39	26	18
College, graduate	7	8	3
Family income (annual)			
Less than $4,000	29	23	31
$4,000 to $7,999	31	44	39
$8,000 to $15,000	30	28	29
More than $15,000	10	5	1
Religious preference			
Baptist	8	4	4
Catholic	10	19	34
Congregational	10	6	4
Episcopal	4	4	2
Jewish	0	0	0
Lutheran (Missouri synod)	5	7	8
Lutheran (other)	23	26	16
Methodist	28	17	14
Presbyterian	6	7	7
Church of Christ	0	1	1
Other	5	6	7
None	1	3	3

Source: same as for Table 10.

than Republicans in rural cooperatives of all kinds, the Farmers Union, and the Knights of Columbus.

The percentage of Catholics is much higher for Democrats than for Republicans. Republicans have higher percentages than Democrats in most but not all of the Protestant denominations.

Summary. In summary, we find some variance over time and space in party strength in gubernatorial elections. In general at the county level, the Republican strongholds are: (1) the Russian-German counties of Campbell and McPherson on the North Dakota border; (2) the Lincoln-Turner-Hutchinson-Douglas corridor in the southeast; (3) the east-central area centering on Brookings and Kingsbury counties; and (4) the Black Hills counties. The Democratic strongholds are: (1) the northeastern corner of the state, including Brown, Marshall, Day, and Roberts counties; (2) the Davison-Aurora-Brule-Charles Mix angle based on the Missouri River in the south-central section; and (3) the Indian reservation area in the southwest-central section.

The counties whose Presidential voting performance conforms most closely with that of the state as a whole are Clark, Hand, Grant, Jackson, Meade, and Walworth, where the percentile differences did not exceed five points in the period 1928-1964.

At the precinct level the cities and towns are notably more Republican and less Democratic than the residual rural areas.

Those who habitually vote Democratic tend to be more liberal (that is, to favor an expanded federal role) than Republican voters on the role of the government in the economy, foreign aid, and the voting rights of minority groups.

As to personal characteristics, Republicans are more numerous than Democrats among lawyers, bankers, realtors, and businessmen, while Democrats lead in the labor and government service categories. Republicans generally have more formal education and somewhat higher incomes than Democrats. Republican membership is notably stronger than Democratic in service clubs, Chambers of Commerce, Masonic lodges, and most Protestant denominations; conversely, Democratic membership is stronger in rural cooperatives, the Farmers Union, the Knights of Columbus, and the Catholic church.

For the most part, these tendencies are in conformity with the findings of studies concerning the national and regional electorates.

ADMINISTRATIVE POLITICS: THE FOCUS OF LEADERSHIP

The Governor is generally the most visible politician in South Dakota, and whether he wishes it or not he is subject to a ceaseless flow of invitations to speak, preside, appear, or officiate which involve him in all sorts of relationships with national, state, and local officials and groups. We are chiefly interested here in the Governor's relations with his party and the voters generally, with the legislature, and with other state constitutional officers. All of these relations are to some extent controlled or conditioned by law, but the really crucial confrontations often depend more upon individual characteristics and quirks beyond the law which make the study of politics so fascinating, unpredictable, and baffling.

The state's election laws and traditions place the Governor in a position of almost complete responsibility to the people. This is a responsibility that transcends all of the state's governmental apparatus and his political party's hierarchy with which he shares most of his working hours. It has been a long time since a party organization as such seriously attempted to dictate to a Governor. The party nominee wins nomination with no party help. The party is stuck with the primary winner as its candidate, and once elected, the Governor is the obvious chief representative of his party. [1]

Party affiliation is chiefly important to the candidate for two reasons, neither of them involving any great degree of party control. In the first place, and in spite of the non-ideological basis of American and South Dakota political parties, it is apparent that many voters are attracted by the party label alone. There is a traditional political disposition at work affecting thousands of voters year in and year out. Candidates will thus avoid offending their own party or any segment thereof. Seldom in South Dakota politics do ideological matters constitute an important part of a campaign. This is not to say that there are no substantive issues, merely that the position of parties and politicians in South Dakota seems to have little to do with a consistent philosophy of government; nowhere is this fact better illustrated than in the Republican party's consistent defense of the state cement plant, an instance of state ownership of production, sometimes referred to as "socialism." [2]

The second reason why party affiliation is important to the candicate is that, through its organizational hierarchy, it collects and allocates campaign money and, to a varying extent from county to county, involves itself in electioneering. The amount of control thus exercised by the party as such is probably not great, because party officials prefer to follow set formulas and thus avoid charges of favoritism in allocating campaign money. Recently, especially in the Republican party, there have been attempts to discourage independent candidate solicitation of funds and to put the fund-raising operations entirely under party auspices.[3] This policy, if uniformly carried out, might well enhance the party's role and diminish the role of individuals and interest groups who have contributed significant sums to particular candidates, but we have no evidence yet that will reveal how firmly the policy is being or will be adhered to.

Republican and Democratic candidates and party officials rely to a differing degree on state and national party sources. The Republicans in South Dakota have long been able to attract a sizable amount of campaign contributions, which has meant that Republican candidates could afford to pay more attention to state than to national party organizations. Republican Congressmen from South Dakota have fared well enough from the GOP Congressional and Senatorial campaign committees, which have little connection with the Republican National Committee. On the other hand, South Dakota Democrats have had to depend to a greater degree than their Republican rivals on funds from outside the state, a fact that has linked South Dakota Democrats with their national organization to a greater degree than the Republicans are linked with their national organization.

The candidate for Governor, in sum, owes his nomination to the voters of his party and his election to the general voters of the state. Republican candidates may be more independent than their Democratic counterparts because it is likely that the national GOP organization imposes fewer strictures on a state enjoying such comparative fiscal and electoral prosperity.

Party control over gubernatorial candidates is lessened further by the fact that candidates can run as Independents by petition. This was a fairly common practice in South Dakota prior to the New Deal.

Gubernatorial succession in South Dakota runs to the lieutenant governor, the speaker of the House of Representatives, the president pro tempore of the Senate, the speaker pro tempore of the

House, and the secretary of state, in that order.[4] The office of Governor has never been vacant[5] and no Governor has ever been impeached.

Political careers in South Dakota have sometimes been affected by fortune. A most notable example of this was the entrance of William J. Bulow into major politics. Bulow's neighbor, Andrew Anderson, the Democratic gubernatorial candidate of 1924, was killed by a roan bull about six weeks prior to the election. The Democratic state central committee chose Bulow as the replacement.

In discussing the beginning of his political career many years later, Bulow pointed out:

"I had always been a Democrat, but for more than twenty-five years had taken no active part in party politics and was not too well acquainted over the state. I made the best campaign that I could make during the available time, and was defeated. . . .

"I attended the Democratic state convention in 1926, and that convention had no difficulty in persuading me to try for the Governorship again. Politics had gotten into my blood. I enjoyed campaigning, traveling over the state, and meeting new people.

"I always maintained that a roan bull was responsible for my political career. It was the roan bull that caused a vacancy on the Democratic ticket for the office of Governor. If there had been no vacancy my name would never have been entered on the ticket, and I never would have been elected Governor. If I had not been elected Governor I never would have been elected to the United States Senate. Full credit or blame for my career as a politician must be given to a roan bull. The bull did not act with malice aforethought; had no premeditated designs, but acted upon the spur of the moment, without contemplating results. That roan bull shaped the political future of one South Dakotan even though he did not know what he was doing."[6]

It is possible to make too much of the roles of roan bulls and other irrational forces in the origin of political careers, but the preponderance of available evidence strongly suggests that such forces are more determinant of political success in South Dakota than are the official actions of political party leaders and groups acting in their official capacities. This is especially true in the recent period when party groups as such only rarely have the power to nominate persons for the top positions on the November ballot.

The relations of the Governor and the legislature are most crucial in determining whether a governor is strong or weak. The strength of an American President is commonly measured in terms of his relations with Congress, and similar analysis will be useful here. Some Governors have exerted forceful leadership, others have played a passive role, while many have fluctuated between the two extremes.

The key formal relationship involves the partisan affiliations of the Governor and the legislative majority. Most of the time the two branches have been controlled by the same party. In the more than thirty legislative sessions since statehood, party control of the administrative and legislative branches has been split on only five occasions. In 1899, a Republican legislature confronted Populist Governor Andrew Lee, and in both 1927 and 1929 Governor Bulow had to contend with Republican legislatures. Because of a general similarity of governmental philosophy, the latter association was not difficult; but Lee had considerable trouble. [7] Partial splits occurred in 1937 and 1959 when the Democrats controlled the Senate and the Republicans the House. Both Governors involved, Republican Jensen and Democrat Herseth, served but one term. Otherwise, the Republicans controlled both the Governorship and the legislature, except in 1897 when the Populists and in 1933 and 1935 when the Democrats were in control of both branches.

The relationships between Governor and legislature, beyond mere partisanship, are more difficult to analyze because they depend on the individual characteristics of the chief executive and the more prominent legislators. To some extent, these informal relationships can be interpreted from official documents such as the Governor's messages. The Governor can recommend specific actions to alleviate current problems and can aggressively exercise his powers to force compliance; this positive approach was characteristic of such administrations as Lee's, Crawford's, Norbeck's, McMaster's, and Berry's. [8] Or he can make his recommendations and then absent himself from the decision-making process. [9]

Finally, consider the relationships between the Governor and the elected state officials serving under him, namely the lieutenant governor, secretary of state, state auditor, state treasurer, commissioner of school and public lands, superintendent of public instruction, and attorney general. [10] Though some citizens view the administrators as a sort of elective state cabinet, the comparison with the national administration cannot be accurately pursued very far. In the first place, the powers of the elective officials are not very broad, although the authors of the South Dakota Constitution "considered these positions to be the most important in the administration of state affairs."[11] None of them supervise a very large staff, not comparing in size (and for the most part not comparing in significance) to such administrative agencies as the Highway, the Game, Fish, and Parks, the Public Welfare, or the Unemployment Compensation departments.[12] In the second place, the persons involved are elected individually; they are not members of a cohesive official family and need not be in agreement with the Governor on policy matters.

The principal function of the lieutenant governor, other than being available in the event of gubernatorial vacancy, is to preside over the Senate. The secretary of state is the official record keeper, recording gubernatorial appointments, articles of incorporation and franchises, maintaining election statistics, and performing a number of similar functions. The state auditor is responsible for the payment of accounts and claims against the state, while the state treasurer is responsible for all public monies paid into the state treasury. The commissioner of school and public lands, together with the non-partisan superintendent of public instruction,[13] has responsibilities in the field of education.

The duties of the attorney general are somewhat more important than those of his colleagues. He is the chief legal officer of the state and consequently gives written opinions on questions of law submitted by other state officials; he is responsible for prosecuting or defending all actions in the Supreme Court in which the state is interested as a party; he has important responsibilities in connection with the prevention, detection, and prosecution of crime; and, as industrial commissioner for the state, he is responsible for the administration of workmen's compensation statutes and supervises the division of labor.[14]

For the most part, the lesser officials have been members of the same party as the Governor under whom they have served. The exceptions can be quickly noted, and generally they occur in conjunction with the Governor-legislature splits already noted. The Populist Governor Lee had only one Populist elected with him in 1896 and none at all two years later. Governor Bulow was the only Democratic administrator elected in 1926 and in 1928. Governor Jensen in 1936 was elected with only one other Republican, the lieutenant governor. Governor Herseth came into office after the 1958 election with four fellow Democrats and two Republicans. Complete uni-party slates resulted from the remaining 32 elections in the state's history, the Republicans being victorious 30 times and the Democrats twice (1932 and 1934).

It can be said that the Governor's relations with his presumed administrative inferiors occur on two levels. There are relations on a purely administrative level involving the more or less routine functions of the officials concerned. Beyond this, there are relations on a political level where the decisions depend to a greater extent on the discretion of the officials and where, presumably, there is more likelihood that the decisions will significantly affect the politician's future political career. This is not to say that all matters are either administrative or political. It would doubtless be possible to identify some administrative and some political aspects in any matter. But it is well to keep in mind that there are differences in the kinds of problems coming before administrative officials and that these differences will condition the responses to be made. Of great importance in the disposition of any matter is whether or not the decision will be made in such a way as to be visible to the general public. The laws of the state tend to put the administrative decision-making process on a visible basis, but often there are not the journalistic resources or the general interest necessary to develop an informed public criticism of administrative actions.

Only two of the six partisan elective administrative positions under the Governor have been significant as stepping stones to the Governorship. Six persons have moved from the lieutenant governorship to the chief executive's position, Herreid in 1901, Byrne in 1913, Norbeck in 1917, McMaster in 1921, Gunderson in 1925, and Boe in 1965. At one time in the state's history, then, it is apparent that the second position on the ballot was a crucial choice.

Four Governors had prior service as attorney general. Crawford was attorney general a decade prior to his gubernatorial term commencing in 1907, as had been Sharpe prior to his term beginning in 1943. Sharpe's two immediate successors, George Mickelson and Sigurd Anderson, each served two terms as attorney general directly prior to their terms, which began in 1947 and 1951, respectively.[15] Two other attorneys general, Buell Jones (1923-29) and Phil Saunders (1955-1959), received the Republican party's gubernatorial nomination but were defeated in the general election. The current attorney general, Frank Farrar, is generally considered to be a potential gubernatorial candidate.[16]

In earlier days, gubernatorial candidates often emerged from the party heirarchy. Crawford, Jensen, Bushfield, and Sharpe may be mentioned as examples of Governors who had previously exerted considerable direct influence in the formal party leadership. But since World War II, there has been less connection between high party position and the Governor's office. Mickelson and Anderson served as attorney general when they ran for Governor. The four most recent Governors all had been prominent legislators prior to their gubernatorial candidacies. Perhaps the Legislative Research Council, instituted in 1951, has indirectly helped legislators with latent gubernatorial ambitions by exposing them to and giving them more competent experience with general statewide problems that are the Governor's lot, as compared with the more local problems of their particular legislative constituencies.

The Roles of the Governor. The fourth article of the state's constitution defines the basic powers of the Governor. In order of importance, those powers are:
1. To take care that the laws be faithfully executed;
2. To report to and recommend action to the legislature;
3. To make appointments to and remove officials from public office;
4. To carry out certain interstate and intergovernmental functions.

Connected with the Governor's role as legislative guide is his power to call special sessions and to veto legislation. He also serves as commander-in-chief of the military and naval forces of the state, exercises the pardoning power, may require the opinion of judges of the Supreme Court, and performs a number of tasks resulting from statutory action.

But to be Governor means much more than to carry out the letter of the law. It seems more realistic to consider the roles of the Governor in more general terms, following the practice of a number of commentators on the American Presidency. Five major roles that pervade the experience of every Governor of South Dakota are these: (1) chief officer of the state and its official representative with other states and the federal government; (2) head of the administrative apparatus of state government, including more than seven thousand state employees; [17] (3) head of his political party; (4) legislative leader; and (5) guardian of the state's economy. The first two roles are broadly outlined by the constitution and statutes of the state, and they need not be dwelt on here. Comments elsewhere have, it is hoped, emphasized the author's belief that party leadership resides in the Governor's mansion (or possibly in the Senate Office Building in Washington, depending on the locus of the issue or the appointment involved). For most of the state's Governors, the best way to study their legislative leadership, or lack thereof, is through their inaugural addresses and messages and the few journalistic comments that are still available. [18] Though there has been little concern about the Governor's role in economic affairs, one is struck by the frequency with which almost every Governor has bothered himself about the condition of the state's economy, notably farm income; this is a recurring theme in the messages of Republican and Democratic, rural and urban, and progressive and conservative Governors alike.

Characteristics of the Governors. The composite South Dakota Governor is a lawyer by occupation, a Protestant, was born outside the state but educated at the University of South Dakota, is a Republican (very likely with a progressive bent), is in his early fifties at his inauguration, and resides in a small town in the eastern part of the state (see Table 12).

Of the 23 Governors that have served South Dakota, 11 have been lawyers, six have been farmers or ranchers, and the remainder have been businessmen, inventors, bankers, or engineers.

Eight were born in South Dakota, Norbeck having been the first to claim this distinction. Of the 15 born elsewhere, four came from Iowa, three from Wisconsin, two each from Norway (Lee and Anderson) and Indiana, and one each from Kansas, Nebraska, Ohio, and Vermont. This reflects the midwestern origins of the early settlers of the state.

Seven received their terminal college education at the University, while seven others attended Big Ten schools. DePauw and North Dakota State each claim one South Dakota Governor among their alumni. The remaining seven had no college education whatsoever.

Nineteen of the Governors were Republicans, three were Democrats, and one (Lee) was a Populist.

At their inauguration, two were in their sixties, eleven in their fifties, and ten in their forties. The oldest at inauguration was Green (62), the youngest Foss (40).

Twenty of South Dakota's Governors came from the eastern half of the state, while three (Berry, Jensen, and Sharpe) resided west of the Missouri river at the time of their election. Only two Governors (Foss and Boe) resided in the state's largest city, Sioux Falls, and both have served within the last ten years. The state's second city, Rapid City, has never been honored as the residence of a

TABLE 12

THE GOVERNORS OF SOUTH DAKOTA

Name	Residence	Life Span	Age at Inauguration	Years in Office	Party	Occupation	Terminal College Education
Arthur C. Mellette	Watertown	1842-1896	47	1889-1893	Rep.	Lawyer	Indiana U.
Charles H. Sheldon	Pierpont	1840-1898	53	1893-1897	Rep.	Farmer	None
Andrew E. Lee	Vermillion	1847-1934	50	1897-1901	Pop.	Businessman	None
Charles N. Herreid	Eureka	1857-1928	44	1901-1905	Rep.	Lawyer	U. of Wisconsin
Samuel H. Elrod	Clark	1856-1935	49	1905-1907	Rep.	Lawyer	DePauw U.
Coe I. Crawford	Huron	1858-1944	49	1907-1909	Rep.	Lawyer	Iowa U.
Robert S. Vessey	Wessington Springs	1858-1929	51	1909-1913	Rep.	Real Estate	None
Frank M. Byrne	Faulkton	1858-1928	55	1913-1917	Rep.	Real Estate	None
Peter Norbeck	Redfield	1870-1936	47	1917-1921	Rep.	Businessman	U. of South Dakota
William H. McMaster	Yankton	1877-1962	44	1921-1925	Rep.	Banker	Beloit College
Carl Gunderson	Mitchell	1864-1933	61	1925-1927	Rep.	Engineer	U. of South Dakota
William J. Bulow	Beresford	1869-1960	58	1927-1931	Dem.	Lawyer	U. of Michigan
Warren E. Green	Hamlin county	1869-1945	62	1931-1933	Rep.	Farmer	None
Tom Berry	Belvidere	1879-1951	54	1933-1937	Dem.	Rancher	None
Leslie Jensen	Hot Springs	1892-1964	45	1937-1939	Rep.	Lawyer	U. of South Dakota
Harlan Bushfield	Miller	1882-1948	57	1939-1943	Rep.	Lawyer	U. of Minnesota
Merrill Q. Sharpe	Kennebec	1888-1962	55	1943-1947	Rep.	Lawyer	U. of South Dakota
George T. Mickelson	Selby	1903-1965	44	1947-1951	Rep.	Lawyer	U. of South Dakota
Sigurd Anderson	Webster	1904-	47	1951-1955	Rep.	Lawyer	U. of South Dakota
Joe Foss	Sioux Falls	1915-	40	1955-1959	Rep.	Businessman	U. of South Dakota
Ralph Herseth	Houghton	1909-	50	1959-1961	Dem.	Farmer	U. of South Dakota
Archie Gubbrud	Alcester	1910-	51	1961-1965	Rep.	Farmer	North Dakota State
Nils Boe	Sioux Falls	1913-	52	1965-	Rep.	Lawyer	U. of Wisconsin

Much of the data for Governors Mellette through Anderson are taken from a table in Dalthorp, South Dakota's Governors (Sioux Falls: Midwest Beach Company, 1953) p. vi. However, Governor Byrnes occupation has been changed from "farmer" to "real estate."

Governor. Further, only five other Governors came from cities with a 1960 population of more than five thousand; these include Mellette from Watertown, Lee from Vermillion, Crawford from Huron, McMaster from Yankton, and Gunderson from Mitchell.

The foregoing paragraphs involve easy categorizations based on data that is objective and tangible. It is much more difficult, perhaps impossible, to categorize the Governors of the state as to strength or weakness. Any such categorization is and should be open to serious question and debate. There is not only a shortage of quantitative data that might assist in the measurement, there is a question of what constitutes executive strength and what constitutes executive weakness. The author, sharing what is probably a prevalent tendency, equates strength with imagination, willingness to experiment, forthrightness, and adherence to a positive philosophy of government. On these generalized bases, and restricting our judgment to a period decently removed from the contemporary, it seems that the names of Andrew Lee, Coe Crawford, Peter Norbeck, William McMaster, and George Mickelson should be placed on the list of strong Governors, with William Bulow, Tom Berry, and M. Q. Sharpe as additional possibilities. [19]

If we accept the view that South Dakota's political system operates in such a way as to progressively winnow out the weak, the corrupt, the unjust, and the inept, and to push forward the strong, the honest, the just, and the competent, then we must conclude that South Dakota's Governors have been as able a group of men as have made themselves available for the state's highest public office.

A Comparison with Other State Governors. A study of the relative amount of power potentially available to American state Governors provides a convenient basis for a summary comparison of the power of South Dakota Governors in relation to their fellow Governors. [20] Schlesinger investigated four aspects of gubernatorial discretion—namely, his tenure potential, his appointive power, his budget power, and his veto power.

As to tenure, the longer the term and the fewer restrictions on reelection, the more power the Governor was thought to possess. Maximum strength was accorded to the Governors of states such as California, Illinois, Montana, New York, and Wyoming, where the gubernatorial term is four years and there is no restraint on re-election. South Dakota and New Mexico, with their two-year term and one re-election limitation, rated in the lowest category. [21]

As to the appointment power, a detailed formula based on the Governor's power to name officials in 16 fields produced for South Dakota a comparatively low index of 39 (based on a maximum potential of 100). This compares with 79 for Tennessee (the highest index) and 15 for Colorado (the lowest). Neighboring states had indices both above and below South Dakota's: Minnesota, 51; Iowa, 49; Nebraska, 46; Wyoming, 42; Montana, 39; Wisconsin, 38; and North Dakota, 18. [22]

As to budget control, the Governor's full responsibility in South Dakota gave him the highest rating, also earned by 28 other Governors. [23]

As to the veto power, South Dakota's Governor ranked in the second strongest category. [24]

In summary, the Schlesinger study gives the South Dakota Governor a combined power index of 11 (based on a maximum potential of 20), compared to a national median of 13, a high of 19 for New York, and a low of 7 for Mississippi, South Carolina, Texas, and North Dakota. Among other neighboring states, these combined indices were recorded: Wyoming and Montana, 16; Minnesota, 14; and Iowa, Nebraska, and Wisconsin, 12. [25] By these standards, the office of Governor in South Dakota is slightly weaker than in neighboring states with the exception of North Dakota.

Summary. The political system in South Dakota is such that the Governor of the state is controlled only to a small extent by officials in the party hierarchy. Neither party has enough full time professional staff members of sufficient experience, prestige, and connections to exert a strong controlling influence on the actions of the Governor. In some cases, such controls may be exerted by representatives of certain interest groups, particularly where campaign funds and similar sanctions are involved.

The state's election laws, in intent and in fact, do make the Governor amenable to popular control. He is nominated and elected by popular vote; the party is not expected to support a particular candidate in its primary election, and it is expected to throw its resources behind its primary victor in the subsequent general election. Thus its role in candidate choice is limited.

Some party control may be exerted through the party's nomination to fill the elective positions subordinate to the Governor. However, the interests of party harmony are usually such that the Governor will have a voice in the selection of candidates. Further, except for the lieutenant governor and the attorney general, the elective positions do not wield a significant amount of power and it is not likely that the decisions of these officials will often be such as to embarrass or endanger the Governor's position.

In the Governor's office, and perhaps more so in his person, is located the main hope for political leadership in South Dakota. The Governor is dependent on the general public for his position to a greater degree than in most American states; therefore in his negotiations with legislators elected by parts of the state or with individuals and groups representing special interests in the state, he might well be particularly aware of the potentialities of his role as an active leader for the statewide public.

Unquestionably, the Governor of South Dakota does have a large amount of administrative confusion and duplication to overcome in his efforts to urge state government to act. We have mentioned a few conditions that limit his ability to govern the state's administrative bureaucracy. But burdensome and frustrating as the limitations may be, they can be overcome by diligent application of the Governor's great and largely untapped reservoir of personal, party, public, and constitutional power.

The continuing test of the South Dakota executive, and perhaps of South Dakota government generally, will be whether the Governor can lift himself above the personal ambitions and bureaucratic struggles beneath him and, in the pure clear air above, define the larger problems facing the state and address himself to formulating and achieving their solution.

VII

LEGISLATIVE POLITICS: EVERY MAN A POLICY-MAKER

The legislative branch of government is the formal arena for the process of making state policy. This is in keeping with the general theory of representative, democratic government and with American practice as well. Laws are made by a body of persons elected by and responsible to the people over whom the government has jurisdiction.

Powers of the Legislature. The legislative power in South Dakota is vested in a bicameral legislature composed of a Senate whose membership may not exceed 35 and a House of Representatives whose membership may not exceed 75.[1] In comparison with the first section of Article I of the U. S. Federal Constitution, which vests in Congress only "all legislative powers herein granted," the South Dakota Constitution appears at first to grant very general and inclusive powers to the legislature. The legislative article states that the "legislative power of the state shall be vested in a legisature. . . ."[2]

However, this general grant of legislative power was soon delimited by the adoption in 1898 of a constitutional amendment reserving to the people the right to initiate and to refer laws. Occasions on which laws have been initiated by or referred to the people have been fairly frequent (see Table 13), and as a consequence the real legislative powers of the legislature itself have been somewhat weakened. Use was made of the initiative and referendum more frequently in the early decades, but the three referred laws of 1964 testify to the continuing vitality of direct legislation in South Dakota. Many of the most controversial measures, such as Congressional redistricting, local liquor option, primary election legislation, establishment of state-owned banks, and the creation or dissolution of various state agencies or institutions, have involved the use of the state's initiative and referendum machinery.[3]

The state constitution confers on the legislators powers, rights, and duties (such as privilege from arrest and privilege of debate) that are comparable with those specified in the Federal Constitution and in most state constitutional documents. The constitution also

Table 13

POPULAR PARTICIPATION IN THE LEGISLATIVE PROCESS:
FREQUENCY OF INITIATED AND REFERRED LAWS IN
SOUTH DAKOTA

Years	Initiated Laws			Referred Laws		
	Voted on	Passed	% Passed	Voted on	Defeated	% Defeated
1900-1908	1	0	0.0	3	0	0.0
1910-1918	7	2	28.6	10	7	70.0
1920-1928	6	0	0.0	6	6	100.0
1930-1938	0	0	-	5	3	60.0
1940-1948	1	0	0.0	4	3	75.0
1950-1958	1	0	0.0	1	1	100.0
1960-1964	0	0	-	3	3	100.0
	16	2	12.5	32	23	71.9

Source: Adapted from Clem, South Dakota Political Almanac, op.
cit., pp. 36-40, supplemented by data from the 1962 and 1964 elections.

reflects an interest in keeping the legislative process both democratic
and open.[4] Bills may originate in either house. Ordinarily, laws
take effect three months after the adjournment of the session at
which they were passed; they go into effect immediately on the
Governor's signature if an emergency clause is affixed to the bill,
which requires a two-thirds vote of all members. This means that
a party majority in excess of two-thirds is significant to the progress
of the majority party's legislative program and to the legislative
strategy of the minority party as well. Given the present number
of members of each house, the emergency clause would require the
support of 24 of the 35 senators and 50 of the 75 representatives.
The majority party, in each case Republican, has held such a two-
thirds edge 10 times in the Senate and 11 times in the House of
Representatives in the 14 sessions since 1938, when the present
membership limits were established.

The constitution, following the broad phrasing of the grant of
legislative power in Section I noted above, goes on to place a number
of restrictions on the legislative power. The legislature may not
enact any "private or special laws" involving divorce, the location
of a county seat, the regulation of county or township affairs, the
incorporation of cities, towns, and villages, the authorization of
ferries across streams wholly within the state, and a number of other
matters.[5] Further, the legislature may not release or extinguish
the indebtedness, liability, or obligation of any corporation, individual, or municipality; it may not authorize any game of chance,

lottery, or gift enterprise "for any purpose whatever;"[7] and it may not
delegate to any special commission, private corporation or association, any power to make municipal improvements, levy taxes, select
a capital site, or perform any municipal functions.[8]

A problem commonly identified with American state legislatures
is the lack of knowledge and experience of members. Few if any
legislators depend on their legislative salary as a major source of
income, and therefore few legislators can devote full-time to their
official business. As one legislator put it in a recent letter to the
author: "I was so inadequately prepared to vote on some of the
issues that I had to seek information. It is difficult to get the
necessary, unbiased, and correct information in such a short time. . . .
I read that article in the past *Reader's Digest*, 'Our Horse and Buggy
Legislatures.' I believe the title was very true and shockingly correct.
We are just not well enough informed."

If knowledge is power, then it is evident that the amateur, part-time
status of most South Dakota legislators deprives them of some
of their effectiveness and authority by limiting the amount of time
they can spend locating and evaluating facts and opinions bearing
on the current legislative business.[9] Groups and lobbyists are quick
to make use of this informational vacuum, but evidently neither
political party has considered attempting to fill the gap. The legislature itself has had, since 1951, a Legislative Research Council
which has organized and published interim studies and which
serves in a reference and drafting capacity during legislative sessions.

Comments by a recent director of the Council bear repetition
here in a discussion of legislative powers.

"The legislature ought to work harder to avoid 'selling itself short.'
It is the first among equals in the three branches of government:
the executive must have legislative acts to administer, and the
courts must have laws to adjudicate. It has been my experience,
however, that the legislature has not had sufficient pride in many
instances, and because of its failure to realize its own importance,
many good plans have been laid aside, and the work of the legislature and the Council has suffered.

"Related to the point above is the necessity, in my opinion, for
the legislature to operate independently of executive direction when
it appears that the legislative approach is superior to the
executive's."[10]

Composition and Terms. Terms of both state Senators and Representatives are set at two years. Until 1963, the legislature met on a biennial basis, beginning the session in early January of the year following the biennial general election in November. In 1962, a constitutional amendment was approved which provided for annual legislative sessions, the first of which was held in 1964.

Prior to 1963, the legislative session was limited to 60 legislative days by the constitution. The 1962 amendment provided for a session in odd-numbered years of 45 legislative days and a second session in even-numbered years lasting 30 legislative days. Thus the total number of sitting days allowed the legislature under the new dispensation is considerably increased over the old, although each session is still severely limited as to the number of days it may remain in session.

George M. Platt has reached several conclusions from the brief experience the legislature has had with annual sessions: "One possible deduction is that the session of 1964 was worth six million dollars to the state, i.e., funds were made available for new or expanded programs deemed necessary to satisfy recognized needs. South Dakota legislators can now maintain much closer communications with the requirements and desires of the people. Certainly a large corporation would not invoke a year's delay in making six million dollars worth of necessary internal improvements merely because its board of directors had not been scheduled to meet." [11]

Platt also commented that the demands placed upon individuals by the annual sessions might cause some changes in legislative personnel and that the annual sessions will have the effect of spreading the legislative load more evenly over the months.

Although members of both houses are elected from districts, fewer than half represent single-member districts. In the lower house, only 17 of the 75 representatives are elected from single-member districts under the new 1965 reapportionment law. The situation is different in the Senate, where 26 of the 35 members come from single-member districts. The multi-member districts result because the legislature has respected county boundaries in drawing legislative districts. Therefore Minnehaha county, which elects nine Representatives and four Senators, elects them all on an at-large basis with each party presenting a slate of candidates to fill all the seats. Similarly, Pennington county elects six Representatives and three Senators, and Brown county elects four Representatives and two Senators. In sum, this practice tends to help the Republican party more than the Democratic, since Sioux Falls and Rapid

City are Republican bulwarks which regularly produce all-Republican delegations for the state legislature.

In the event of vacancy in a legislative seat, the Governor has the power to appoint a replacement.[12] Under the constitution, both houses must apportion their membership "in accordance with the last federal census prior to the legislative session at which such apportionment shall be made."[13] The constitution also states that reapportionment shall take place in the session following the publication of each federal census "and at no other time."[14] But the latter restriction did not prevent the 1965 legislature from enacting a general legislative reapportionment of both houses in conformity to the U.S. Supreme Court's series of decisions.[15]

Subsequent to the constitutional apportionment of legislative seats, and prior to 1960, the legislature passed major reapportionment acts in 1891, 1897, 1907, 1911, 1917, and 1937. That the legislature in the mid-thirties was able to drastically reduce the number of legislative seats may have been due to the fact that the New Deal elections had resulted in an unusually large percentage of Democratic legislators with little tenure. Less extensive adjustments were made in 1903 and 1951. The general pattern of these reapportionments has been to reflect the increasing population in the West River area (see Table 14).

The 1965 reapportionment is generally quite equitable in both houses.[16] Only four districts, two in the House and two in the Senate, have populations which deviate by more than 15 percent from the norms of 9,074 for House districts and 19,443 for Senate districts.[17]

Characteristics of Legislators. The basic characteristic of a legislator is, of course, that he is sufficiently interested in government and politics to devote a great deal of time, often at considerable financial sacrifice, to taking part in the solution of public problems. Perhaps for most legislators, political ambition is an important part of their motivation for legislative service. The status of state legislator itself is one of some honor, and membership in the legislature exposes the legislator to many politicians and groups who concern themselves with locating and enticing potential candidates for the Governorship.

Of the state's twenty-three Governors, fourteen had previous service in the legislature. A fifteenth, Herreid, moved up from the position of lieutenant governor and so had served as presiding office of the state Senate. Nine consecutive Governors, from Crawford through Berry (1907-1937), came out of the legislative ranks. The four most

TABLE 14

SECTIONAL REPRESENTATION IN THE LEGISLATURE,
1889-1967

Law of[a]	Senate Seats				House Seats			
	SE	NE	W	Total	SE	NE	W	Total
1889	20	20	5	45	53	57	14	124
1891	20	19	4	43	37	36	10	83
1897	20	19	6	45	40	36	11	87
1907	19	19	7	45	46	44	14	104
1911	17	18	10	45	36	42	24	102
1937	13	13	9	35	28	28	19	75
1965	13	13	9	35	29	26	20	75

[a] The original apportionment (1889) was contained in the
Constitution. In addition to the laws indicated here, minor reapportionments of legislative seats occurred in 1903, 1951, and
1961. The 1965 law for the first time produced districts that
crossed sectional boundaries (the Missouri River and the Brook-
ings-Moody County boundary extended West to the Missouri). Split
districts are awarded to the section having the majority of the
population.

recent Governors, Foss, Herseth, Gubbrud, and Boe, were former
legislators. Three (Mickelson, Gubbrud, and Boe) had been speakers
of the House.

Compared to the fourteen who had served in the legislature, six
Governors had been lieutenant governor (five of these had also served
in the legislature), four had served as attorney general, five had held
elective county office, and one (Lee) had been a mayor.[18] The
legislature is widely perceived as a stepping-stone to greater political
power.

Table 15, concerning all members of the legislature serving in the
period 1935-1965, categorizes the legislators in terms of (a) occupational background, (b) religious affiliation, (c) terminal educational
institution, (d) age at entrance, (e) number of terms served, (f)
section of the state, and (g) size of community. The data is broken
down by party.

Occupation. The number of legislators with an agricultural background is striking. Nearly half of the legislators in the recent period
have come from the farms and ranches of the state. The second
largest group is business. Law and real estate banking have a sub-

stantial number among the legislature. One would expect that a state legislature with such agricultural and business domination would be markedly unresponsive to suggestions for change and growth in state government, a supposition which would find much support. Considering the property basis of the state's tax structure, it is not surprising that the legislature has not enthusiastically endorsed expensive state programs.

As long as the state legislature is not a full-time, full-pay job, it is not likely that the occupational background of those who have the time to serve will change.

Table 15 shows that farmers and ranchers constitute a much larger portion of Democratic members than of Republican. Just as Democrats are more numerous among rural than among city voters, so are they more numerous among rural than among city legislators. The ratio of businessmen is about equal for the two parties, but in both law and real estate-banking the Republican ratio is much higher. Persons from the field of education are more numerous in the Democratic contingent than in the Republican.

Religious Affiliation. Fewer than half of the legislators indicated their religious preference, but of those who did, the Lutherans and Methodists together constitute slightly more than half. Trailing in order are Presbyterians, Congregationalists, Roman Catholics, and Episcopalians. There is a Protestant bias, then, which is perhaps insignificant because of the very size of the Protestant majority. From the standpoint of party, the Catholics are notably stronger among Democrats than Republicans, while the Methodists and Presbyterians are slightly stronger on the Democratic side. Conversely, the ratio of Lutherans, Congregationalists, and Episcopalians is higher among Republican legislators than Democratic.

Terminal Education. Almost half of the legislators attended a four-year college. Half of these took their terminal college work in the state, with ten percent finishing their formal education at the University, seven percent at the agricultural school at Brookings, and eight percent at smaller colleges. As a group, the Republicans received considerably more formal education. Fifty-two percent of the Republicans attended college, compared to only 37 percent for the Democrats. Notably higher percentages of Republicans than Democrats are to be found among University of South Dakota graduates and graduates of colleges outside the state.

TABLE 15

PERSONAL CHARACTERISTICS OF LEGISLATORS, 1935-1965

	Republican N	%	Democrat N	%	Total N	%
Occupation						
Agriculture	184	36	101	55	285	41
Business	140	28	44	24	184	27
Law	71	14	10	5	81	12
Real Estate, banking	62	12	8	4	70	10
Journalism	15	3	3	2	18	3
Education	6	1	7	4	13	2
Public Service	8	2	3	2	11	2
Healing Arts	12	2	3	2	15	2
Other, DK, NA	9	2	4	2	13	2
Totals	507	100	183	100	690	101
Religion						
Lutheran	68	13	22	12	90	13
Methodist	40	8	19	10	59	9
Catholic	11	2	20	11	31	4
Congregational	29	6	4	2	33	5
Presbyterian	26	5	12	7	38	6
Episcopalian	14	3	2	1	16	2
Baptist	4	1	0	0	4	1
Other	18	4	5	3	23	3
DK, NA	297	59	99	54	396	57
Totals	507	101	183	100	690	100
Age at Entrance						
Less than 35	37	7	17	9	54	8
35-39	53	10	21	11	74	11
40-44	67	13	21	11	88	13
45-49	77	15	34	19	111	16
50-54	74	15	23	13	97	14
55-59	69	14	30	16	99	14
60-64	60	12	18	10	78	11
65 & over	52	10	14	8	66	10
DK, NA	18	4	5	3	23	3
Totals	507	100	183	100	690	100

	Republican N	%	Democrat N	%	Total N	%
Terminal Education						
USD	61	12	10	5	71	10
SDSU(Brookings)	35	7	10	5	45	7
Other SD College	40	8	14	8	54	8
Other College	128	25	35	19	163	24
High School	102	20	39	21	141	20
Grade School	59	12	48	26	107	16
Other, DK, NA	82	16	27	15	109	16
Totals	507	100	183	99	690	101
Terms Served						
1	149	29	72	39	221	32
2	161	32	49	27	210	30
3	76	15	28	15	104	15
4	59	12	20	11	79	11
5	32	6	7	4	39	6
6	12	2	2	1	14	2
7	7	1	2	1	9	1
8	4	1	0	0	4	1
9 or more	7	1	3	2	10	1
Totals	507	99	183	100	690	99
Section						
East	364	72	153	84	517	75
West	143	28	30	16	173	25
Totals	507	100	183	100	690	100
Community Size						
City over 25,000	48	10	3	2	51	7
City 2,500-24,999	98	19	38	21	136	20
Town under 2,500	176	35	45	25	221	32
Rural	185	36	97	53	282	41
Totals	507	100	183	101	690	100

Source: Compiled from biographical sketches in various editions of the South Dakota Legislative Manual, 1935-1965.

Age at Entrance. The median age-at-entrance category is 50-54, but the spread is quite even in all categories, ranging between eight for the youngest category and 16 for the 45-49 group. There is a tendency for Democrats to be elected at an earlier age than their Republican colleagues.

Terms Served. Well over half of the legislators served two terms or less, and only five percent served more than five terms. Seniority does not necessarily or automatically enhance the power of a legislator in South Dakota, although there is little question that legislative experience is useful to the veteran legislator. A much higher percentage of Democrats than Republicans served only one term, while the Republicans generally are more numerous in the categories of longer tenure.

Section. The breakdown of legislators between East and West is precisely that of the state's population as a whole; there are three East River legislators for every one West River legislator. This is a reflection of the sectional equitability of South Dakota's legislative apportionment over the years. Relative to their total numbers, Democrats are more numerous east of the Missouri and Republicans to the west.

Community Size. The rural community is the one which is best represented, in terms of numbers at least, in the legislature. The ratio (41) of rural residents is the same as that of agriculture in the occupational breakdown discussed above. More than half of the legislators come from cities and towns with populations less than 25,000. Only seven percent have been elected to represent the 16 percent of the state's population residing in the two largest cities, Sioux Falls and Rapid City. This is a dirct reflection of the underrepresentation suffered by these two cities prior to the 1965 and (more especially) the 1961 reapportionments. On the basis of parties, the Republican ratio is much higher than the Democratic in the big city and small town categories, while the Democratic ratio is much higher than the Republican in the rural category. The GOP ratio of 19 and the Democratic ratio of 21 for cities between 2,500 and 25,000 population are roughly equivalent.

Over the entire period, 507 (73 percent) of the 690 legislators were Republicans and 183 (27 percent) were Democrats.

In an attempt to come to grips with the implications and ramifications of personal characteristics among the legislators, a survey was conducted among members of the 1965 legislature asking them to respond to questions involving political ideology, role perception, and major sources of pressure on the legislative process.[19] Responses in these three areas were tabulated in such a way as to allow conclusions as to the chamber, party, section, and size of community of the legislators.

On the ideology question, the Democratic group rates most liberal and the Republican group most conservative. Thus of all the variables, that of party seems most crucial in determining political ideology. If the perfect liberal index were 100, the perfect conservative index zero, and the moderate index 50, the Democrats would show a group index of 47 and the Republicans 24. The fact that Democratic legislators fall short of the halfway mark on the liberal scale should not be overlooked. Almost as crucial in ideology is the variable of section. The liberal index of eastern legislators is 37, of western legislators 26. Neither size of community nor chamber seems to make much difference; none of the ratios in these categories is higher than 35 nor lower than 32. The overall ideological index of the 1965 legislature, based on the members' own evaluation, is 34.

More variations are found when role perception is considered. Here, state Representatives are more likely to describe themselves as "delegates" or "politicos", while state Senators are more likely to describe themselves as "trustees".[20] This is perhaps due to the fact that there are fewer state Senators than Representatives; their larger districts may result in a feeling of less direct contact with their constituents. As to party, a larger proportion of Democrats than of Republicans describe themselves as "politicos." On a sectional basis, "delegates" are more numerous in the eastern part of the state, and "politicos" are more numerous in the west. As to size of community, "politicos" are more numerous among city and town legislators, while "trustees" and "delegates" are more numerous among the rural group.

In the general view of the responding legislators, their entire constituency and their own personal predispositions and attitudes are by far the most important sources of pressure or influence on their actions. Each of the 110 legislators was asked by the author in the summer of 1965 to distribute seven points as he saw fit among the seven suggested pressure sources. The most often cited pressure source was the "entire constituency," given a score of 119 by the 55 respondents. "Personal predispositions and attitudes" received 108 points, followed in order by "internal legislative influences," 44 points; "political party," 42 points; "interest groups in the constituency," 26 points; "state administrative agencies," also 26 points; and "colleagues from the same area," 20 points. The relatively low importance attached to the political party as a source of pressure seems especially significant.[21]

Some notable variations in the perception of pressure sources should be mentioned. Representatives were more aware of constituency sources than were Senators, while the latter were more aware of party sources and their own predispositions. Republicans were more aware than Democrats of the state administrative agencies, probably due largely to the fact that the state administration in 1965 was in the hands of the Republican party. Democrats were more aware than Republicans of their own predispositions. Westerners were more aware than easterners of pressures from the constituency, probably a reflection of the self-consciousness of the West River area in South Dakota politics. Easterners were more aware of their own personal predispositions than were their western colleagues.

Legislative Voting Behavior. Unlike the legislatures of some other states, that of South Dakota has been subjected to little scientific analysis of the voting behavior of its members. This section of the study is therefore something of a pioneering effort, designed to ascertain what generalizations can be made about patterns and degrees of cohesion among the various categories of legislators.

The first question to be dealt with is the relationship of roll call results to party control. Do close voting divisions occur more frequently when the party division is close? The four legislative sessions in the period 1953-1959 provide a satisfactory setting in which to investigate this question. In 1953, the GOP controlled all 35 Senate seats and 73 of 75 House seats, an almost unanimous situation. In succeeding sessions, the Democrats steadily reduced the Republican margin, until in 1959 it was able to establish control of the Senate.[22]

Now, in these four sessions in the two chambers, what happened to the ratio of close voting divisions? As Table 16 shows, there is considerable variation in the percentage of close voting divisions in the Senate as the party control ratio changes. In the upper chamber, the ratio of close voting divisions was as low as it ever was when one party held all the seats (1953). There was very little change in the ratio of close voting divisions when the minority party gained six Senate seats in 1955. But in 1957, when the Senate had an almost even 18 to 17 party split, the ratio of close voting divisions increased

TABLE 16

VOTING DIVISIONS IN THE SOUTH DAKOTA LEGISLATURE,
1953-1959

Senate Session	Party Division Rep. Dem.		Unanimous Votes (%)	Votes with 1-9 Dissents (%)	Votes with 10 or more Dissents (%)	Total Roll Call Votes (N)
1953	35	9	73	20	8	684
1955	29	6	73	21	5	600
1957	18	17	57	32	10	706
1959	15	20	57	29	14	662

House of Representatives Session	Party Divison Rep. Dem.		Unanimous Votes (%)	Votes with 1-19 Dissents (%)	Votes with 20 or more Dissents (%)	Total Roll Call Votes (N)
1953	73	2	53	34	13	688
1955	57	18	52	38	10	628
1957	48	27	55	35	10	724
1959	43	32	50	38	12	655

Source: Compiled from the Journals of the South Dakota Senate and House of Representatives, 1953, 1955, 1957, and 1959. Percentages are rounded.

sharply. There was a further increase in the most divisive categories in the 1959 Senate when the Democratic party took control.

In the larger chamber the division ratios from session to session were remarkably consistent, being lowest in 1959 when the chamber was most closely contested between the parties. But it should be noted that the minority party never came very close to control of the House in the sessions investigated here. In general, as the party division approached equality, the ratio of close voting divisions has tended to increase, suggesting that in at least some degree divisive votes are a function of close party competition.

A more searching inquiry into the consequences of party control on roll call voting behavior can be made by grouping legislators into categories based on their party, section, community size type, and occupation, separating the voting data by session. In Table 16, all recorded roll call votes were the subject of analysis; here, the concern is limited to about 15 selected roll call votes in each session on significant issues where there was substantial voting opposition to the matter at issue. The percentages for all legislators vary within only six percentiles, reaching a high agreement index of 64 in the 1955 Senate and a low of 58 in the 1957 Senate when the party division was closest. Republican majoritarian voting in the House was weakest in 1957 when their majority was greatest; similarly, Republican majoritarianism in the Senate was strongest in 1957 when their majority was most closely challenged. When the Democrats won control of the Senate in 1959, they promptly began to vote with the majority much more frequently than they had in the past. In other words, members of the majority party in a closely divided chamber voted on the majority side of an issue more frequently than did members of a minority party or of an overwhelming majority party.[28]

The other categories bear some further investigation. Variations by section are similar to the party variations just discussed. The westerners showed a consistently if only slightly higher majoritarian voting index until the 1959 Senate, when they for the first time fell below the 50 percent mark. This suggests that the Democratic majority of that year was perceived by the westerners to be attuned to eastern South Dakota interests; in the same session, the easterners scored their highest majoritarian voting ratio.

The community size categories show generally that the legislators from cities and towns are much more likely to vote on the majority side than are the rural legislators. The only significant exception again occurred in the 1959 Senate, when the city legislators' ratio skidded to 47 and that of the small town legislators to 49.

As to occupation, the five non-agricultural categories are above the average in terms of the percentage of times their members voted with the majority, while the farm-and-ranch legislators never exceeded, and only once equalled (in the 1959 Senate), the overall majoritarian voting index. Thus, while the rural areas are abundantly represented in terms of numbers in the South Dakota legislature, as has been shown, the rural legislators were less frequently found on the winning side on divisive, significant roll call votes. When the chips were down, the rural representatives have been able to call the shots less frequently than have the business and professional legislators from the cities and towns of the state.

Thus far, this discussion of legislative voting behavior has concerned itself with the voting majority of the entire chamber without regard to how a majority of members of the two parties voted. Let us now turn our attention to the 1965 legislature and consider the question of how often each legislator voted with the majority of his own party. In the first place, as Table 17 shows, party voting was not very strong by external standards in the 1965 legislature. On just over half of the 48 selected significant and divisive roll calls, the ratio of legislators voting with their party majority was greater than 80. This suggests that party membership is not terribly crucial in determining how a legislator will vote. Party loyalty was notably higher in the House than in the Senate. In terms of specific issues, party loyalty was at its lowest in the Senate on release of oil and gas leases, township road assessment,

TABLE 17

PARTY LOYALTY ON SIGNIFICANT, DIVISIVE ROLL CALLS, 1965 LEGISLATURE, BY CHAMBER

Number of Roll Calls in Various Party Loyalty Percentile Categories

	0-19%	20-39%	40-59%	60-79%	80% & over	Total Selected Roll Calls
House	2	4	2	3	13	24
Senate	1	4	10	2	7	24
Totals	3	8	12	5	20	48

Source: Compiled from the Journals of the South Dakota Senate and House of Representatives, 1965.

county home rule, and school transportation; and in the House on school tuition rates, municipal welfare payments, motor vehicle licenses, sales tax, and delinquent personal property taxes. Greatest party loyalty tended to occur on more general statewide issues such as election registration, sales tax rate, university buildings, Congressional reapportionment, and profits of the state cement plant.[24]

There are no extreme variations when party loyalty is analyzed on the basis of several obvious categories (Table 18). The party loyalty quotient is higher for Republicans than Democrats in the House, but higher for Democrats than Republicans in the Senate. In both chambers, the party loyalty quotient is higher among westerners than easterners. Community size makes little difference in the Senate, but more in the House, where city legislators have a higher overall party loyalty quotient than rural legislators, who in turn rate higher than small town legislators in terms of party loyalty.

The occupational results are irregular; in the House, lawyers and bankers and real estate men rank highest in party loyalty, while in the Senate the latter category ranks lower even than the agricultural category.

On an individual basis, the highest party loyalty quotient (100) was recorded by two Democrats, Senator C. E. Boehrs of Eagle Butte and Representative Dale Gullickson of Lake Preston. In both chambers, Republicans recorded the lowest party loyalty quotients, Senator G. Robert Bartron of Watertown (63) and Representative John Buehler of Emery (54).

A national survey of American state legislatures now more than ten years old indicates that party cohesion in South Dakota is only moder-

TABLE 18

PARTY LOYALTY IN THE 1965 SOUTH DAKOTA
LEGISLATURE FOR VARIOUS GROUPS, BY CHAMBER

Party	House		Senate	
	N	PLQ	·N	PLQ
Republican	45	86	19	78
Democrat	30	80	16	82
Section				
East	56	83	25	78
West	19	85	10	84
Community Size				
City	24	87	12	81
Town	16	81	7	80
Rural	35	83	16	80
Occupation				
Agriculture	37	83	15	80
Business	17	84	9	84
Lawyer	7	89	7	76
Banking & real estate	8	87	3	84
Public Service	4	81	-	-
Other Professional	2	86	1	63

Note: PLQ indicates "Party Loyalty Quotient," that is,
the percentage of roll calls on which the legislator voted
in agreement with the majority of members of his party. The
figures in the table above are average PLQs for all legislators
in the various categories.

Source: Compiled from the Journals of the South Dakota
Senate and House of Representatives, 1965.

ately strong. This summary placed South Dakota in the same category
with New Hampshire, Vermont, and Wisconsin. In the neighboring
state of North Dakota, which like South Dakota was categorized as a
modified one-party state, strong factional cohesion was located within
the dominant party, but party cohesion there was described as "weak".[25]
The same study described pressure politics in the South Dakota legislature as "moderate", with local issues producing "moderate" cohesion
and national issues "weak" cohesion. For all the states, the Zeller
survey found pressure politics to be the most frequently cited substi-
tute for party divisions in the legislature, followed in order by local
issues, intraparty factionalism, rural/urban splits, sectionalism, combi-
nations on particular issues, conservative/liberal splits, administration/
anti-administration splits, and personalities.[26]

Summary. Two things militate against the unilateral exercise of power by the legislature itself in making laws for South Dakota. In the first place, the people have in the initiative and referendum processes reserved considerable legislative discretion to themselves. As noted above, many of the most significant legislative acts in the state's history have been accomplished by the general voting citizens of the state rather than by the legislative branch of state government. Secondly, the comparative shortness of the legislative sessions has made its machinations less visible to the general public and thus lessened the legislature's role as the locus of public pressure on the poicy-making process.

This latter limitation is increased by the comparative lack of sophistication of the South Dakota press and by the comparative geographical isolation of the capital in Pierre from the state's population, educational, and economic centers. Even though the sessions have recently been placed on an annual basis, the limitation to 75 legislative days over the two-year period militates against the full and proper development of public interest in and involvement with the legislative process.

As the behaviorial investigations have demonstrated, party affiliation is not the crucial determinant of voting patterns in the legislature. Perhaps this is to be expected where partisan politics are non-ideological and somewhat removed from national issues and politics. This divorcement between national and state politics is not necessarily a bad thing, but it does have implications on the responsibilities of the legislature as a representative body. If the voters are only vaguely informed with respect to national issues and candidates, how much less are they informed as to the situations at the state and local level? When compared with the interest generated by the concurrent Presidential, gubernatorial, and Congressional elections, the typical legislative campaign in South Dakota is almost invisible. Few if any questions are asked of the legislative candidates, either by the party whose voters nominate him, by the press, or by the voters who evaluate him and his opponent in November. A small percentage of the people develop real awareness of the legislature. The personalities and issues are so local that they receive little attention outside the immediate constituency or in the news media.

Legislators are elected from small districts to serve in the legislative chambers in Pierre; they are to represent the interests of their locality and, at the same time, to take part in the process of setting state policy. Party officials are generally unwilling (and perhaps unable) to exert control in the selection of their local legislative candidate, and this inevitably reinforces the legislator's impression that he is in fact a free agent. The controls that exist on the selection of the legislator are generally not such as will affect his crucial actions in the legislative corridors, committee rooms, and chambers far away in Pierre. In this respect, the state legislator is similar to the four Congressmen elected by the voters of South Dakota to represent their interests in Washington. But Congressmen may behave more in line with the thinking of their constituents than do legislators simply because the state press gives more attention to those who serve in Washington than to those who serve in Pierre. This comparative lack of systematic and authoritative review of and control over the legislator is one obvious reason for the relatively low degree of party cohesion in the South Dakota legislature.

VIII

CONGRESSIONAL POLITICS: THE WASHINGTON SCENE

So much of a Congressman's attention and energy is focused on Washington and the national political scene that he stands apart in state politics.[1] Yet at the same time he cannot afford to leave the shortest section of his political fences at home in poor repair, for his continuance in office depends on a distressingly frequent vote of approval from his constituents. In discussing Congressional politics, therefore, the observer should keep both the Washington and South Dakota political fields within his vision if he is to adequately cover the subject. Even though the two fields are intimately related, it is helpful to separate them for the purpose of organizing the present inquiry.

Our first concern will be comparatively elementary, emphasizing the constituency point of view and the personal characteristics of South Dakotans who have served in the American Congress. Later, this chapter will concentrate on the Washington environment, studying the role of South Dakota Congressmen in the national policy-making process and their relative ideological orientations.

South Dakotans in Congress. Evidence suggests that Congress is the pinnacle of a South Dakota political career. Whereas many prominent politicians holding elective office under the state have sought Congressional office, no South Dakotan once in the Congress has ever left the U. S. Senate or House for the purpose of seeking political office in the state. Once a South Dakotan has reached Congress, his principal political objective has been to stay there.

The pre-eminence of Congress in the minds of South Dakota politicians can be tested by inquiring into the termination of their Congressional careers. Nineteen have been defeated for re-election — five (Representative Lucas and Senators Moody, Pettigrew, Kittredge, and Gamble) in party conventions or in legislative elections, six in party primary elections, (Representatives Hall and Dillon and Senators Crawford, Sterling, Bulow, and Gurney) and eight (Representatives Kelley, Knowles, Gandy, Christopherson, Williamson, Werner, and Lovre and Senator McMaster) in general elections. Five (Representative Parker and Senators Kyle, Norbeck, Bushfield, and Case) died in office. Twelve retired from office voluntarily. In this latter category are three Representatives who successfully sought election to the Senate (Gamble, Mundt, and Case) and three other Representatives who were unsuccessful in Senate bids (Burke, Hildebrandt, and McGovern). The remaining Congressmen who retired voluntarily were Representatives Royal Johnson, Gifford, Jolley, Pickler, and Martin and Senator Edwin Johnson.

Three South Dakota Congressmen, Crawford, Philo Hall, and Royal Johnson, had served as attorney general of the state prior to their Congressional service. Five moved to the U. S. Senate directly from the Governor's mansion — Crawford in 1908, Norbeck in 1920, McMaster in 1924, Bulow in 1930, and Bushfield in 1942. Four other Governors unsuccessfully attempted to win election to the Senate—Berry in both 1938 and 1942, Jensen in 1938, and Anderson and Foss, who were formal candidates for the Republican nomination in 1962 following the death of Senator Case. Four persons, Gamble, Case, Mundt, and McGovern, moved to the Senate from the House of Representatives; as noted earlier, McGovern was defeated by Mundt in 1960 but was successful in his 1962 Senate bid.

A characteristic of South Dakota's modern Congressional delegation is that it has had little previous experience in elective positions. While in the earlier period the state's Congressmen commonly ran for Congress after service in prominent political positions in the state, three of the four members of the state's present delegation (Mundt, McGovern, and Reifel) never ran for another elective office.

Actions of many state officials have been conditioned in part by their ambitions for Congressional office.[2] Relations between national and state officials have sometimes been strained by the potential rivalry of the individuals concerned, perhaps most notably the relations between Governor Bulow and Senator McMaster prior to 1930 and those between Governors Anderson, Foss, and Boe on the one hand and Senator Mundt on the other more recently. In such situations, the Governor has some obvious advantages and disadvantages. On the positive side, the Governor is closer to the press and the citizens of the state, not only geographically but in terms of the issues he resolves. On the negative side, the same geographical and political propinquity can work to the Governor's disadvantage; his decisions are more visible to the journalists and voters of the state and therefore potentially more damaging to himself. The effect of this seems to be, on occasion, to discourage forceful acts by the Governor and by other state officials. In these same terms, Congressmen are encouraged to

TABLE 19

MEMBERS OF THE U.S. HOUSE OF REPRESENTATIVES FROM SOUTH DAKOTA, 1889-1967

Name	Party	Life Span	House Service	Age at Entrance	Occupation	Terminal Formal Education	Residence	District
O.S. Gifford	Rep	1842-1913	1889-1891	47	law	Beloit	Canton	AL
J.A. Pickler	Rep	1844-1910	1889-1897	45	law	Michigan	Faulkton	AL
John J. Jolley	Rep	1840-1926	1891-1893	51	law	Eastman Bus. College	Vermillion	AL
William V. Lucas	Rep	1835-1921	1893-1895	58	journalism	high school	Hot Springs	AL
Robert J. Gamble	Rep	1851-1924	1895-1897 1899-1901	44	law	Lawrence	Yankton	AL
John E. Kelley	Pop	1853-1941	1897-1899	44	journalism	high school	Flandreau	AL
Freeman Knowles	Pop	1846-1910	1897-1899	51	journalism	high school	Deadwood	AL
Charles H. Burke	Rep	1861-1944	1899-1907 1909-1915	38	law	high school	Pierre	2nd AL
Eben W. Martin	Rep	1855-1932	1901-1907 1909-1915	46	law	Michigan	Deadwood	AL 3rd
Philo Hall	Rep	1865-1938	1907-1909	42	law	high school	Brookings	AL
William H. Parker	Rep	1847-1908	1907-1908	60	law	George Washington U.	Deadwood	AL
Charles H. Dillon	Rep	1853-1929	1913-1919	60	law	Indiana	Yankton	1st
Harry L. Gandy	Dem	1881-1957	1915-1921	34	journalism	Tri-State College	Rapid City	3rd
Royal C. Johnson	Rep	1882-1939	1915-1933	33	law	U. of South Dakota	Aberdeen	2nd
C.A. Christopherson	Rep	1871-1951	1919-1933	48	law	Sioux Falls Bus. C.	Sioux Falls	1st
William Williamson	Rep	1875-	1921-1933	46	law	U. of South Dakota	Oacoma	3rd
Fred H. Hildebrandt	Dem	1874-1956	1933-1939	59	labor	high school	Watertown	1st
Theo B. Werner	Dem	1892-	1933-1937	41	journalism	high school	Rapid City	2nd
Francis H. Case	Rep	1896-1962	1937-1951	41	journalism	Northwestern	Custer	2nd
Karl E. Mundt	Rep	1900-	1939-1949	39	teaching	Columbia	Madison	1st
Harold O. Lovre	Rep	1904-	1949-1957	45	law	U. of South Dakota	Watertown	1st
E. Y. Berry	Rep	1902-	1951-	49	journalism	U. of South Dakota	McLaughlin	2nd
George S. McGovern	Dem	1922-	1957-1961	35	teaching	Northwestern	Mitchell	1st
Ben Reifel	Rep	1906-	1961-	55	civil service	Harvard	Aberdeen	1st

Source: Biographical Directory of the American Congress, 1774-1961, (Washington: Government Printing Office, 1961).

Note: This table does not include John R. Gamble, who was elected in 1890 but died before taking his seat.

TABLE 20

MEMBERS OF THE U. S. SENATE FROM SOUTH DAKOTA, 1889-1967

Name	Party	Life Span	Senate Service	Age at Entrance	Occupation	Terminal Formal Education	Residence
Gideon C. Moody	Rep	1832-1904	1889-1891	57	law	high school	Deadwood
Richard F. Pettigrew	Rep	1848-1926	1889-1901	41	law	Wisconsin	Sioux Falls
James H. Kyle	Pop	1854-1901	1891-1901	37	clergy	Oberlin	Aberdeen
Robert J. Gamble	Rep	1851-1924	1901-1913	50	law	Lawrence	Yankton
Alfred B. Kittredge	Rep	1861-1911	1901-1909	40	law	Yale	Sioux Falls
Coe I. Crawford	Rep.	1858-1944	1909-1915	51	law	Iowa	Huron
Thomas Sterling	Rep	1851-1930	1913-1925	62	law	Illinois Wesleyan	Vermillion
Edwin S. Johnson	Dem	1857-1933	1915-1921	58	law	high school	Platte
Peter Norbeck	Rep	1870-1936	1921-1936	51	business	U. of So. Dak.	Redfield
William H. McMaster	Rep	1877-1962	1925-1931	48	banking	Beloit	Yankton
William J. Bulow	Dem	1869-1960	1931-1943	62	law	Michigan	Beresford
J. Chandler Gurney	Rep	1896-	1939-1951	43	business	high school	Yankton
Harlan J. Bushfield	Rep	1882-1948	1943-1948	61	law	Minnesota	Miller
Karl E. Mundt	Rep	1900-	1949-	49	teaching	Columbia	Madison
Francis H. Case	Rep	1896-1962	1951-1962	55	journalism	Northwestern	Custer
George S. McGovern	Dem	1922-	1963-	41	teaching	Northwestern	Mitchell

Source: Biographical Directory of the American Congress, 1774-1961, (Washington: Government Printing Office, 1961).

Note: This table includes only those persons elected to regular terms. Thus excluded are three persons appointed by the governor to fill vacancies (Herbert Hitchcock, 1937-1938, Vera C. Bushfield, 1948, and Joseph H. Bottum, 1962) and one person elected for a two-month term (Gladys Pyle, 1938).

act more positively since this is the most likely method of convincing the federal government to expand its programs in the state.

Representatives from the eastern and western districts are generally cooperative and agreeable with one another for the simple reason that they are not likely to become rivals for the same position. Relations between Representatives and Senators, however, can become as touchy as those between Senators and Governors, again because of the potential for direct political rivalry in the future. There is a tendency for the state's Representatives to feel inferior to the Senators and to follow their lead, even though South Dakota is one of the few states whose Senate and House delegations are of equal size. The principal reason for this is probably that year in and year out the Senators generally have more Congressional seniority and national prestige than do the Representatives.

Perhaps the closest involvement between Congressmen and state political party officials comes with the allocation of campaign funds. It is in this matter that the Congressmen feel most urgently the need to keep the folks at home happy. In a sense, recent efforts to regularize the collection and allocation of these funds is traceable to a feeling that the Congressmen should be held more strictly accountable to the party.

Congressmen naturally act as something of a go-between in negotiations involving federal and state governments and federal and state party organs. This has been true even though the state's Presidential nominating delegations have not on several recent occasions included members of the Congressional delegation. Though the three Republicans in Congress were not members of the 1964 delegation in San Francisco, they met regularly with the delegates there and Mundt and members of his staff were particularly active in keeping the channels of communication open between the Goldwater camp and the South Dakota delegation.

Relations between Congressmen and local officials and pressure groups vary widely depending on party affiliation, occupational background, and ideology.

Personal Characteristics. What kinds of people have the voters elected to represent them in Washington? The typical member of Congress from South Dakota was in his forties when first elected, had some college education outside the state, was a lawyer, and came from a city or town.

Twenty-four South Dakotans have served in the U.S. House of

Representatives.[3] Of these 24, 10 served one or two terms, six served three or four terms, and eight served five terms or more. The average tenure in office has been 7.33 years. Extended tenure for South Dakota Representatives has occurred in three periods. The first period began at the turn of the century and lasted until the beginning of World War I; the incumbents for most of this period, except for the two Progressive Republicans nominated by the Crawford-dominated Republican convention of 1906, were Charles Burke of Pierre and Eben Martin of Deadwood. The second period ran from World War I until the 1932 election, when two Republicans were defeated and the third, Royal Johnson, voluntarily retired on the occasion of the state's loss of one of its Congressional seats; the incumbents for this period were Johnson of Aberdeen, C. A. Christopherson of Sioux Falls, and William Williamson of Oacoma. The third period began in the late 'thirties, when the Republicans returned to power, and lasted until the mid-fifties when Democrat George McGovern was elected. The incumbents for the first part of this period were Francis Case of Custer and Karl Mundt of Madison. When they moved on to the Senate in 1951 and 1949 respectively, they were replaced by E. Y. Berry of McLaughlin and Harold Lovre of Watertown.

Five of the 24 Representatives were in their thirties when first elected, 12 were in their forties, and seven were over 50. Johnson was the youngest at first election, 33, and William Parker of Deadwood and Charles Dillon of Yankton the oldest, 60.

As to education, four received their terminal work at the University of South Dakota, 12 at colleges outside the state, and eight did not pursue their formal education beyond high school.[4]

Thirteen of the state's Representatives were lawyers by occupation and seven were newspapermen. Two (Mundt and McGovern) were college professors, one (Reifel) a federal civil servant, and one (Hildebrandt) a railroad workman.

Fifteen of the 24 Representatives resided in the eastern half of the state, nine in the West River area. Nineteen came from cities with a population in excess of 2,500 and five from smaller towns. Of the nineteen city residents, two Democrats (Gandy and Werner) were from Rapid City and one Republican (Christopherson) from Sioux Falls.

Sixteen South Dakotans have been elected to regular U.S. Senate terms.[5] Of these, Mundt has been elected four times and Norbeck three times; seven were elected twice, and seven were elected once. The average tenure in office for Senators has been 9.75 years.[6]

Of the 16 Senators, one (Kyle) was first elected in his thirties, six were first elected in their forties, six in their fifties, and three in their sixties. The oldest at election were Sterling and Bulow, both 62.

Only one Senator received his terminal college education in the state, and that was Norbeck who attended the University. Thirteen others attended college outside the state, and two (Johnson and Gurney) completed their formal education at the high school level.

By occupation, eight Senators were lawyers, two (Johnson and Mc-Master) were in banking, two (Norbeck and Gurney) were business-men, two (Mundt and McGovern again) were college professors ', one (Kyle) was a clergyman, and one (Case) was a newspaperman.

Fourteen Senators were residents of the eastern half of the state, only two coming from the West River area. This East River senatorial dominance may have been the result of a sort of informal political agreement, since from 1932 until the 1965 redistricting, the sparsely populated West River area elected one of the state's two representatives; when the Republican state central committee nominated Bottum for the Senate following the death of Case in 1962, Bottum's supporters argued with effect that the West River area was traditionally accorded one of the Senate seats. However, the "tradition" actually extended no farther back than Case's own service. The only other West River Senator had been Moody, so that for a span of 60 years, from 1891 to 1951, both South Dakota Senators had been residents of the eastern half of the state.

As to size of community, twelve Senators came from cities with 1960 populations of more than 2,500 and the remaining four came from smaller towns. Sioux Falls was the residence of two early Republican Senators, Pettigrew and Kittredge. Three Senators (Gamble, McMaster, and Gurney) lived in Yankton.

The Senators have a longer average tenure by two years and are four years older on the average; the average age-at-entrance for South Dakota Senators is 50.4 years, and for Representatives 46.3 years. A higher ratio of Senators are college-educated; the ratio is seven-eighths for Senators and two-thirds for Representatives. Law is the profession for most of both groups; a comparatively large number of Representatives were newspapermen, while in comparative terms a large number of Senators were bankers or businessmen.

Concerning residence, as noted above, the sectional arrangement is more equitable with respect to population for Representatives than for Senators. For both groups, the urban characteristic is strong. No South Dakotan primarily concerned with agriculture as a vocation or living on a farm or ranch has ever been elected to serve in the

Congress! In this respect the Congressional delegation is different from the group of men who have served as Governors, for in the latter group are a number of farmers and ranchers (see Chapter VI, and Table 12 above). On the other hand, the paucity of residents of the state's two largest cities, Sioux Falls and Rapid City, is notable for the Congressional delegation and for the inhabitants of the Governor's mansion as well.

Of the state's 23 Governors, five later served in Congress. In the past generation, the cycle of gubernatorial and Senatorial terms has not always encouraged an outgoing Governor to consider running for Congress. As a matter of fact, the last time that a Governor moved directly to Congress was in 1942 when Bushfield defeated ex-Governor Berry, who had in turn defeated the incumbent Democrat, Senator Bulow, earlier in the year. Aside from Bushfield and Bulow, the others to serve as both Governor and Senator were Crawford, Norbeck, and McMaster. Governor Foss, a popular figure, after his two terms in 1958 challenged Congressman McGovern for the First District seat, but was unsuccessful. Other recent Governors either did not express interest in Congressional service or were diverted by Presidential appointments to federal positions; Herseth and Gubbrud fell into the former category, Mickelson and Anderson into the latter.

Congressional Committees. The committee assignments held by South Dakota Congressmen have generally reflected the interests of the middle west. The state held several committee chairmanships in the period prior to the Congressional reorganization of 1946 which drastically reduced the number of standing committees. In the earlier period, Senators held as many as ten standing committee assignments, as Senator Sterling did in the 64th Congress. In the modern period, the average number of committee assignments in the Senate is less than five, with minority members generally assuming a heavier burden because of the necessity of getting some minority party representation on every standing committee.

South Dakota assignments have been heavily weighted toward domestic problems such as agriculture, reclamation, resources, Indians, and transportation. Several South Dakotans held assignments to committees on Indian Affairs, Public Lands, Indian Depredations, Railroads, Improvement of the Missouri River, Transportation Routes to the Seaboard, Irrigation and Reclamation of Arid Lands, Forest Reservation and Protection of Game, and Mines and Mining.

Probably the most significant of the committee chairmanships held by South Dakota Congressmen have been Norbeck's six-year chairmanship of the prestigious Senate Banking and Currency committee, Bulow's ten-year chairmanship of the Senate Civil Service committee, and Gurney's two-year chairmanship of the Senate Armed Services committee. Most of the chairmanships in the earlier period, when there was a much larger number of Congressional committees, were comparatively unimportant.

The state's present Senators have never held a major committee chairmanship. Mundt served for 12 years on the Senate Agriculture and Forestry committee but left that assignment when offered a position on the Foreign Relations committee in 1965. He also serves on the Appropriations and Government Operations committees, having been the ranking Republican member of the latter since 1957. McGovern, comparatively new in the Senate, in 1966 ranked sixth of ten Democrats on the Agriculture and Forestry committee and ninth of eleven Democrats on the Interior and Insular Affairs committee. Needless to say, in this period of national Democratic supremacy, it is more difficult for a Democrat to acquire a strong committee assignment in the first place or to ascend the ladder to a committee chairmanship subsequently. Then too, promotion comes faster on the lesser committees. Case, for example, was first assigned to the District of Columbia committee in the 82nd Congress and served as its Chairman in the 83rd Congress in the first two years of the Eisenhower administration. On the other hand, Mundt was first appointed to the Appropriations committee in the 83rd Congress and was at that time the ninth-ranking of 12 Republican members. Since then he has been on the minority side and in the 89th Congress had advanced to the third position among nine Republicans. In the 90th Congress, with the retirement of Senator Leverett Saltonstall of Massachusetts, Mundt became the second-ranking Republican.

While Mundt has never served as chairman of a standing committee, three appointments deserve mention. In 1948, in the last months of his service in the House of Representatives, he was acting chairman of the Committee on Un-American Activities during most of the Alger Hiss investigations. Congressman Parnell Thomas of New Jersey, the chairman at the beginning of the 80th Congress, had been removed by committee members who felt that questionable financial dealings involving his Congressional office made it inappropriate for Thomas to serve. As mentioned in Chapter I, Mundt was also chairman of another key investigating committee, the select committee of the Senate which conducted the "Army-McCarthy" hearings in 1954. Finally, Mundt was also chairman of the Alexander Hamilton Bicentennial Commission; he had introduced the bill to organize the commemorative activities and it may have seemed appropriate for a Republican to chair the remembrance of the great Federalist.

A number of Senators have served on important committees and have thus been in a position to play a crucial role in national policy formulation. Pettigrew, Gamble, Norbeck, Hitchcock, Gurney, and Mundt have served on the powerful Appropriations committee. Seven (Crawford, Johnson, Norbeck, Bulow, Bushfield, Mundt, and McGovern) have served on the Agriculture and Forestry committee. Gurney and Mundt served on Foreign Relations, Bushfield on Finance, and Norbeck on Naval Affairs. In addition to these important assignments, there have been some relatively insignificant ones, such as Ventilation and Acoustics, Investigation of the Condition of the Potomac River Front at Washington, and Interoceanic Canals (of which Kittredge was chairman).

Fewer South Dakotans on the House side have served as committee chairmen, but a goodly number of Representatives have been members of important committees. Representatives Pickler, Gamble, Kelley, Gandy, Williamson, Werner, Case, Mundt, and Berry served on the Interior and Insular Affairs committee, or comparable committees in the earlier period. Four (Jolley, Lovre, McGovern, and Reifel), served with the Agriculture committee, and three (Burke, Martin, and Dillon) were members of the Interstate and Foreign Commerce committee. Mundt and Berry have served with the Foreign Affairs committee, Case and Reifel with the Appropriations committee, and Christopherson with the Judiciary committee.

South Dakotans and National Policy-Making. Although South Dakota policies have not produced a person who has achieved as much national attention as Bryan or Norris of Nebraska, Stassen or Humphrey of Minnesota, Wheeler or Mansfield of Montana, or even Langer of North Dakota,[3] members of the state's Congressional delegation have at times played leading roles in certain specific policy matters. A basic reason for this lack of national leadership may be related to the formal democratization and socialization of the South Dakota polity resulting from the Populist and Progressive periods. The initiative and referendum and the direct primary have tended to discourage small group control of political offices. State ownership and regulation of many enterprises have made less crucial the issues with which it has been called upon to deal. Another basic reason may simply be the consequences of a small population. The major positive thrust of South Dakota politics on the nation was contained in the tempestuous Populist agitations of the 1890's and the Progressive and pacifist movements of the World War I era. This brief generation also encompassed the period in which the state constituted a significant part of the nation's population growth. Rural recession followed immediately upon the Great War and discouraged immigration into South Dakota, a situation which in turn tended to weaken the state's political and economic vigor.

South Dakota has not produced powerful national spokesmen. Senators Kyle and Pettigrew, the former a Populist and the latter a Republican, were something of mavericks, and both virtually reversed their party allegiances in their second terms.[9] Both earned rather modest reputations in Washington. Their successors, Republican Stalwarts Robert Gamble and Alfred Kittredge, are chiefly remembered for their long and bitter struggles over patronage matters, which distressed both Presidents Roosevelt and Taft.[10] When Progressive Republican Coe Crawford replaced Kittredge in 1909, he and Gamble quickly found themselves at odds over the fight to expel Senator William Lorimer of Illinois on the grounds that his election in 1908 was fraudulent.[11] This was but one aspect of the continuing rupture within the Republican party caused by the long-standing feud between the Stalwart and Progressive factions. The problem finally caused the defeat of several prominent Republicans of both sides. Gamble was defeated in the 1912 primary by Republican Thomas Sterling. But two years later the Stalwarts gained revenge when they successfully backed U. S. Representative Charles Burke, who had served as GOP whip in the House, against Crawford in the latter's bid for a second term in 1914. Crawford in turn urged the defeat of Burke and thus helped to secure the November election of Democrat Edwin Johnson.[12]

Peter Norbeck's long Senate service placed him in the public spotlight on a number of occasions. He was a close associate of many of the leading Progressives, including Norris and Hiram Johnson of California.[13] A recognized leader in conservation matters, Norbeck once attempted to invoke cloture during Senate debate on migratory bird refuges legislation.[14] He was a chief leader in the fight to establish the Mt. Rushmore memorial and to develop the Black Hills and Badlands of western South Dakota.[15] He was similarly interested in conservation programs all over the United States and Alaska, and worked mightily for the establishment of Teton National Park in Wyoming.[16] Throughout the 'twenties, Norbeck was also a leader in midwestern Republican attempts to ameliorate the effects of the farm recession.

Norbeck was probably the most effective spokesman South Dakota ever had in Washington. His "strength and influence in the Senate reached its highest peak during the Seventy-second Congress (1931-1933)".[17] There, in the waning months of the old order just prior to the advent of Franklin Roosevelt's "New Deal," he was chairman of the Senate Banking and Currency committee and supervised its well-publicized investigations of the stock market and the banking and insurance industries. He took to the radio networks twice in the spring of 1932 and as a result attracted much comment from all parts of the country. Though the investigations were criticized at times by both sides, reformers generally calling for more speed and dispatch and the vested interests calling for more careful consideration, he carried the matter through. The investigations, particularly effective after Norbeck's appointment of Ferdinand Pecora as chief counsel for the committee in January of 1933, eventually formed the basis for federal regulation in the Securities Act of 1933, the Securities and Exchange Act of 1934, and the Public Utilities Holding Company Act of 1935.[18]

Norbeck's protege, William McMaster, in his one Senate term attracted considerable attention when he carried by a vote of 54-34 a resolution to lower tariffs over the vigorous opposition of Senator Reed Smoot of Utah.[19]

Bulow's two Senate terms were most noteworthy for his long chairmanship of the Civil Service committee. As a pre-1932 Democratic Senator, Bulow was in a promising position to exert national leadership, but his Senate service was chiefly notable for obstructionism. He cheerfully "incurred the displeasure of the New Deal administration"[20] and, after supporting Roosevelt in 1932 and 1936, turned away from the New Deal as a self-confessed isolationist.[21] His defection from FDR was an issue in his defeat by Tom Berry in the 1942 Democratic primary.

Gurney, as we have seen, chaired the Armed Services committee during the 80th Congress. He generally supported President Truman's postwar foreign aid policy, and his defeat by Representative Case in the 1950 Republican primary election was widely interpreted as a blow to Truman's position.[22]

At least one maneuver in Case's long Congressional career has attracted scholarly attention. This occurred in 1946 when Case's proposal to deal with industrial and labor disputes received a rule from the Rules committee without consideration by the Education and Labor committee. "The haste with which the Rules committee acted was matched only by the decisive vote by which the House passed the rule, 258 to 114. This was the only case in twenty years when the committee reported a rule which a legislative committee had not requested." [23] This is an isolated instance of South Dakota influence, and Case's success was probably chiefly due to general Congressional support for the proposal and not any inherent influence possessed by Case or his state.

In the contemporary period, South Dakota Republicans in Congress have been generally conservative and its one Democratic Congressman, George McGovern, has been vocally liberal. McGovern received a considerable amount of national attention as a member of President Kennedy's administration, where he served as Food for Peace director after his unsuccessful attempt to defeat Karl Mundt in 1960 and prior to his successful Senate bid against Joe Bottum in 1962. McGovern in 1965 found himself discussed on front pages all over the nation when he attacked President Johnson's foreign policy with respect to the Far East and Caribbean areas. [24]

In the sum, it seems fair to say that South Dakota Congressmen, despite a few isolated instances of national leadership, have never cut a really large swath in Congressional deliberations, certainly not of a dimension to compare with the activities of several Congressmen from neighboring states.

Congressmen and the Folks at Home. Influence and prestige are related to the degree to which a representative speaks for a large number of people in his constituency and in the nation at large. It is safest for Congressmen to speak for their constituents rather than for the nation if there appears to be a difference in attitudes in the two groups. The positive influence of many recent Republican Congressmen from South Dakota has been limited by the governmental philosophy they have adopted which calls for less government activity and involvement in the social and economic order, particularly at the national level. Illustrative of the conservative statements are the following remarks by Representative Berry:

"I have steadfastly opposed the drift toward a bigger more powerful centralized government in Washington . . .

"I have favored those programs which would result in less federal interference in local affairs . . .

"Where fiscal matters are concerned, I have fought for balanced budgets and reduction in the national debt, opposing the philosophy now in vogue of "planned deficits" during a time of relative peace and normal economic conditions . . .

"As long as I continue as a Member of Congress, I shall fight to preserve constitutional government, the strengthening of the free enterprise system, more business in government and less government in business, stabilization of the dollar through balanced budgets, and return of government into the hands of the people instead of the hands of the Washington politicians where it has been drifting for the past 30 years." [25]

To a considerable extent, the public statements of Congressmen tend to reflect their committee assignments, which in turn usually have some connection with their personal background or with the economy of their district. Congressmen use their regular newsletters to keep the citizens at home informed on Washington developments with particular reference to the peculiar interests of the constituency. Thus it is not surprising to find, as Table 21 shows, that the most popular topic in the South Dakota Congressional newsletters has been agriculture. Committee assignments and philosophy explain the high ranking given fiscal affairs. Foreign policy rates high with Mundt and Berry, who are both members of their chamber's foreign policy committee, and with McGovern as an outspoken critic of recent U.S. policy. Reifel has ignored the topic in his newsletter. Mundt and McGovern have mentioned defense policy many times. Mundt and Reifel have mentioned natural resources more often than have their colleagues. McGovern is the only one who has not dwelt on the topic of civil rights, and Mundt is the only one who has publicly worried in his newsletters about the threat of Communism.

The careful reader of Congressional newsletters and similar public relations devices can gain a fuller understanding of the Congressman's philosophy and objectives. Possibly the topics discussed are ones which his readers will be most interested in; certainly, the topics will be discussed in such a way as to enhance the figure of the author. Newsletters provide insights on congressional personality. Mundt's breezy "Your Washington and You" columns suggest nothing so much as informal daily columns on the sports page; the Senator, obviously an old pro who knows his way around Washington, dashes off short vignettes about committee meetings and conferences he has attended and usually adds a more extended essay on a patriotic theme, sometimes quoting clergy, professors, or prominent public officials at length. He was as apt to chide President Eisenhower as he more recently

TABLE 21

TOPICS OF NEWSLETTERS ISSUED BY CONGRESSMEN, JAN. 1, 1963 - JULY 1, 1965

	Agriculture	Fiscal Policy	Foreign Policy	Welfare	Defence	Natural Resources	Civil Rights	Education	Communism	Labor	Transportation	Business Regulation	Total
Senators													
Mundt	14	7	13	2	7	8	3	1	5	-	1	2	63
McGovern	7	-	4	1	7	1	-	4	-	-	-	-	24
Representatives													
Berry	10	13	8	8	2	2	2	1	-	1	-	-	47
Reifel	19	8	-	9	3	5	5	4	-	3	1	-	57
Totals	50	28	25	20	19	16	10	10	5	4	2	2	191

Note: Excluded from computation are several items that did not lend themselves to this issue-by-issue categorization, particularly the listing of office visitors or travel itineraries and references to good citizenship, patriotism, etc. It should be noted that some items are treated at considerable length, up to 500 words, while some are passed off with as few as 50 words. And note also that this table does not indicate which side of the issue was presented by the congressmen. The purpose of the table is to show the frequency with which each congressman felt called upon to discuss a particular topic with his constituents.

Source: Mimeographed or processed newsletters issued by the respective congressional offices and mailed to interested South Dakota citizens and news outlets. This compilation was made by the author from newsletters filed in the Governmental Research Bureau library at the University of South Dakota.

chided Presidents Kennedy and Johnson; but through it all there is little if any rancor and most of the characters in his sketches are reasonable and likeable, if perhaps somewhat fuzzy-minded, gentlemen. McGovern's "Senator George McGovern Reports" columns are more serious, giving fuller attention to fewer topics. The tone of Reifel's column, despite its catchy title of "Reifel Shots", is closer to McGovern's than to Mundt's in the sense that it gives more details of the congressional procedures involved in the policies being discussed. The newsletters of Mundt, McGovern, and Reifel are comparatively non-partisan and non-ideological; Berry on the other hand is more inclined to criticize the administration and the bureaucracy.

This persistent negativism makes Berry's newsletter unique among the South Dakota Congressional reports.

Congressional Behavior. Systematic analysis of the behavior of public officials can reveal much that is of use not only to the political scientist but also to the general citizen and the officials themselves. But there are a number of limitations in behavioral research that should condition the methods of analysis and may restrict somewhat the utility and significance of the numerical indices produced. When a given act made by a number of officials is given the identical numerical value, it is being forced into a tight compartment with the apparent assumption that the action was performed by all officials for the same reasons and represented the same values for all officials behaving in that way.

For example, we may look at the roll call votes "yea" and "nay" on an appropriations bill providing five million dollars in military aid to a far eastern nation faced with overt Communist aggression. We find that Representatives A and B vote in favor of the appropriation and that Representatives Y and Z vote against it. Yet A may well be a conservative midwestern Republican and B a conservative southern Democrat who generally oppose foreign aid and who supported this particular appropriation out of an overriding desire to strengthen any regime confronted by Communist encroachment. On the other side, Y may be a liberal midwestern Democrat and Z a liberal eastern Republican who generally support foreign aid but oppose this measure because the regime involved does not represent to them any significant improvement over the aggressors. In short, on the specific issue involved in any roll call vote, different ideological or party orientations may dictate identical votes while similar ideological or party loyalties may dictate different votes.

Admitting these and similar methodological difficulties, behaviorists still insist that meaningful and confident conclusions can be made if sufficient care is employed in choosing the roll call votes or other recorded actions on which to base the analysis, and if a sufficient number of cases are studied. In the previous chapter, because so little has been published on the behavior of South Dakota legislators, the author had to choose the roll calls to be used for analysis of legislative politics. In the present chapter's discussion of congressional behavior, however, the observer can draw on a number of studies made by national interest groups. Obviously such groups have special interests to serve; they conduct and publish their analyses for the main purpose of identifying "friends" and "enemies" in the Congress so that the organization and its members can have more concrete information on the Congressmen who favor and oppose the group's position. This bias does not hinder the present purpose of determining the degree to which South Dakota Congressmen adhere to the position of liberal (AFL-CIO Committee on Political Education, National Farmers Union) and conservative (Americans for Constitutional Action, American Farm Bureau Federation) non-party groups in American politics.

The evidence available on recent members of Congress shows that South Dakota Republicans have been consistently oriented on the conservative side of the ideological continuum. The one South Dakota Democrat in Congress has been consistently liberal. Table 22 gives index scores for South Dakotans who have served in the Congress since 1950. The Republicans vote in general agreement with the Farm Bureau and ACA and in general disagreement with the Farmers Union and COPE; McGovern's behavior is reversed.

TABLE 22

AGREEMENT INDICES FOR SOUTH DAKOTANS IN CONGRESS, 1950-1964

	COPE 1947-1964	NFU 1959-1960	NFU 1961	NFU 1963-1964	AFBF 1963-1964	ACA 1963-1964
Mundt	14	61	24	28	64	70
McGovern	97	96	--	94	0	2
Case	19	52	18	--	--	--
Berry	7	30	20	4	100	100
Lovre	17	--	--	--	--	--
Reifel	9	--	29	25	88	81

Figures show the percentage of votes cast in the period indicated by each Congressman in agreement with the position of the group at the head of the column.

Sources: COPE---How Your Senators and Representatives Voted, 1963-1964 (Washington: AFL-CIO Committee on Political Education, n.d.). NFU---"Selected Roll Call Votes" for sessions indicated, (mimeographed), National Farmers Union, Washington, D. C., September 15, 1960, November 1, 1961, December 31, 1963, and October 1, 1964. AFBF---The American Farm Bureau Federation's Official Newsletter, September 14 and 21, 1964, pp. 146-148, 151-152. ACA---ACA-Index, Second Session, 88th Congress, 1964: An Analysis of the Voting Record of Each Member in the Congress of the United States, (Washington: Americans for Constitutional Action, 1964).

Berry has been consistently more "conservative" (that is, in agreement with the Farm Bureau and ACA) than his House colleagues. Mundt and Case were quite close in their voting patterns, with Case slightly less in agreement than Mundt with the liberal side in the indices given in Table 22. As one would expect, there is a large difference in the indices listed for Mundt and McGovern. The Senate indices are consistently more liberal than those for the House, but it should be noted that the various indices are computed from different votes in the two chambers and thus conclusions as to ideological differences between chambers should be made carefully if at all.

ACA data have been adapted by the author to allow comparisons with congressmen from other parts of the nation. The Senate data covering the period 1955-1964 show that Mundt, while in the top one-fifth in terms of conservatism for all senators, is at the midway point in conservatism for Senate Republicans. Extremes for Republicans are Tower of Texas (100) and Goldwater of Arizona (98) on the ultra-conservative side, and Case of New Jersey (30) on the liberal side. Mundt's conservative index of 75 is identical with that of his party leader, Dirksen of Illinois. McGovern, with an ACA index of 2, is in the midst of a large Democratic liberal group; 11 other Democrats score zero or one to "out-liberal" the South Dakotan. The Democrats, it should be noted, show an even greater ideological range than the GOP, with Byrd of Virginia at 93 and four others higher than Mundt's index of 75.

The differential of 73 between the Mundt and McGovern indices is great, but the senators of six other states have even greater differentials. The largest differential (93) is claimed jointly by Texas and Wyoming. The states of Ohio and South Carolina both had index differentials of 60, in spite of the fact that in 1964 both pairs of senators were Democrats. The median index differential for the 50 states (19) was recorded by Connecticut.

The House of Representatives data show substantially the same thing. On a national basis, most Republicans are more conservative than most Democrats, and vice versa. Again, Democrats show greater variation, with members in all ideological score categories, while the Republicans have no members in the three most liberal groups. Berry is in the most conservative category with a score of 92 and Reifel, with 77, is in the third group. The 40 most conservative Democrats, each with an index of over 50, are all from southern or border states. One of the 11 most liberal Republicans, those below the 50 mark, is from Wisconsin; the others are from the East. The index range for Democrats extends from 95 (Marsh of Virginia and Waggoner of Louisiana) to zero, and for the Republicans from 100 to 31 (Halpern of New York). The Democratic median score is 11 and compares with a Republican median index of 85.

The ideological orientation of the South Dakota Congressional delegation in recent history has been determined by the member's party affiliation. Republicans have been conservative, the one Democrat liberal. This generally holds true of midwesterners,[26] but this clear party/ideology pattern is much more confused when data from other sections of the country are presented. There are in the East Republicans as liberal as many Democrats, and in the South Democrats as conservative as most Republicans. Suffice it to say here that as far as Congressional politics are concerned, South Dakota Congressmen behave consistently with the national norms of Republican conservatism and Democratic liberalism.[27]

Summary. The state's four seats in the Congress constitute the apogee of political life in South Dakota. No Congressman has retired from his position to seek non-Congressional political office at the disposal of the voters of the state.

The state's Congressmen act in a political field far removed from South Dakota's parochial interests, and yet they are as dependent as the Governor or the legislators on continuing support from the people of the state.

In terms of the interests they represent, it is significant that no South Dakotan primarily concerned with agriculture as an occupation has ever been elected to Congress. Only five have resided in the state's two largest cities.

South Dakotans have not been among the top leadership in Congress, even though a few have held committee chairmanships, and even though on rare occasions a few have taken a leading role in the formulation of specific important policies.

Analysis of recent roll call voting indicates that South Dakotans in Congress have behaved consistently with national and regional norms for members of their respective parties; that is, the Republicans have been on the conservative side and the one recent Democrat has been definitely liberal.

IX

CONCLUSION: THE PAST, PRESENT, AND FUTURE

Many of the findings of this book tend to confirm hypotheses that have long been held without empirical proof; some of them, it is hoped, will awaken readers to facts they have not known or concerned themselves about previously.

In comparison with its neighbor states (Chapter II), South Dakota, while less firmly Republican in the mid-1960's than she had been in the 1900's or the 1940's, is by almost every measure more consistent in its Republican loyalty. In some of these states, a condition of consistent Republicanism has been replaced by intense two-party competition if not by consistent Democratism.

The appraisal of long-term trends (Chapter III) shows that extended public service in major offices at the disposal of South Dakota voters is associated with the Congress. The titans in terms of political longevity—Karl Mundt, Francis Case, Royal Johnson, and Peter Norbeck—spent all but six of their total of 98 public years in the Congress. Comparatively little power on the national political scene has ever been exerted by South Dakotans; the nature of their constituency has not encouraged the state's Congressmen to adopt important stands on national issues. The Republican party has dominated state politics with the exception of four brief challenges (Populist, Nonpartisan, New Deal Democrat, McGovern Democrat), in all of which rural agitation and rural votes worked against Republican candidates. The agrarian radical movements have been dramatic but impermanent. The Republican and Democratic parties are not rigidly ideological; there have been liberals and conservatives among the leadership and membership of both parties.

Party organizations (Chapter IV) as such have seldom played a crucial role in South Dakota politics since the establishment of the direct primary in the second decade of statehood. Prior to that, however, factions within parties, particulary Stalwarts versus Progressives in the Republican party, did usually determine the state's political leadership and the policies that the state would pursue. Groups with access have used the parties principally as a means of keeping the elective officials from a particular course of action inimical to them.

As to voting behavior and political disposition of the electorate

(Chapter V), areas of Republican and Democratic strength among the precincts of the state are irregularly spaced. Republican candidates consistently receive a better vote in the cities and towns, while Democrats conversely do better in the rural precincts. In the earlier period, the Republican strength was somewhat more pronounced in the eastern half of the state than in the west; more recently Republican strength has been somewhat more apparent in the west. Democratic voters are in general more liberal than Republican voters on the issues of the government's role in the economy, foreign aid, and civil rights. The economic, social, and religious characteristics of party members are in general conformity to those of the national and regional electorates.

As to the Governor (Chapter VI), he has not been dominated by a single man or by an identifiable small group in the party heirarchy, largely because of the shortage of experienced and respected professional staff members. The voters, rather than the party leadership, choose the party's nominee, and the party as a matter of course backs the candidate chosen in its primary. The Governor's control of the state's administrative apparatus is somewhat diminished by the fact that several of his presumably subordinate officers are also elected on a statewide ballot, but this is mitigated by two considerations. First, except for the attorney general and perhaps the lieutenant governor, these officers have little power. Second, the Governor often takes a hand in helping the party's state convention decide who shall be nominated for these positions.

As to the legislature (Chapter VII), its law-making powers have been considerably restricted by the state's early adoption of the initiative and referendum processes and by certain specific constitutional restrictions. In common with many state legislatures, it has also been hampered by disorganization and by a lack of ready information; the latter problem has been partly solved by the creation of the Legislative Research Council in 1951. Among recent legislators, Republicans have a comparative preponderance of lawyers and bankers, while Democrats have been relatively much more numerous among farmers and ranchers. Republicans are likely to be a little older at entrance and to serve more terms than Democrats; a higher percentage of Republicans than Democrats come from the West River area, big cities, and smaller towns, while Democrats are more numerous on a percentage basis in the eastern half of the state and in the rural areas. Republicans are more likely than Democrats to describe themselves as "conservative" and to vote accordingly. Partly affiliation is not a particularly significant determinant of voting behavior in the legislature.

As to the Congressional delegation (Chapter VIII), this is the high point of South Dakota political careers. Several persons have moved from office in the state, including that of Governor, to run for the Congress, but no South Dakotan in Congress has ever voluntarily retired in order to run for non-Congressional office in the state. No South Dakotan primarily concerned with agriculture as an occupation has ever been elected to the Congress. On occasion, a South Dakotan has taken a leading role in Congressional deliberations, but as a group the state's delegation has not exerted influence that would compare with that wielded by politicians from Minnesota, Montana, and Nebraska. Contemporary Congressmen from the state are ideologically oriented with their fellow party members in the midwest — Republicans are generally conservative and the one Democrat is liberal.

Popular Control, Diffused Power. All of these summary statements suggest that a high degree of popular control over government officials exists in South Dakota. Party control is minimal. Political strength seems to reside in individual candidates rather than in a party heirarchy, although one must keep in mind the predominance of Republican voters and the resultant enhanced chances for election of a Republican. Political power is diffused in the state. The voters retain a comparatively large share of it, a result of the direct primary system that affects Congressional, gubernatorial, legislative, and county candidates. Political power is comparatively impermanent. Governors are now in effect restricted to two terms or a total potential incumbency of only four years.[1] Political power is severely limited as well, both by law and by a continuing popular inclination, which may be changing. The power of the legislature to make laws is limited by specific constitutional restrictions and by the initiative and referendum; the power of the Governor to administer laws is restricted by a vast array of boards, commissions, departments, agencies, committees, and the like, over which he has a varying amount of control. In short, the situation is one of diffuse, impermanent, and limited political power. The experienced politicos have an advantage over their less sophisticated fellow citizens in the ease with which they locate and apply pressure to the power structure. For the most part, groups who have gained access have tended to favor restricting the role of government, while groups who have tended to favor significant expansions or changes in that role have not been able to realize their demands as effectively.[2]

Tied up with all these factors is the geographical isolation of the nerve center of state government. The capital city of Pierre lies within ten miles of the geographical center of South Dakota and roughly halfway between the state's two largest cities, Sioux Falls at the eastern edge of the state and Rapid City on the slopes of the Black Hills to the west; the capital was originally placed in Pierre principally because western interests were not willing to see it located any farther east. Between the James River 80 miles to the east and the Black Hills 140 miles to the west, South Dakota is principally arid, sparsely-populated rangeland. It is in the midst of this vast sea of grass that the nerves of state government are collected. Those nerves are thickly insulated by the vastness of the prairie from popular pressures, and as a result the response of state government to many needs and wishes has often been relatively slow. It is natural to associate the isolation of Pierre from the bulk of the state's population with the state's isolation and resultant sense of withdrawal and disassociation from the nation as a whole.[3] A comparatively underdeveloped press further contributes to the lack of communication between the people and their governmental officials. There are signs, however, that the continuing expansion and improvement of transportation and communications facilities are changing the situation by making Pierre's geographical isolation less pronounced.

Political leadership in such circumstances is difficult to exert. The repressive drag of inertia can be overcome only by a great expenditure of political resources on the part of individual political leaders or groups. Thus progress, where it has been achieved, has come in response to fairly mature and obvious needs. Government in South Dakota has seldom anticipated such needs, whether at the state or local level. This has meant that politicians at both levels have generally, on assuming office, been faced with an imposing set of urgent problems that have cried for immediate attention; further, many less obvious problems have not been dealt with until they in turn have become serious. This lag is one result of the comparatively large degree of popular control in South Dakota government. The masses are not known for their ability to perceive present problems touching a small number of citizens or institutions, let alone the future problems. State and local programs and budgets reflect yesterday's and today's problems, seldom tomorrow's. Here again, however, the observer can see signs of a new awareness; recently the Governor has

been provided with a budget officer with responsibilities over coordi-
nating agency requests and forward fiscal planning.

Democratic Government and the Party System. Democratic government means government in which the citizens participate meaningfully by making discreet, free choices not subject to human criticism,
review, or sanction.

The people can participate directly in government by voting on
policy questions themselves, as in the direct democracy of a New England town meeting. South Dakota makes considerable use of direct
democracy forms, in the initiative and referendum processes at the
state level and in a variety of issues at the local level, such as bond
issuances, changes in forms of government, and home rule.

Popular participation can take the form of electing candidates to
public office; thus the citizen is represented by a policy-maker held
responsible through the election system. Governors, legislators, and
county and municipal officers are elected by the people. The indirect
democracy of our representative government is, in effect, a continuing and recurring check on the performance of our elective officials
in office. In general, it is this system with which South Dakota
citizens are most familiar.

A third form of democracy involves the citizen in the selection of
a group which in turn makes the final election. The American electoral college is an example of this even more indirect democracy, and
reflects to this day the reluctance of the Founding Fathers to expose
the nation to the perils of complete democracy. Another example of
this third form is the process of selecting leadership in South Dakota
political parties. When it comes to organizing their political parties,
the people are restricted by state law to electing intervening committees to which is reserved the power of selecting leadership. County
chairmen are elected by county committees, which meet irregularly
if at all, and state chairmen are elected by the state party convention.
In these circumstances, real party leadership is discouraged. The
status quo tends to be preserved. The party as such in South Dakota
contributes little imagination or initiative to the state's political life.

Citizens of South Dakota control their government directly, but
make little real use of the party system except as convenient agencies
for separating candidates into opposing groups. Responsibility for
governing the state resides in individual office-holders, with the parties
playing a very limited role. Might not the political parties take a more
active and useful position with respect to candidates and policies?

The question suggests the value of an assessment of South Dakota political parties in terms of some major concerns expressed by political scientists.

Scholars are not united on the utility of American parties. As Samuel Eldersveld puts it in his recent study of party functions: "Some students of the American party today feel that the party system is adequate, effective, viable. Others claim that atrophy, incoherence, and dysfunction predominate."[4] The first view holds that our party system must be given some of the credit for the general success of the American system of government, certainly at the national level if not in South Dakota itself. While accepting this viewpoint, the responsible citizen will want to consider and reform the signs of party weakness and ineffectiveness that are visible, for surely the best human mechanism needs careful attention if it is to do the job intended. With this in mind, let us pursue the criticisms made regarding our party system so that we can arrive at some judgments and recommendations by way of summary.

One of the principal conclusions of Key's *American State Politics* is that party government in American states should be encouraged and strengthened:

"The proposition seems axiomatic that if party as party is to fulfill its role, a more effective organization of its leadership is in order . . .

"An enlivened, more representative, and active party organization could easily earn its keep by searching out, encouraging, and financing likely candidates for elective offices ranging all the way from legislative seats to the governorship. It remains a serious question whether party organization can exist and function effectively in the promotion of candidates if it must work through the pure form of the statewide direct primary, save perhaps under the most exceptional circumstances . . . Wide-open primaries tend both to shatter party organization and to leave it without much of anything to do. In the absence of working party organization or its equivalent, the direct primary often produces almost unbelievable sorts of nominations."[5]

Another scholar has been impressed by the need in America to give more attention to the purely institutional aspects of popular control:

"As Americans mature it is their sovereign responsibility to exact higher types of leadership and to give that leadership better structures in which local egoisms yield more readily to a patriotism which, while deeper than ever, has attained a new breadth. Realization of self-interest can no longer have less than planetary perspective and implementation. But the instruments of the ablest leaders must be basically institutional. Our new professions at the world level will not be in fact reassuring except as we demonstrate that we have learned to conduct our own institutional affairs in sufficiently whole-nation terms." [6]

Key's commentary gets at the heart of the obstacles to real party control over the politics of South Dakota. In achieving popular government, the state has discouraged a responsible party system. The same problem exists at the county level, although here there is seldom primary competition for county office. Party controls are almost completely non-existent in municipal politics, which are non-partisan under state law. As Key says:

"The preachings of several generations have diverted quantities of civic energy away from partisan activities. The systematic depreciation of partisanship perhaps both depresses impulses to community leadership as well as pushes activity into nonpartisan channels. However that may be, the party system, which lies at the heart of the governing process, often is left by default in a weakened position. The evangel who wishes to strengthen states in the governing process needs to work out ways and means to bring to the service of party a larger share of the energies and abilities of the potential resources for leadership." [7]

These and similar studies suggest a crucial question about the role of the political party in the government and politics of South Dakota. Should we be content with the present situation wherein political parties, as such, are unable or unwilling to involve themselves decisively and intimately with the processes of candidate selection and policy determination? In this situation, the major candidates, with the rare exceptions noted earlier, are chosen directly by the voters and are thus accountable to the general party public more than to the party heirarchy. Policies are determined by legislators and Governors acting virtually on their own without any significant degree of direction or restraint from party officialdom. To add significantly to the power of the party hierarchy and thus encourage party action would radically change the nature of South Dakota politics. It would certainly make state government more responsive to certain interests and groups in the public. Any proposal to enhance the role of parties should be made with the possible rearrangements of power and influence in mind.

Reforming Party and Government. To achieve what many scholars interested in an enlarged role for the political party have suggested, South Dakota might consider a number of changes. An attempt might be made to draw tighter the loose lines of party responsibility in the legislature. Formal party decisions might be further encouraged in legislative caucuses, which already exist, for the purpose of exerting a higher degree of loyalty either internally by the party-in-the-legislature or externally by the state party itself. The collection and distribution of party funds might be further formalized and centralized, with the chief objective of discouraging collections by individual candidates and disbursements by special interest groups. The party organizations at the county, district, and state levels might be given more power in nominations, either by allowing the organization to nominate candidates directly or by indicating on the ballot the preference of the party organization. This would diminish the rather negative and diffused control now possessed by the generality of party voters in primary elections and would thus change South Dakota's traditional habits of direct primary election.

Efforts might be directed toward making party leadership positions more visible to the general public. The state party chairmen might be chosen by the party's gubernatorial nominee, a situation which pertains between the national party's chairman and Presidential nominee; this would make the state chairmanship more distinctly a state-based office rather than one depending on support from the inexperienced and local-oriented state convention. The members of the national committees might be elected by the party voters, as was previously done. The state convention might be combined with the state central committee to eliminate needless duplication of effort and to focus party responsibility at the state level. County chairmen might be selected directly by the general voters of the party in the primary election rather than leaving the selection of local leadership to the county central committee, or perhaps appointed by the state organization with the advice and consent of the local members. These reforms would seem to encourage a more imaginative and competitive party leadership, two conditions so desperately lacking in South Dakota party politics generally.

One problem encountered many times in this study is that quite often power has not been exercised in the visible, formal arenas of government or even of party politics. Political parties have as a critical function the sharpening of lines of political conflict so that the people may understand why certain things are done and why certain other things are not done by their government. If parties neglect their duty by failing to take meaningful stands on policy questions or by failing to force a degree of conformity to party positions on the part of party members aspiring to or holding political office, then one is left to wonder whether the party has any really useful function at all to perform. Party irresponsibility hinders the advancement of responsible, democratic government. Without party responsibility on crucial policy matters, the polity is missing a link in the power chain which, presumably at least, connects the wishes of the people with the decisions of their government.[8] If political parties are nothing more than agencies for organizing candidates and collecting votes, without any power or inclination to make an impression on policy-formulation, then it is little wonder that so few citizens are willing to contribute time or money to them.

As a means of encouraging meaningful party positions and channeling party efforts, the political parties of South Dakota might consider the erection of policy committees, made up of well-known people with general backgrounds and interests, which would have the power (1) to formulate, on behalf of the party, certain general principles of action to guide their voters and elected officials alike, and (2) to give meaningful support, through campaign contributions and preferential designation on the primary ballot, to candidates who have supported or seem likely to support party policy. Platform statements need not be strictly ideological, but they should face up to the problems confronting the state. The present statutory party agencies, the state conventions and the state central committees, are too large and meet too seldom to provide effective leadership.[9] Such a policy committee should act as the permanent council of the party under the leadership of the state chairman and should meet with more frequency than once a year. It might be elected in the primary election and should probably number no more than 15. It should prepare its agenda carefully and should keep records of its proceedings, for the edification of the party members and the general public. It should hire and have general authority over the professional staff of the party, supervise the distribution of party funds, authorize and publish studies on governmental policy, and oversee, praise, or criticize, the actions of members of its own and the opposing party; in short, it should provide intelligent and constant leadership to the party. If such reforms could be accomplished, then party politics in South Dakota would mean more than they do today.

It should be understood that these and similar changes designed to give the party a heightened role to play in South Dakota politics would not necessarily guarantee better, wiser, or more honest government. Most South Dakotans probably believe that their political parties as such wield more power than they actually do; and in this sense, changes to strengthen the party would produce a more rational system, since then the parties would have the power most citizens erroneously believe them to have. The power structure and access thereto would be clearer to the average citizen and would coincide with his comprehension of his own political environment.

Explicit party control would, of course, affect many relationships. We might therefore expect that proposals for a greater degree of party authority would be opposed by those officials, groups, and interests benefiting from the present power arrangement, and favored by those who believe their demands on government are not now receiving sufficient attention. How many citizens fall into either of these two groups is uncertain. If, as the author suspects, most citizens fall into neither group but are rather unconcerned about parties and politics, then the likelihood of significant changes being adopted is slim indeed.

Aside from the purely party changes discussed so far, what of reforms in the structure of state and local government?

The legislature could be strengthened by: (a) adoption of the unicameral form so as to concentrate legislative power and responsibility and allow the policy-making branch of state government to speak and act more coherently and quickly in its relationships with administrators and the general public; (b) more liberal provision of staff support and office equipment for the individual legislator; (c) removing many of the constitutional strictures on the legislature's powers and schedule; and (d) increasing the legislators' salary to encourage candidates and to increase the probability that legislators can devote adequate time to the study and resolution of state problems.

The executive could be strengthened by: (a) giving the Governor a freer hand in choosing the chief officers of the state administration and allowing him more discretion over the officials on whose performance so much of his reputation depends; (b) giving the Governor more freedom in reorganizing the administrative structure which is now endangered by excessive power diffusion and irresponsibility, in common with the situation in many sister states; and (c) extending the Governor's term of office.

Local government could be strengthened by: (a) consolidation of

units (counties, school and special districts, etc.) and functions
(property assessment, records maintenance, law enforcement, welfare,
health and sanitation, etc.) of local administration; (b) hiring of pro-
fessionally trained administrators such as county and city managers;
and (c) placing municipal government on a partisan basis to involve
both parties and citizens more intimately with the local policy making
process.

Much of the zeal for governmental and party reform originates in a
desire for more active and progressive government. On the other
hand, the diffused authority and confused organization that charac-
terize so much of South Dakota politics, which have been discussed
here repeatedly, have resulted from widely held convictions to the
effect that "government is best which governs least." Thus the abstract
idea of reform will draw support from those desiring systemic change
and at the same time will offend others who prefer things as they are.
The hope is that the great majority of citizens, irrespective of any
reformist or stabilistic tendencies, will be willing to consider and
support sensible reforms that will put the government and politics of
South Dakota on a more rational, efficient, and democratic basis.

These suggestions for reform are made sincerely and after due
thought, but they remain the suggestions of one individual and will
not necessarily impress the majority of observers. If these suggestions
encourage constructive thought on the problems they are meant to
attack, they will have made some contribution. Needless to say, if
any of these or similar reforms are to be put into effect, concerted
effort by a large number of interested and articulate citizens will be
required.

It should not be forgotten that South Dakota's political system as
it exists today is itself the result of previous reforms designed to correct injustices of an earlier period. The minor role played by party
organizations in choosing major state and county candidates had its
origins in a period when abuses in decisions made by the party
hierarchy indicated the desirability of making nomination processes
more visible and popular.[10] The indirect control of party chairmanships at the state and county level makes it more difficult for vested
interests to gain permanent control over the party. The initiative and
referendum laws allow the public to take part in legislative decisions
and to more directly review the performance of the legislature. The
cyclic nature of political reform suggests that reformers should be
careful to avoid producing a new situation where additional reforms
become necessary.

The Spirit of Citizenship. In the beginning, this study was concerned with the question of whether or not wise government is compatible with popular control. The question is somewhat dissociated from the empirical data presented here, and yet the question should be one of deep and continuing concern. In the answer to this question is wrapped the future of enlightened self-government. It is obvious that, at times, the majority will make a decision which is unwise from one standpoint or another. Many citizens have candidate and issue preferences which are rejected by the majoritarian process. To those who believed in the relative superiority of Thomas Dewey, Adlai Stevenson, Richard Nixon, or Barry Goldwater, to use familiar examples, the electoral results of this generation were not as wise as they might have been.

Political wisdom in an immediate context is impossible to identify certainly. In terms of our democratic tradition and environment, wisdom may be defined as those candidates or policies that are most popular. But whether these majority-favored candidates or policies will produce the best results, whether they are truly wisest in some objective sense, is a different matter. This impossibility of being authoritative about wisdom is part of the rationale of democracy. If we cannot be certain of the wisest course for government to pursue, then what more satisfactory solution is there than to let the people allocate political responsibility to individual leaders through the free and recurring electoral process?

Although wisdom and democratic government are not necessarily related, still the public should concern itself about the wisdom of the policies its government undertakes in response to popular pressures. If the people are not inclined to worry much about the long-range results of governmental action or inaction, this role must be assumed by political officials if the state is to maintain itself. The decision-makers ought to be reasonably confident that a given course of action is wise in terms of the community of the future as well as popular in terms of immediate acceptance by the people of the present.

The proper goal of government is to produce general satisfaction while protecting individual rights. According to a general view of American history to which the author subscribes, our democracy, while it may have been wrong on occasion, has produced a workable and popular government. In the best Burkean view, successful usage has hallowed the American institution of democratic government, and has suggested that democracy is no enemy of enlightened self-government.

For the future, some reforms would certainly have a favorable effect on the governmental process in South Dakota. But the state's future, like its past, will depend only in part on the formal organizations of government and party. Structural defects are only part of the problem. Basically, the success of state government will depend as much on the spirit of the citizenry as on the impersonal rules and organizational devices by which the people regulate themselves and their government. Crucial to the future will be the intelligence, honesty, imagination, and public conscience of the state's citizens and their elected representatives in seats of power. There will continue to be an imperative need for general education, communication, and discussion, to the end that problems can be identified and brought before the proper tribunals for wise and democratic settlement.

REFERENCES

CHAPTER I

1. The point that similar options have been available to all Presidents can be pushed too far. For example, it is probably too much to say that President Hoover had the same breadth of options available to him that were possessed by President Franklin Roosevelt. Hoover's responses to the Depression were limited by his political affiliation and the ascendancy of vested interests in the business world. Roosevelt was under some controls by similar interests but, in the deepening emergency, was able to call on vast popular resources that Hoover could not or would not tap.

2. The situation in South Dakota local government, where candidates run on a non-partisan ballot, is even more irresponsible since the candidates and officials are removed from even the minor strictures of policy control from local party officials and voters.

3. Leslie Lipson, *The Democratic Civilization*, (New York: Oxford University Press, 1964), p. 309.

4. Kenneth Heller, "Mental Illness and the North Dakota Depressive Reaction," a paper presented at the 1961 national convention of the American Psychological Association, New York, (mimeographed), pp. 1-2.

5. Herbert S. Schell, *History of South Dakota*, (Lincoln: University of Nebraska Press, 1961), pp. 383-8.

6. *Ibid.*, p. xi.

7. *Ibid.*, p. xi.

8. A handy and thought-provoking condensation of the hearings is David T. Bazelon (ed.), *Point of Order!: A Documentary of the Army-McCarthy Hearings*, (New York: W. W. Norton, 1964). Mundt's position was characterized by his opening statement, "Presiding over these hearings is a responsibility which I do not welcome." *Ibid.*, p. 18.

9. His opponent in the 1966 Republican primary, a former member of the John Birch Society in California, criticized Mundt's "liberal" record on education. Mundt, accepting the advice of many supporters, simply ignored this and similar charges and received 83 percent of the primary election vote to win his fourth consecutive Senatorial nomination.

CHAPTER II

1. More detailed attention to these developments will be given in Chapter III.

2. See the discussion of the politics of statehood proposals in Herbert S. Schell, *History of South Dakota*, (Lincoln: University of Nebraska Press, 1961), pp. 217-222.

3. The People's Party of 1896 and the Fusion Party in 1898 were essentially alliances of Populist and Democratic sympathizers. See Schell, *op. cit.*, Chapter

16, and Clem, *South Dakota Political Almanac*, (Vermillion: Governmental Research Bureau, 1962), pp. 13-16.

4. Samuel Lubell has said that isolationism is "most presistent in areas of cultural insularity." *The Future of American Politics*, second edition, revised, (New York: Doubleday, 1956), pp. 155-156. See also Heller's comments in Chapter I.

5. Clem, "Characteristics of South Dakota County Officers," *Public Affairs*, November, 1962. In 1963-64, of the 488 county officers in the state's sixty-four organized counties, 277 (61.8%) were Republicans and 156 were Democrats (the remaining fifteen offices were vacant or held by persons with no declared party affiliation).

6. Robert L. Morlan, *Political Prairie Fire: The Nonpartisan League, 1915-1922* (Minneapolis: University of Minnesota Press, 1955), p. 124. Morlan's point is reminiscent of Stuart Rice's findings in his study of variations in the voting behavior of adjacent precincts. "A state or county total of the votes cast . . . usually conceals the differences existing among subordinate groupings . . . This was the case in Minnesota, where by segregation of the votes in the small villages, leaving the open country as a residuum, I was able to disclose sharp differences in political attitude between farmer and villager. In one election, in the same territory, 'rural' by census definition, less than a fifth of the villagers but more than a half of the farmers voted for the Nonpartisan League candidate." Rice, "Measurements of Social Attitudes and Public Opinion," a paper presented at The Institute of Methods of Rural Sociological Research, Washington, D. C., December 31, 1929- January 4, 1930 (mimeographed).

7. The ranking is based on the sum of the Republican percentages in the ten elections. South Dakota's average presidential Republican average is 53.8, compared to Nebraska's 55.6.

8. Minnesota also now has a four-year governor term, 1964 being the first election in which that state did not hold a gubernatorial election on a biennial basis.

9. Note that for the sake of simplicity these summarizations discuss Republican strengths. The converse of the statement would hold true for the Democrats.

10. Daniel J. Elazar, *American Federation: A View from the States*, (New York: Thomas Y. Crowell, 1966), pp. 85-116. Patterson argues that the "organizing notion of political culture" can enhance the contributions of comparative analysis of state politics. Samuel Patterson, "The Political Cultures of the American States," Report No. 4, The Laboratory for Political Research, University of Iowa, 1966, p. 1.

11. Elazar, *op. cit.*, p. 88.

12. Compare the comment of Arthur Bromage that "Some councilmen follow the rule that to lead on too many (or any) issues may engender intense reactions." Arthur W. Bromage, "Mayors, Councilmen and Citizens," *Governmental Affairs Bulletin*, (Boulder: Bureau of Governmental Research and Service, June, 1966). It might be added that Professor Bromage, from the moralistic state of Michigan, was speaking to an audience in the moralistic state of Colorado.

13. Elazar, *op. cit.*, p. 93.

14. *Ibid.*, p. 97.

15. *Ibid.*, p. 108. Compare Riker's statement that morality in English government is "almost entirely contemporaneous with the development of English democracy." William H. Riker, *Democracy in the United States*, (New York:

Macmillan, 1953), pp. 314-5. Further, "the democratic system does much more [than to eliminate bribery and graft] because it provides a constant spur to official action." *Ibid.*, p. 315.

16. Not to mention the last decade of the Nineteenth Century when the Republicans often constituted only a minority segment opposed by shifting alignments of Farmers Alliance, Independent, Populist, Fusionist, and Democratic groups.

17. Joseph A. Schlesinger, "A Two-Dimensional Scheme for Classifying the States According to Degree of Inter-Party Competition," *American Political Science Review*, December, 1955, pp. 1120-1128. For other analyses of relative state electoral performance, see Austin Ranney and Willmoore Kendall, "The American Party System," *American Political Science Review*, June, 1954, pp. 477-485; and Duane Lockard, *The Politics of State and Local Government*, (New York; Macmillan, 1963), pp. 179-189. Lockard, basing his conclusions on the Presidential and gubernatorial vote, 1944-1960, characterized South Dakota, North Dakota, and Nebraska as "less competitive, Republican dominant" states and Iowa, Minnesota, Montana, and Wyoming as "competitive" states.

CHAPTER III

1. Major reliance has been placed on the following works: for the Populist era, John D. Hicks, *The Populist Revolt: A History of the Farmers' Alliance and the People's Party*, (Lincoln: University of Nebraska Press, 1961); for the Progressive period, Robert L. Morlan, *Political Prairie Fire: The Nonpartisan League, 1915-1922*, (Minneapolis: University of Minnesota Press, 1955); for Crawford, Calvin Perry Armin, *Coe I. Crawford and the Progressive Movement in South Dakota*, unpublished Ph.D. dissertation, University of Colorado, 1957; for Norbeck, Gilbert C. Fite, *Peter Norbeck: Prairie Statesman*, (Columbia: University of Missouri Studies, 1948). Herbert Schell's definitive *History of South Dakota* (Lincoln: University of Nebraska Press, 1961) covers the period to 1960, as does the present author's essentially statistical *South Dakota Political Almanac* (Vermillion: Governmental Research Bureau, 1962).

2. President Grover Cleveland signed a bill creating four new states, including South Dakota, on February 22, 1889. A constitutional convention in Sioux Falls in September did not fundamentally change the constitution approved in 1885, confining its work to specific items questioned by Congress. The voters approved the Constitution on October 1 and President Benjamin Harrison formally proclaimed admission November 2. Schell, *op. cit.*, pp. 219-222.

3. Election returns in this chapter are taken from biennial editions of the *South Dakota Legislative Manual*. A number of evident errors in reporting returns limit the usefulness of the *Manuals*. For a discussion of the problem of recording errors, see Clem, *Precinct Voting*, (Vermillion: Governmental Research Bureau, 1964), pp. 244-247, and Clem, *West River Voting Patterns*, (Vermillion: Governmental Research Bureau, 1965), pp. 89-94. Data on legislative partisanship are taken from Clem, *South Dakota Political Almanac, op. cit.*, pp. 24-28.

4. The state presently has 67 counties, of which three comprising Indian

reservations in the West River area are unorganized. All forty-four East River counties were laid out at the time of statehood. The other six counties were in the Black Hills area, which had a substantial population well before statehood. For illustrations of the shifting voting pattern by counties, see the maps in Chapter 5 and the Appendix.

5. Schell, *op. cit.*, p. 227.

6. Hicks mentions the claim resulting from this early meeting that South Dakota, rather than Kansas, was the real birthplace of Populism. Hicks, *op. cit.*, p. 157.

7. *South Dakota Senate Journal*, 1891, p. 238.   8. *Ibid.*, p. 256-7.   9. *Ibid.*, p. 420.   10. *Ibid.*, p. 480.   11. *Ibid.*, p. 514.   12. *Ibid.*, p. 512-514.

13. Hicks, *op. cit.*, p. 258.

14. Hicks, *op. cit.*, p. 236, and Schell, *op. cit.*, p. 231.

15. Schell, *op. cit.*, p. 231.

16. Hicks refers to signs of Democratic-Populist union in 1894. Hicks, *op. cit.*, p. 328.

17. Schell, *op. cit.*, p. 233-234. Key states that western silver interests allied themselves with the Democratic party. Key, *Politics, Parties, and Pressure Groups*, 5th Ed., (New York: Crowell, 1964), p. 235.

18. The fact that modern major American political parties do not consistently adhere to a specific line or segment of the ideological spectrum, so unsettling to many scholars and citizens, owes much to the complex re-alignments of politicians and socio-economic interests that accompanied Bryan's victory over the Democratic convention of 1896. Since then, both permanent major parties in South Dakota have frequently had factional disputes often largely based on ideological differences. On the national level, Key states that the realignment of 1896 brought a sharper contrast in the policy orientation of the major parties. Key, *op. cit.*, p. 257.

19. Voting was not by slate; each voter had four votes to dispose of among four Republican, four Populist, and four Prohibitionist electors. See Clem, *South Dakota Political Almanac*, *op. cit.*, p. 12.

20. For a discussion of some confusing data on these races in various editions of the *South Dakota Legislative Manual*, see Clem, *West River Voting Patterns*, *op. cit.*, pp. 92-94.

21. Schell, *op. cit.*, pp. 234-235.   22. Schell, *op cit.*, p. 237.

23. Hicks, *op. cit.*, p. 377.   24. Hicks, *op. cit.*, p. 395.   25. Schell, *op. cit.* p. 239.

26. The words are those of Walter Prescott Webb. Webb, *The Great Plains*, (New York: Ginn and Company, 1931), p. 503. The serious student of radical agrarian politics will read with profit his short section entitled "Why Is the West Politically Radical?" Webb, *op. cit.*, pp. 502-505.

27. Schell, *op. cit.*, p. 241.

28. Senator Kyle, whose second term was scheduled to run until 1903, died July 1, 1901. To succeed him, Governor Herreid appointed Alfred B. Kittredge, a former Republican national committeeman. The legislature elected Kittredge to a full Senate term commencing in 1903.

29. Schell, *op. cit.*, p. 241.

30. Fite says that "the Progressive movement in South Dakota was little

more than the realization of some of the Populist demands by the Progressive wing of the Republican party." Fite, *op. cit.,* p. 29.

31. Schell, *op. cit.,* p. 258-259. Crawford had harbored hopes for the Senatorial appointment after Kyle's death in 1901. Fite calls Crawford "the man largely responsible for inaugurating a real progressive movement in South Dakota. . . ." Fite, *op. cit.,* p. 30.

32. Schell, *op. cit.,* pp. 260-261; Fite, *op. cit.,* p. 30; and Chapters V and VI in Armin, *op. cit.,* pp. 74-121.

33. Fite, *op. cit.,* p. 32.

34. The 1908 Republican state convention, where the Progressives held a 266-223 edge over the Stalwarts, had earlier (April 7) endorsed Crawford for Senator, Vessey for Governor, and Taft for President. Armin, *op. cit.,* pp. 180-181; and Schell, *op. cit.,* p. 262.

35. Two other Progressives, Lieutenant-Governor Howard C. Shober and State Senator Frank Byrne, had been mentioned for the gubernatorial nomination, but under Crawford's aegis all were able to unite behind Vessey's candidacy. Armin, *op. cit.,* pp. 223-224.

36. Fite, *op. cit.,* p. 39.   37. Armin, *op. cit.,* pp. 270-272.   38. Armin, *op. cit.,* pp. 272-274.

39. Key states that many prominent GOP Progressives found themselves removed from positions of national power after the abortive Bull Moose movement. Key, *op. cit.,* pp. 264-265.

40. Armin, *op. cit.,* p. 293.   41. Fite, *op. cit.,* p. 47.   42. Armin, *op. cit.,* p. 303.   43. Fite, *op. cit.,* p. 49.

44. Morlan, *op. cit.,* p. 212. For a more detailed study, see Fite, "Peter Norbeck and the Defeat of the Nonpartisan League in South Dakota," *Mississippi Valley Historical Review,* 33: 217-236, September, 1946.

45. Morlan, *op. cit.,* p. 124.

46. Pacifist agitation in the state is discussed in Morlan, *op. cit.,* pp. 174-175, and Schell, *op. cit.,* pp. 271-273.

47. Morlan, *op. cit.,* pp. 212-214.

48. National issues played an inconspicuous role in South Dakota's 1920 election. Norbeck was not enthusiastic about Harding. Fite, *op. cit.,* p. 95. Nor was Crawford, who supported the Cox-Roosevelt Democratic ticket. Armin, *op. cit.,* p. 210.

49. Schell, *op. cit.,* pp. 274-275.

50. *Ibid.,* p. 275. The gas war between the state and the oil companies continued intermittently until a decision of the Supreme Court in 1925 ended the state's retail gasoline venture.

51. In the same election, the voters rejected a plan to move the state university from Vermillion to Sioux Falls by the highest percentage ever recorded in a South Dakota statewide referendum. The idea was heavily rejected not only in Vermillion but also in Sioux Falls, where a number of private institutions were trying to establish themselves. Clem, *South Dakota Political Almanac, op. cit.,* p. 35.

52. Samuel Lubell points out that during the 1920's the Progressive Republicans came from the Midwest, but that by the 1950's they came from the East. Lubell, *op. cit.,* p. 245.

53. In 1924 Nonpartisan League candidates ran under the Farmer-Labor banner.

54. Norbeck's role in McMaster's victory alienated an old Redfield friend, S. W. Clark, who was a law partner of Sterling's. This would have repercussions eight years later. Fite, *op. cit.*, p. 184.

55. *Ibid*, pp. 121-122. Norbeck seldom found himself in agreement with the personalities or policies of the three Republican presidents whose terms coincided with his. With strict impartiality, he opposed the nomination of each, as well as that of Landon in 1936.

56. Norbeck and Senator Nye of North Dakota were the only Republican Senators in the entire Midwest to be re-elected in 1932. Fite, *op. cit.*, p. 189.

57. Senator Norbeck rather half-heartedly supported Borah's Presidential ambitions. *Ibid.*, p. 203. Norbeck had not followed Senator Norris of Nebraska, Borah of Idaho, Hiram Johnson of California and young LaFollette of Wisconsin in publicly voting for Roosevelt in 1932. *Ibid.* p. 188.

58. *Ibid.*, p. 206.

59. Election to the Office of Superintendent of Public Instruction was put on a nonpartisan basis for the 1938 election.

60. A reapportionment of the state legislature passed by the 1937 legislature reduced the total membership of the two houses from 148 to 110.

61. Since Case had been nominated by the Republican primary before his death, the vacant nomination under South Dakota law had to be made by the party's state central committee.

62. For a detailed discussion of the committee proceedings, see Clem, *The Nomination of Joe Bottum*, (Vermillion: Governmental Research Bureau, 1963).

63. It should be noted that Hubert Humphrey was born and raised in South Dakota.

64. Senator McGovern's controversial stand in 1965 with respect to U. S. policy in Viet Nam seems to have been an exception.

65. The GOP controlled the 80th Congress, 1947-48, and the 83rd Congress, 1953-54. See the comments of Charles O. Jones, "South Dakota in Washington: Profile of a Congressional Delegation," *Public Affairs*, No. 24, February, 1966.

Considerable importance attaches to seniority no matter which party controls the legislative body, notably in a member's original committee assignment and later in subcommittee and conference committee appointments. But, unless unusual personalities or circumstances are involved, the chances of influencing national policy are greater when a member is on the majority side than when he is with the minority.

66. Quoted in Webb, *op. cit.*, p. 502. Italics supplied. The climate is seen as an important condition affecting rural government as well as individual behavior. "Because a very fickle rain is ruler of this country [the northern Great Plains], it follows that flexibility is a prime desideratum of governmental as well as of agricultural operations. It may therefore be that a first element in any plan for viable local government would be a foresighted scheme of flexible public finance. The kind of flexibility typical of the past—marked by starvation of public services, widespread delinquency and forfeitures, and near-bankrupt financing expedients— seems too costly and cruel. The manageable limits of public borrowing are too quickly reached." Herman Walker, Jr., and Peter L. Hansen, "Local Government

and Rainfall: The Problem of Local Government in the Northern Great Plains,"
American Political Science Review, December, 1946, pp. 1113-1123, at p. 1123.
See also John D. Barnhart, "Rainfall and the Populist Party in Nebraska," *American Political Science Review,* August, 1925, pp. 527-540. Local government is
further discussed in Chapter IV.

CHAPTER IV

1. Key, *op. cit.,* pp. 163-5.
2. *The Works of the Right Honourable Edmund Burke* (Boston: Wells and
Lilly, 1826), Vol. I, pp. 422-4.
3. William Goodman, *The Two-Party System in the United States,* second edition, (Princeton: D. Van Nostrand, 1960), p. 6.
4. See Chapter III.
5. See Table 2, Clem, *South Dakota Political Almanac, op. cit.,* pp. 19-21.
6. *South Dakota Code,* 16.0102.
7. *Ibid.,* 16.0201.   8. *Ibid.,* 16.0209.   9. *Ibid.*
10. *Ibid.,* 17.0211.   11. *Ibid.,* 16.0241.   12. *Ibid.,* 16.0240.
13. It is unfortunate that so little systematic study has been given to the mechanics of these major party election processes. About all there is to rely on,
aside from the observations of participants, are the few accounts in daily newspapers. Consider the 1963 selection of Henry Moeller of Vermillion as Republican
national committeeman. His election took eleven ballots and involved a four-man race among the victor and Jerry Simmons of Sioux Falls, Charles Howard
of Aberdeen, and Stan Adelstein of Rapid City. Why did several of Howard's
votes go to Simmons on the second ballot, and of Adelstein's to Moeller on the
fourth? On the remaining ballots, why did Moeller pick up most of Howard's
votes? What things about the various candidates most impressed the convention
members? Answers to these and related questions would help us to better understand our politics.
14. Compare the comments of Duane Lockard: "It is often assumed that the
closer power is to the people the greater will be their interest in and control
over it. This assumption runs into difficulty when we begin to test it empirically.
Is the public in fact more interested in state and local government than about
the more remote national government? . . . By ordinary tests of public attitudes
it would appear that even among citizens who show any interest at all in public
affairs—and many do not, of course—a greater proportion concern themselves with
national than with state or local matters." Lockard, *The Politics of State and Local
Government,* (New York: Macmillan, 1963), p. 28. See also Ralph H. Smuckler
and George M. Belknap, *Leadership and Participation in Urban Political Affairs,*
(East Lansing, Michigan: Government Research Bureau, Michigan State University, 1956), p. 30. In South Dakota, participation in state and local elections
is regularly less than in national elections; see the data for Presidential, gubernatorial, Congressional, and legislative voting in Clem, *Precinct Voting, op. cit.,*
and Clem, *West River Voting Patterns, op. cit.* Key found similar results and concluded that "The salience of the personalities and issues of national politics ordinarily command the attention of far more people than do the less dramatic questions of state politics." Key, *op. cit.,* p. 579.

15. *South Dakota Code,* 16.0203.

16. *South Dakota Code,* 16.0208. The same provision prohibits nomination of a person for a third successive gubernatorial term.

17. For a discussion of the controversial Richards primary law, see Clarence Berdahl, "Richards Primary in South Dakota," *American Political Science Review,* 1920, pp. 93-105, and Armin, *op. cit.,* pp. 304-305. Among other things, the primary law required an official party publicity pamphlet and public joint debates by gubernatorial candidates on "paramount issues" of their choosing. Schell, *op. cit.,* pp. 273-274.

18. A contingent nomination-by-convention was narrowly averted in the 1950 Republican gubernatorial primary when Sigurd Anderson received 35,601 votes and Joe Foss 33,257 votes out of 100,731 cast.

19. *South Dakota Code,* 16.0501.   20. *Ibid.,* 16.0240.

21. For a detailed discussion, see Clem, *The Nomination of Joe Bottum, op. cit.* The same procedure was used by the Democratic party in 1962 when Thomas E. Poe, Jr., of Vermillion was named to replace William Day of Winner, as the party's nominee for attorney general. The code reference is *South Dakota Code* 16.0243.

22. Armin, *op. cit.,* p. 223. In this connection, see generally Armin, *op. cit.,* Ch. IV, "Break with the Machine."

23. Among the many commentators who have discussed the lack of interest in national policy on the part of local party officials in the United States is Norton Long. "The interests of local party leaderships, when not hostile to Washington, frequently extend no further than a shrewd appreciation of the value of keeping the votes regular. Their pre-occupation is for the most part with local job politics rather than national policy." Long was also concerned about the implications on party activity of the comparatively rudimentary development of a national public opinion. Long, *The Polity,* (Chicago: Rand McNally & Co., 1962), p. 18.

24. *South Dakota Code,* 16.06.   25. *Ibid.,* 16.14.

26. The 1962 party platforms are reprinted in the *South Dakota Legislative Manual* for 1963, pp. 225-235.

27. See the discussion in the chapter on "Administrative Politics" below.

28. George M. Platt, "South Dakota's 1964 Legislative Session," *Public Affairs,* May, 1964.

29. Governor Bulow said of himself: "I was a Democrat of the old school and a firm believer in the democratic doctrines taught by Thomas Jefferson. I believed that the people are best governed when least governed, and, with Jefferson, believed that the federal government is a grant of power that should only be exercised within constitutional limitations, and that all powers not granted to the federal government were reserved to the people . . . I was in opposition to many New Deal activities . . . I was an isolationist and never an internationalist." Bulow, "An Autobiography," in Charles J. Dalthorp (ed.), *South Dakota's Governors,* (Sioux Falls: Midwest-Beach Company, 1953), p. 46.

30. See Chapter V.

31. See Schell, *op. cit.,* pp. 223-265, *passim,* and Armin, *op. cit.,* especially Chapter III.

32. Armin tells us for example that the Homestake Mine was instrumental in the defeat of Senator Crawford in 1914. Armin, op. cit., p. 297. Senator Pettigrew's

important forest land amendment in 1897 was based on the interests of Home-stake. Gifford Pinchot, *Breaking New Ground*, (New York: Harcourt, Brace, and World, 1947.).

33. Clem, "The 1964 Election: Has South Dakota Become a Two-Party State?" *Public Affairs*, February, 1965.

34. Clem, "U. S. Sugar Policy: The View from South Dakota," *Public Affairs*, February 1962.

35. George M. Platt, "South Dakota's 1964 Legislative Session," *Public Affairs*, May, 1964.

36. George M. Platt, "South Dakota's 1963 Legislative Session," *Public Affairs*, May, 1963.

37. The comparative insignificance of South Dakota's strength in the national political picture is illustrated by the obituary of former Democratic National Committeeman C. L. Chase of Watertown wherein Chase's principal contribution is said to have been his tie-breaking vote on the 1960 convention cite committee which caused the Democratic convention to be held in Los Angeles. AP dispatch from Watertown in Sioux Falls *Argus-Leader*, May 24, 1965. On the other hand, of course, South Dakota's political leaders regularly confer with major national party officials and occasionally have made such an impression that they have been remembered. Former Democratic National Chairman James Farley has recalled a meeting with South Dakota National Committeeman Bill Howe during one of Farley's tours in behalf of Franklin D. Roosevelt: ". . . We sat in a lunchroom at Aberdeen on a roasting-hot day. Bill was a canny politician who had been in the game for years; he knew it backward and forward. We sat there for some time, exchanging generalities, without disclosing what either of us really had in mind. Just before it was time to go, Bill plumped his fat fist on the table and growled in a deep voice, 'Farley, I'm damn' tired of backing losers. In my opinion, Roosevelt can sweep the country, and I'm going to support him.'" Farley, "Selling Roosevelt to the Party," *The American Magazine*, August, 1938, p. 98.

38. The code provision is *South Dakota Code* 16.0211. See the historical discussion in T. C. Geary, "South Dakota," in Paul T. David, Malcolm Moos, and Ralph M. Goodman (eds.), *Presidential Nominating Politics in 1952.*, Vol. IV., *The Middle West*, (Baltimore: The Johns Hopkins Press, 1954), pp. 258-278, at pp. 260-262.

39. For a more detailed discussion of the 1952 primary struggles, see Geary, *loc. cit.*, pp. 263-267. Geary concludes that "the rift in the Republican party occasioned by the heated primary did not prove difficult to mend." *Ibid.*, p. 269.

40. Fite says it would have been more consistent for Norbeck had he supported Johnson. Norbeck "expressed an ardent desire to send a progressive Republican to the White House, but he did not support the most progressive candidate, and he even admitted that Wood would probably not be a popular president." Fite, *op. cit.*, pp. 94-95. Norbeck was a leader in securing the vice-presidential nomination of Calvin Coolidge. Paul Bellamy, "Peter Norbeck," in Charles J. Dalthorp (ed.), *South Dakota's Governors*, (Sioux Falls: Midwest-Beach Company, 1953). p. 32.

41. T. C. Geary, "South Dakota", *op. cit.*; Charles O. Jones, "Decision-Making in a Small Delegation: South Dakota Republicans," in Paul Tillett (ed.), *Inside Politics: The National Convention, 1960*, (Dobbs Ferry, N. Y.: Oceana Publications, Inc., 1962), pp. 160-170; and Clem, "No Hits, No Runs, No Errors: Na-

tional Convention Impact on Small State Politics," unpublished manuscript, 1964, 18 pp.

42. Geary, *op. cit.*, pp. 262-263. 43. *Ibid.*, p. 269. 44. *Ibid.*, p. 275.

45. Jones, *op. cit.*, p. 163. The threat of a possible Rockefeller candidacy would most likely have caused the South Dakotans to unite behind Nixon. In 1960 and 1964 among the South Dakota GOP delegation, it is the present author's impression that opposition to Rockefeller was stronger than support for Goldwater.

46. *Ibid.*, p. 165. Italics supplied.　　　47. *Ibid.*, p. 166.

48. Clem, "No Hits, No Runs, No Errors: National Convention Impact on Small-State Politics," *op. cit.*, p. 16.

49. The 1964 Republican experience is illuminating. Senator Mundt had long been a conservative power along with Senator Carl T. Curtis of Nebraska. The latter led the Nebraska delegation to San Francisco and became Goldwater's floor manager. Mundt's lack of status on the South Dakota delegation lessened the possibility that he would take a large part in any of the crucial manipulations.

50. Clem, "Characteristics of South Dakota County Officers," *op. cit.* Other data in this discussion of county officers come from the same source.

51. W. O. Farber, T. C. Geary, and W. H. Cape, *Government of South Dakota,* (Sioux Falls: Midwest-Beach, 1962), p. 174.

52. *Ibid.*, pp. 178-181. See also Eugene Kimmel, *The Abandonment of City Manager Government by South Dakota Municipalities,* (Vermillion: Governmental Research Bureau, 1966) and David A. Gugin, "An Inquiry into Rapid City's Rejection of Home Rule," *Public Affairs,* No. 23, November, 1965.

CHAPTER V

1. Walter Dean Burnham begins a recent article by discussing the "well publicized conflict (that) has arisen between aggregationists and survey researchers." He is optimistic about the scholarly contributions of both groups. Burnham, "The Changing Shape of the American Political Universe," *American Political Science Review,* March, 1965, pp. 7-28, at p. 7.

2. The two periods each include ten gubernatorial elections.

3. Clem, *Precinct Voting, op. cit.*, pp. 7 and 235-236.

4. Samuel Lubell, *op. cit.*, p. 156. The four counties, however, showed a surprisingly weak Republican vote for President Hoover against Roosevelt in 1932. McPherson county is illustrative. The Republican Presidential percentages there dropped from 91 in 1924 to 46 in 1928 and to 19 in 1932, then rose again to 55 in 1936 and to 77 in 1940.

5. Clem, *Precinct Voting, op. cit.*, p. 7.

6. Clem, *Precinct Voting, op. cit.*, pp. 222-232 *passim,* and Clem, *West River Voting Patterns, op. cit.*, pp. 81-88 *passim.*

7. The "city vote" means returns from precincts in cities of more than 2,500 population (1960). The "town vote" means returns from towns of between 100 and 2,500 population. See footnote 2, Clem, *Precinct Voting, op. cit.*, p. 222.

8. Clem, *Precinct Voting, op. cit.*, p. 232.

9. Clem, *West River Voting Patterns, op. cit.,* pp. 82-83.   10. *Ibid.,* p. 83.

11. *Ibid.*

12. Clem, *Precinct Voting, op. cit.,* pp. 235-236.

CHAPTER VI

1. As noted earlier, the party heirarchy does play a more positive role when (1) a candidate for Governor, Senator, or Congressman fails to win 35 percent of the vote in the primary election or (2) when a vacancy occurs in a nomination.

2. Socialism is "a political and economic theory of social organization based on collective or governmental ownership and democratic management of the essential means for the production and distribution of goods." *Webster's New International Dictionary of the English Language,* 2nd ed., (Springfield, Mass.: G. & C. Merriam Co., 1959), p. 2387.

3. County chairmen of the political parties generally prefer solicitation by party representatives only as a means of simplifying their perennial problem of meeting the local quota set by the state party organization.

4. Article IV, Sections 6 and 7. *South Dakota Constitution.*

5. Gubernatorial vacancies occur in many states because the Governor resigns to have himself appointed to fill a vacancy in the U. S. Senate. South Dakota has had four such Senate vacancies, in 1901 on Kyle's death, in 1936 on Norbeck's death, in 1948 on Bushfield's death, and in 1962 on Case's death. Governors Herreid and Berry were thought to have had Senate aspirations, but decided to adopt a more circuitous and democratic (and less successful) route; Governors Mickelson and Gubbrud evidently did not entertain such notions very seriously. The Case vacancy is the subject of Clem, *The Nomination of Joe Bottum, op. cit.*

6. William John Bulow, "An Autobiography," in Dalthorp, *op. cit.,* pp. 45-46.

7. "Lee found himself in constant disagreement with a hostile Legislature." Schell, *op. cit.,* p. 239. " . . . Bulow maintained an air of cordiality with the majority party which he found rewarding in subsequent bids for office." *Ibid.,* p. 281.

8. Referring to Norbeck, Fite concludes that "no other South Dakota Governor has ever exercised such a strong influence upon the legislature and none so impressed his personality upon events during an administration." Fite, *op. cit.,* p. 79.

9. The actions of Governor Sheldon are illustrative. Sheldon had prepared a farewell message for the 1897 legislature in which he complained of his lack of power over his own administration and of the failure of the legislature to extend his power. The Governor was informed that if he tried to read his message a motion to adjourn would be made, and so he did not even present the message. Will G. Robinson, "Charles H. Sheldon," in Dalthorp, *op. cit.,* p. 7.

10. In addition, the three members of the public utilities commission are elected on a statewide partisan ballot.

11. Farber, *op. cit.,* p. 90.

12. Considering the trend toward a larger role by the federal government in so many areas of concern to state government, it is apparent that the power

of state Governors and other policy-makers will be increasingly affected by decisions made in Washington. Elazar makes the point that, in states where power is widely diffused in the administrative branch, federal aid programs have tended to increase the power and responsibilities of the separate executive departments by giving them "new sources of funds outside of the normal channels of state control. . . ." Elazar, op. cit., p. 81.

13. The latter position was put on a non-partisan basis subsequent to the service of Democrat I. D. Weeks, who in 1935 was appointed president of the University of South Dakota by Governor Berry. The Governor was thought to be suspicious of designs on Weeks' part to challenge his position. Weeks for many years had the distinction of being the person with the longest tenure as president of a state university or land-grant college in the United States.

14. See generally Farber, op. cit., pp. 90-94.

15. It should be noted that Mickelosn defeated Sharpe in the 1946 GOP gubernatorial primary while serving as attorney general.

16. For a discussion of political career trends and the major offices in the state, see Clem, South Dakota Political Almanac, op. cit., pp. 12-18.

17. Farber, op. cit., p. 95.

18. For several Governors, biographical studies are available, notably those on Crawford and Norbeck by Armin and Fite respectively, cited elsewhere.

19. It is always particularly difficult to judge an incumbent or others still involved in politics objectively. Two newspaper reports buttress Boe's claim to be listed as a "strong" Governor. One quoted Senator Mundt as saying in a Senate hearing that in South Dakota "we have a Governor with some guts." Associated Press dispatch from Pierre in Sioux Falls Argus-Leader, May 25, 1965. The other revealed that Boe had been named to a "Republican task force on the conduct of foreign relations." Other members of the task force included former Ambassador Robert Hill, former Congressman Walter Judd, Gen. Lucius Clay, former CIA-head Allen Dulles, Professor Gerhart Niemeyer, and Adm. Arleigh Burke. Associated Press dispatch from Washington in the Sioux Falls Argus Leader, May 26, 1965.

20. Joseph A. Schlesinger, "The Politics of the Executive," Chapter 6 in Herbert Jacobs and Kenneth N. Vines (editors), Politics in the American States: A Comparative Analysis, (Boston: Little, Brown and Company, 1965), pp. 219-229. Alaska and Hawaii were excluded from Schlesinger's analysis. For a discussion of the Governor's resources, see Lockard's four factors: (a) personal resources stemming from the Governor's individual personality and background, (b) party resources depending upon basic party strength in the state, (c) publicity resources involving the Governor's ability to communicate with the general public, and (d) legal-constitutional resources which relate to the office itself irrespective of the individual incumbent. Lockard, op. cit., pp. 369-95.

21. Schlesinger, op. cit., p. 220.   22. Ibid., p. 222.   23. Ibid., p. 226.
24. Ibid., p. 227.   25. Ibid., p. 229.

Chapter VII

1. Prior to a constitutional amendment adopted in 1936, the Senate membership had been 45 and the House membership 103. The House fluctuated in size several times during the first quarter-century of statehood.

2. Section 1, Article III, Constitution of South Dakota.

3. Not all laws are subject to referendum. For example, in 1965 rumors were afoot that H. B. 743, Chapter 296 of the 1965 Session Laws, commonly known as the broadened sales tax law, would be referred to the people. Attorney General Frank Farrar, responding to a request from Secretary of State Alma Larson for information as to whether or not the petitions could be filed in her office, said: "I wish to advise you that this enactment cannot be referred to the vote of the people under the referendum provided by Article III, Section I . . . Regardless of the merits of the broadened sales tax, it is a revenue measure to support state government . . . It has been the consistent position of the Supreme Court of this state that revenue measures for the necessary support of the government cannot be referred to the vote of the people . . . I therefore advise you to reject these petitions when they are filed." Official Opinion of the Attorney General, June 11, 1965. It should also be noted that the Constitution may be amended only with legislative action, not by the initiative alone as in Nebraska and North Dakota. Where a constitutional change is contemplated, the popular will is not sufficient, but must be augmented by legislative consent.

4. The actual openness of legislative procedures may be seriously weakened by the last phrase of Section 15, Article III, which states: "The sessions of each house and of the committee of the whole shall be open, unless when the business is such as ought to be kept secret."

5. Section 23, Article III.   6. Section 24, *Ibid.*

7. Section 25, *Ibid.*   8. Section 26, *Ibid.*

9. Lockard, himself once a state Senator in Connecticut, has trenchantly described some of the problems facing the typical freshman state legislator. Lockard, "The Tribulations of a State Senator," *The Reporter*, May 17, 1965, p. 24. Elsewhere he points to: (a) the need to follow the advice of respected and more experienced legislators; (b) the freshman's ignorance of much major legislation — for example, the nonlawyer "faced with the details of a corporation code or a revision of inheritance-estate laws"; and (c) the suprisingly strong interest of certain constituents or lobbyists in evidently trivial matters such as "fishing regulations in a state park, barber licensing, revising the charter of a city at the opposite end of the state, and so on." Further, "The problem of too little time and too many duties result in his emphasizing the major problems that directly encompass many lesser items (the budget or major reforms or a constitutional convention) and selected other questions that arouse his attention . . . It does not take long for the novice to learn that legislative politics is not a lawn party but serious and hard-fought contests over issues that are vital to the contestants. The stakes are high and the players go after their objectives not in the manner of a Sunday afternoon croquet player but with the fire and determination of a World Series shortstop." Lockard, *op. cit.*, pp. 281-2.

10. Dean E. Clabaugh, "Thoughts upon Leaving," *LRC Newsletter and Council Minutes*, (Pierre: State Legislative Research Council, July 1, 1965), p. 6.

11. George M. Platt, "South Dakota's 1964 Legislative Session," *Public Affairs*, May, 1964, p. 7.

12. From 1948, when the constitution was amended to provide for gubernatorial appointment to fill legislative vacancies, through 1963, the Governor made twenty-one such appointments. In at least three instances, the Governor appointed a member of his own party to fill vacancies in seats which had been won by the opposing party in the previous election. T. C. Geary, *Lawmaking in South*

Dakota, Fourth Edition, (Vermillion: Governmental Research Bureau, 1966), p. 2.

13. Section 5, Article III.   14. *Ibid.*

15. Baker *v.* Carr, 369 U. S. 186 (1962) and the six decisions bearing on bi-cameral apportionment, Reynolds *v.* Sims, 84 S. Ct. 1362 (1964) *et seq.* For a pre-Baker discussion of the problem of legislative malapportionment in South Dakota, see the present author's "Legislative Power and Reapportionment in South Dakota," *Public Affairs,* August, 1961. Application to congressional and county commissioner districts is contained in the present author's more recent monograph entitled "Distorted Democracy: Malapportionment in South Dakota Government," *Public Affairs,* November, 1964. Although pockets of malapportionment formerly existed in the state, particularly with reference to Sioux Falls and Rapid City, the state's situation was not as serious as that in many other states, such as Kansas. The South Dakota legislature, which reapportioned its districts in both 1961 and 1965, has been quite responsive to court and citizen demands for more equitable representation at the Congressional and state legislative levels.

16. The problem of defining precise mathematical standards by which to evaluate the equitability of an apportionment has concerned a number of judges and scholars and has not been (and may never be) conclusively solved. See the cautions of Justices Frankfurter and Harlan and the comments of, among others, Arthur L. Goldberg, "The Statistics of Malapportionment," *Yale Law Journal,* November, 1962, 90-106; Glendon Schubert and Charles Press, "Measuring Malap-portionment," *American Political Science Review,* June, 1964, 302-327; and the present author's "Problems of Measuring and Achieving Equality of Representa-tion in State Legislatures," *Nebraska Law Review,* April, 1963, 622-643.

17. Two House districts electing a total of three representatives, Beadle and Clay, are slightly underrepresented. For the Senate, the Lincoln-Union district is slightly underrepresented and the Douglas-Hutchinson district is slightly over-represented.

18. Governors Mellette, Sheldon, and Jensen had held no elective public office in the state prior to their election.

19. Questionnaires were devised, mailed out, and tabulated by the author in July and August of 1965. Of the 110 legislators, fifty-five responded, or exactly half. The representational role categories (trustee, delegate, politico) were sug-gested by John C. Wahlke, Heinz Eulau, William Buchanan, and LeRoy Ferguson, *The Legislative System: Explorations in Legislative Behavior,* (New York: John Wiley & Sons, Inc., 1962). The seven pressure source categories were suggested by Hugh Bone, *American Politics and the Party System,* 3rd edition, (New York: McGraw-Hill, 1965.)

20. The questionnaire definitions: "trustee," one who bases his decisions solely on his own knowledge and judgment irrespective of the opinions of others; "delegate," one who carries out the wishes of his constituents, even if they may conflict with his own principles and preferences; "politico," one who at various times or in various circumstances may partake of both roles listed above. The "trustee" definition is essentially the view associated with the eminent British statesman Edmund Burke, often referred to as the father of modern conservatism.

21. As Bone says, "Party influences therefore conflict with many other interests for the legislator's vote." Bone, *op. cit.,* p. 246.

22. In both the 1957 and 1959 sessions, the Democratic party was in a position

to block emergency appropriations, which require a two-thirds majority. See the discussion above in this chapter.

23. For extended treatment of the strategic consequences of various sizes of majorities, see, among others, William H. Riker, *The Theory of Political Coalitions*, (New Haven: Yale University Press, 1962), and Richard C. Snyder, "Game Theory and the Analysis of Political Behavior," in *Research Frontiers in Politics and Government: Brookings Lectures 1955*, (Washington: The Brookings Institution, 1955).

24. The thrust of this inquiry has been extended in Clem, "Roll Call Voting Behavior in the South Dakota Legislature," *Public Affairs*, May, 1966. Principal attention was given to the voting cohesion of the more obvious partisan, sectional, population, religious, occupational, age, tenure, and educational groupings and to the party loyalty indices of each state senator and representative.

25. Belle Zeller, *American State Legislatures*, (New York: Crowell, 1954) pp. 190-194. See also Austin Ranney, "Parties in State Politics," Chapter 3 in Jacob and Vines, *op cit.*, pp. 87-89; and Malcolm E. Jewell, "Party Voting in American State Legislatures," *American Political Science Review*, September, 1955, 773-791.

26. Zeller, *op. cit.*, p. 193.

CHAPTER VIII

1. The word "Congressman" is used here to designate members of both houses of the national legislature. The words "Senator" and "Representative" will be used when the intent is to distinguish between members of the two houses.

2. However, as noted earlier in Chapter VI, no South Dakota Governor on the occasion of a vacancy in the Senate has adopted the direct route of resigning from office and having his successor appoint him to the Senate.

3. A twenty-fifth, John R. Gamble, was elected in 1890 but died before taking office and is excluded from this analysis. Table 19 is a biographical table for South Dakota Representatives.

4. However, three of the eight who did not attend college read law and were admitted to the bar.

5. Three others, Herbert Hitchcock, Vera Bushfield, and Joseph Bottum, Jr., were appointed to the Senate to fill vacancies and one, Gladys Pyle, was elected for the two-months remaining of the term to which Norbeck had been originally elected in 1932. These four are excluded from analysis here. Table 20 is a biographical table for South Dakota Senators.

6. In its original allocation of Senate terms when it achieved statehood in 1889, South Dakota drew one full six-year term and one two-year term. In Pettigrew's class, prominent successors have been Gamble, Sterling, Bulow, and Mundt. Prominent successors of the Moody class have been Kyle, Crawford, Norbeck, Gurney, Case, and McGovern. South Dakota will elect Senators to regular full terms in 1968 (the expiration of McGovern's first term), 1972 (the expiration of Mundt's fourth term) 1974, 1978, 1980, etc.

7. It should be noted that one of the Senators classified as a lawyer, Sterling, was dean of the University's law school when elected.

8. Senators from North Dakota have served much longer, on the average,

than have those from South Dakota. Only Norbeck and Mundt from South Dakota have been elected as many as three times to the Senate; four North Dakotans (Peter McCumber, 1899-1923; Gerald Nye, 1925-1945; William Langer, 1941-1959; and Milton Young, 1945-present) have served more than three terms and two others (Henry Hansbrough, 1891-1909, and Lynn Frazier, 1923-1941) have served three full terms.

9. Schell, *op. cit.,* pp. 234-237. The Republicans in 1900 "concentrated upon the legislative contest to ensure Pettigrew's defeat and retirement from public life." They were aided by a number of prominent figures who came to South Dakota to fight Pettigrew, including Theodore Roosevelt and Marcus Hanna, both of whom had been bitterly attacked in the Senate by Pettigrew. *Ibid.,* pp. 240-241.

10. Armin, *op. cit.,* p. 264.   11. *Ibid.,* p. 263.   12. *Ibid.,* p. 302.   13. Fite, *op. cit.,* p. 97.

14. *Congressional Record,* LXVII, June 1, 1926, p. 10392.

15. Paul E. Bellamy, "Peter Norbeck," in Dalthorp, *op. cit.,* pp. 32-33. Norbeck's strong loyalty for Theodore Roosevelt is said to account for the Rough Rider's visage on Mount Rushmore, along with those of Washington, Jefferson, and Lincoln. Thomas A. Bailey, *Presidential Greatness,* (New York: Appleton-Century-Crofts, 1966), pp. 12-13.

16. *Ibid.,* p. 35.   17. Fite, *op. cit.,* p. 184.   18. *Ibid.,* pp. 168-183.

19. Harry Robinson with Therman Wetteland, "William H. McMaster," in Dalthorp, *op. cit.,* pp. 38-39.   As militant members of the Farm Bloc, Norbeck and McMaster were proud to be included in the group of "Wild Jackasses of the Prairie." *Ibid.,* p. 38.

20. Schell, *op. cit.,* p. 311.

21. Bulow, *op. cit.,* p. 46. Bulow was especially critical of FDR's attack on the Supreme Court; he opposed and helped defeat President Roosevelt's attempt to pack the court with additional judges of his own choosing. *Ibid.,* p. 47.

22. "Gurney Defeat Means Truman Administration Loses a Vote on Foreign Aid, Military Spending," *U. S. News and World-Report,* XXVIII, June 16, 1950, pp. 16-17; and "Too Busy to Win," *Time,* LV, June 19, 1950, p. 21.

23. James A. Robinson, "The Role of the Rules Committee in Arranging the Program of the U. S. House of Representatives," *Western Political Quarterly,* XII, September, 1959, p. 658. Case received considerable national attention when he dramatically announced that an oil company lobbyist had attempted to bribe him during Congressional consideration of the natural gas bill in 1955-56. Case's action was a major factor in President Eisenhower's subsequent decision to veto the bill because of what he termed "arrogant lobbying." Edith T. Carper, *Lobbying and the Natural Gas Bill,* (University, Alabama: Inter-University Case Program, 1962).

24. "McGovern, Church Urging Negotiation on Viet Nam," *Aberdeen* (S.D.) *American-News,* February 28, 1965, p. 9.

25. *Congressional Record,* CX, No. 167, September 1, 1964, pp. 20555-20557.

26. In the eleven states of the midwest, the highest index for a Democratic Representative is 35 (Secrest of Ohio). O'Konski of Wisconsin at 43 is the only Republican Representative below 50; the next lowest Republican index is 64 (Broomfield of Michigan.)

27. Professor Charles O. Jones, using data from the *Congressional Quarterly,*

finds much the same results in his recent contribution to the study of the state Congressional delegation. Jones, "South Dakota in Washington: Profile of a Congressional Delegation," *Public Affairs,* February, 1966. Jones is also concerned about committee assignments and chairmanships, the work of the Congressional staff, and "congruity" between the party affiliations of the South Dakota delegation and national leadership.

CHAPTER IX

1. Lipson is concerned about the limitation involved in the two-year Congressional and gubernatorial terms. Lipson, *op. cit.,* p. 299.

2. Key makes several important summarizations of the political situation in American states. "Within the states, conditions have come to exist that make most difficult the organization of popular leadership. Instead of political sensitivity we often have political stalemate. Instead of ready and easy ways for the expression of popular will we have confusion and obstruction. Instead of the alertness and sensitivity described by the political orators, the actual situation discourages the maintenance of a party leadership and a party competition that might provide dynamic forces necessary for the fulfillment of the mission of the states. At times, in fact, obstructions to political initiative within the states divert to Washington activities that might as well be handled at state capitals." Key, *American State Politics,* (New York: Alfred A. Knopf, 1956), pp. 4-5. Duane Lockard has a similar conclusion: "There is a great deal of timidity, confusion, and evasion of responsibility in state politics . . ." Lockard, *op cit.,* p. 207.

3. See the discussion in Chapter 2 above.

4. Eldersveld, *Political Parties: A Behavioral Analysis,* (Chicago: Rand McNally & Co., 1964), p. 23.

5. Key, *op. cit.,* pp. 287-8.

6. Paul Appleby, *Citizens as Sovereigns,* (Syracuse: Syracuse University Press, 1962), p. 200.

7. Key, *op. cit.,* p. 289.

8. See the quotation from Lipson, Chapter 1 above. Compare Lipson's comments on the functions of party with the following: "It is well to recall, as Sorauf reminds us in his study of Pennsylvania, that the party seldom presents a comprehensive legislative program to the voters, that local parties and legislative candidates pay little attention to issues, and that most voters have only a vague awareness of whatever policies are advocated." Malcolm E. Jewell and Samuel C. Patterson, *The Legislative Process in the United States,* (New York: Random House, 1966), p. 449.

9. One recent critique of the performance of South Dakota party hierarchies is the present author's *The Nomination of Joe Bottum, op. cit.* One question raised was whether the large and diverse committee was capable of acting in the best interest of the party in making a crucial nomination. "The committee was a group with numerous and complicated internal associations, about to embark on a task which few if any of its members had ever taken part in before or even considered prior to the death of Senator Case a few weeks before." *Ibid.,* p. 44. Referring to elective state central committees, Key concludes that "rarely is the level of voter-interest in these choices much more than nominal.

The committees are virtually self-designated . . . the general impression that
most of them are virtually dead is probably not far wrong. A few have continuing staffs active in the business of the party. Others have an avid concern
about the spoils of politics and present, for that reason alone, an appearance of
internal cohesion and strength . . . In some way other elements, and often more
dynamic elements, of the leadership echelons could perhaps be brought into the
formal apparatus of party leadership. The elder statesmen, the major contributors
to party funds, the eggheads — Republican advertising men and Democratic
academicians —, spokesmen for interests associated with the party, and other
types of party influentials might very well be worked into the formal organs of
party leadership in one way or another." Key, *op. cit.*, p. 287.

10. See Berdahl, *op. cit.*

APPENDIX

WINNING CANDIDATES IN MAJOR
GENERAL ELECTIONS IN SOUTH DAKOTA, 1889-1966

Year	Governor	U.S. Senators "A"	U.S. Senators "B"	U.S. Representatives "1"	U.S. Representatives "2"	U.S. Representatives "3"
1889	Mellette	Pettigrew	Moody	Pickler	Gifford	--
1890	Mellette	--	Kyle	Pickler	Jolley	--
1892	Sheldon	--	--	Pickler	Lucas	--
1894	Sheldon	Pettigrew	--	Pickler	Gamble	--
1896	Lee	--	Kyle	Knowles	Kelley	--
1898	Lee	--	--	Burke	Gamble	--
1900	Herreid	Gamble	--	Burke	Martin	--
1902	Herreid	--	Kittredge	Burke	Martin	--
1904	Elrod	--	--	Burke	Martin	--
1906	Crawford	Gamble	--	Hall	Parker	--
1908	Vessey	--	Crawford	Burke	Martin	--
1910	Vessey	--	--	Burke	Martin	--
1912	Byrne	Sterling	--	Burke	Martin	Dillon
1914	Byrne	--	Johnson	Johnson	Gandy	Dillon
1916	Norbeck	--	--	Johnson	Gandy	Dillon
1918	Norbeck	Sterling	--	Johnson	Gandy	Christopherson
1920	McMaster	--	Norbeck	Johnson	Williamson	Christopherson
1922	McMaster	--	--	Johnson	Williamson	Christopherson
1924	Gunderson	McMaster	--	Johnson	Williamson	Christopherson
1926	Bulow	--	Norbeck	Johnson	Williamson	Christopherson
1928	Bulow	--	--	Johnson	Williamson	Christopherson
1930	Green	Bulow	--	Johnson	Williamson	Christopherson
1932	Berry	--	Norbeck	Hildebrandt	Werner	--
1934	Berry	--	--	Hildebrandt	Werner	--
1936	Jensen	Bulow	--	Hildebrandt	Case	--
1938	Bushfield	--	Gurney	Mundt	Case	--
1940	Bushfield	--	--	Mundt	Case	--
1942	Sharpe	Bushfield	--	Mundt	Case	--
1944	Sharpe	--	Gurney	Mundt	Case	--
1946	Mickelson	--	--	Mundt	Case	--
1948	Mickelson	Mundt	--	Lovre	Case	--
1950	Anderson	--	Case	Lovre	Berry	--
1952	Anderson	--	--	Lovre	Berry	--
1954	Foss	Mundt	--	Lovre	Berry	--
1956	Foss	--	Case	McGovern	Berry	--
1958	Herseth	--	--	McGovern	Berry	--
1960	Gubbrud	Mundt	--	Reifel	Berry	--
1962	Gubbrud	--	McGovern	Reifel	Berry	--
1964	Boe	--	--	Reifel	Berry	--
1966	Boe	Mundt	--	Reifel	Berry	--

INDEX

administrative agencies, 97, 108, 135
administrators, 2, 91, 143
AFL-CIO Committee on Political Education, 131
agrarian radicalism, 6, 9, 22, 27, 45, 100
agriculture, 121, 122, 128, 129, 133, 136
Alaska, 125
Alexander Hamilton Bicentennial Commission, 124
Alliance-Republican party, 22
American Farm Bureau Federation, 57, 131-132
American Medical Association, 62
Americans for Constitutional Action, 131-132
Anderson, Art B., 39, 52
Anderson, Sigurd, 11, 40, 42, 53, 91-94, 116, 122
anti-Republicanism, 45
appointment power, 96, 159
apportionment, legislative, 4, 36, 57, 101-102, 160
Army-McCarthy hearings, 8, 124
Attorney General, 12, 89-92, 97, 103, 116, 135
Ayres, Tom, 33, 35, 36

Badlands, 5, 125
Bailey, Thomas A., 162
banks, state-owned, 34, 98
Bartron, G. Robert, 111
Bates, Mark P. "Roy," 33, 35
Benson, Ezra Taft, 11
Berry, E. Y., 19, 40-42, 44, 117, 120, 124, 127-132
Berry, Tom, 8, 11, 36-39, 55, 59, 89, 93-95, 102, 116, 122, 126, 157, 158
Black Hills, 5, 65, 66, 85, 125, 137
Boe, Nils, 19, 42, 43, 48, 53, 91, 93, 94, 103, 158
Boehrs, C. E., 111

Bohemian groups, 81
Bone, Hugh, 160
Borah, William, 37, 60, 152
Bottum, Joseph H., 39, 40, 42, 52, 53, 59, 118, 121, 127, 161
Bromage, Arthur W., 148
Brown county, 66, 101
Bryan, William Jennings, 9, 25, 124
budget, 96, 137
budget officer, state, 38
Buehler, John, 111
Bull Moose party, 10, 151
Bulow, William J., 8, 10, 19, 34-38, 44, 45, 55, 56, 59, 88-90, 94, 95, 115, 116, 118, 121-124, 126, 154, 157, 161
Burke, Edmund, 47, 160
Burke, Charles H., 26-31, 44, 116, 117, 120, 124, 125
Bushfield, Harlan, 38, 39, 44, 91, 94, 115, 116, 118, 122, 124
Bushfield, Vera C., 118, 161
business regulation, 57, 129
Byrd, Harry F., 132
Byrne, Frank, 29-32, 91, 94

cabinet, Governor's, 89
California, 18, 95
campaign funds, 2, 48, 50, 87, 96, 119, 141, 142
Campbell county, 63, 66, 85
candidates, 2-4, 7, 11, 52, 58, 64, 102, 113, 140, 163
Caribbean area, 127
Case, Clifford, 132
Case, Francis H., 11, 35, 37-44, 52-53, 115-118, 120-121, 123-124, 126-127, 131-132, 134, 157, 161, 162
Catholics, 73, 85
cement plant, state-owned, 8, 86
census, 29, 36
Chamber of Commerce, 57, 62, 83, 85

167

Chamberlin, Robert, 41, 43
chairman, party, 49, 50, 64, 138,
141,142, 157
Charles Mix county, 63
Chase, C. L., 155
Christopherson, Charles A., 32, 33,
36, 37, 39, 44, 59, 115, 117, 120,
124.
Church, Louis L., 9
citizen, 1-5, 7, 116, 143, 146
citizenship, spirit of, 145-146
city councilmen, 148
city manager government, 64, 144
civil rights, 57, 128-129, 135
Clem, Alan L., 160, 161, 163
Cleveland, Grover, 9
climate, 5-6, 26, 152
cloture, 125
coal mine, state, 34
Colorado, 96
committee, party, 42, 49-50, 53, 58,
87, 121, 141, 142, 149, 152, 163
committee assignments, Congressional, 122, 123, 128
committee chairmanships, Congressional 123, 133
committeemen, national, 53, 141,
153
Communism, 128, 129
Congress, 2, 16, 89, 98, 115-133, 134
Congressional careers, 115
Congressional Delegation, 31, 32,
116, 119, 122, 124, 133, 136
Congressional districts, 17, 29, 98
Congressional leadership, 44
Congressional newsletters, 128-130
Congressional reorganization, 122
Congressmen, 2, 87, 114-116, 119
Connecticut, 132
conservative and conservatism, 6, 7,
8, 10, 27, 34, 35, 44, 54, 82.
conservation, 125
consolidation of governmental
units, 143-144
constituency, 43, 92, 107-108, 114-
115, 127, 134
constitutional amendments, 26, 32,
33

Constitution: federal, 98; South
Dakota, 21, 89, 92, 98, 99, 102
conventions: state party, 28, 36, 39,
49, 50, 53, 88, 115, 120, 135, 138,
141, 142, 151; national party, 25,
30, 35, 42, 60-61, 119
Coolidge, Calvin, 34, 35, 59, 60
corn belt, 5
county government, 63
county officers, 63, 148
court-packing effort, 162
Cox-Roosevelt ticket, 151
Crawford, Coe I., 7-8, 10, 25, 28-31,
44-45, 55, 89, 91, 94-95, 102,
115-116, 118, 120, 122, 124-125,
161
cross pressures, 4
Cummins, Albert B., 32, 59
currency system, 25
Curtis, Carl T., 156

decision-making process, 10, 89, 91
defense policy, 128, 129
"delegate" (legislative role), 107,
160
delegates to state and county conventions, 49
delegations, national convention,
42, 49, 58, 61-62, 156
democracy, 3-5, 138-140, 145, 148
Democratic strongholds, 85
depression, 7, 38, 147
Dewey, Thomas, 39-40, 60, 81-82, 145
Dillon, Charles Hall, 30-32, 35, 115,
117, 120
Dirksen, Everett, 132
districts, single-member, 101
Downing, J. Hyatt, 6
Douglas county, 73

East River, 12, 36, 66, 79, 121
economic conditions, 5, 43
economy, government role in, 10,
82-83,85,135
education, 57, 81, 83-85, 104-105,
129
Egan, George W., 29, 30, 31, 35
Eisenhower, Dwight D., 11, 13, 40-41,

59-61, 81-82, 123, 128, 162
Elazar, Daniel, 17, 18, 158
Eldersveld, Samuel, 139
elections, 12; at large, 101; Congressional, 14-15, 22; county officer, 63; general, 45-50, 115;
gubernatorial, 14, 19; laws, 96;
returns 149; primary, 7, 28, 29,
31, 35, 39, 48, 50-51, 53, 60, 62,
98, 115, 124,134-136, 139, 142;
state and local, 153; state
comparisons, 16
electioneering, 87
electoral college, 138
electoral process, 145
electric cooperatives, 58
Elrod, Samuel H., 28, 29, 35, 94

factions, 64, 82, 112, 150
Far East, 127
Farley, James, 155
farmers, 26, 57, 58
Farmer's Alliance, 22, 24
Farmer-Labor movement, 35, 46, 49
farm price supports, 57
fiscal affairs, 127-129
Fite, Gilbert, 150-151, 155, 157
Food for Peace program, 42, 127
foreign aid, 57, 82-83, 85, 126, 135
foreign policy, 127-129
forest land amendment, 155
Foss, Joe, 8, 40-42, 53, 56, 59, 61,
93-94, 103, 116, 122
Founding Fathers, 138
Free-silver party, 27
French descendants, 81
frontier, 6
Fusion party, 7, 9, 25-27, 49

Gamble, John R., 22, 117, 161
Gamble, Robert J., 25-27, 30, 44,
115-118, 121, 124, 161
Game, Fish and Parks department,
4, 90
Gandy, Harry L., 19, 31, 33, 115,
117, 120, 124
Garland, Hamlin, 6

German-Russian immigrants, 22
Gerrymander, 14
Gifford, Oscar S., 21, 116-117
Goldwater, Barry, 1, 42, 48, 59,
61-62, 119, 132, 145, 156
Good Government ticket, 49
governmental process, 146
Governmental Research Bureau, 129
Governor, 2, 12, 16, 86-97, 102-103,
116, 119, 122, 133, 135-137, 140,
143, 158; and legislature, 88;
messages and addresses of, 89, 93;
nominee for, 141; office of, 88;
power of, 92, 95, 136; roles of, 92;
succession, 87
grasshopper plague, 6, 26
Green, Warren E., 36, 52, 59-60,
93-94.
Gubbrud, Archie M., 42, 45, 59, 94,
103, 122, 157
Gullickson, Dale, 111
Gunderson, Carl, 34-36, 52, 91,
94-95
Gurney, J. Chandler, 37-40, 44, 115,
118, 121-122, 124, 126, 161

hail insurance program, 34
Halleck, Charles, 61
Hall, Philo, 28, 29, 115-117
Hanna, Marcus, 162
Harding, Warren G., 151
Harrison, Benjamin, 24
Hayden, Carl, 45
Herreid, Charles N., 27, 28, 91, 94,
102, 157
Herseth, Ralph, 41, 42, 56, 89-90,
94, 103, 122
Highway department, 34, 90
Hildebrandt, Fred H., 36, 37, 59,
116-117, 120
Hiss, Alger, 123
Hitchcock, Herbert, 59, 118, 124,
161
Holum, Kenneth, 40, 41
home rule, 64
Homestake Mine, 57, 154
Hoover, Herbert, 13, 35, 36, 147
Howe, Bill, 155

Humphrey, Hubert H., 59, 60, 124, 152
Hutchinson county, 85
hydro-electric development, 34

Idaho, 26
ideology, 45, 54-55, 131-133; of Congressman, 115; of legislators, 107
Illinois, 18, 95
immigration, 17-18, 125
impeachment, 88
Independent party, 9, 22, 33, 48-49, 52, 87
Indians and Indian affairs, 56, 58, 73, 81, 85, 122
Indiana, 93
individualistic political culture, 17
industrial commissioner, 90
Ingalls, John J., 46
initiative and referendum, 7, 26, 27, 32, 33, 98, 99, 113, 124, 135, 136, 138, 144.
Iowa, 5, 13-19, 21, 93, 96
irrigation systems, 32
isolation, 5, 6
isolationism, 11, 126, 148, 154
issue orientation, 82-83
Izaak Walton League, 62

James river, 65, 66, 73, 137
Jefferson, Thomas, 154
Jensen, Leslie, 11, 37-38, 89-91, 93-94, 116
Jewell, Malcolm E., and Samuel C. Patterson, 163
John Birch Society, 147
Johnson, Edwin S., 18, 30-31, 116, 118, 121, 124-125
Johnson, Hiram, 34, 59-60, 125, 152, 155
Johnson, Lyndon B., 1, 42, 48, 59-60, 127, 129
Johnson, Royal C., 29, 31, 33, 36, 43-44, 49, 116-117, 120, 134
Jolley, John L., 22, 116-117, 124
Jones, Buell F., 35, 91
Jones, Charles O., 61, 162, 163

Judd, Walter, 61, 158

Kansas, 26, 46, 93
Kefauver, Estes, 40, 59-61
Kelley, John E., 25, 26, 115, 117, 124
Kennedy, John F., 3, 42, 80-82, 127, 129
Key, V. O., Jr., 47, 139-140, 150, 153, 163, 164
Kittredge, Alfred B., 28, 115, 118, 121, 124-125
Knights of Columbus, 84-85
Knights of Labor, 27
Knowles, Freeman, 25-27, 115, 117
Krause, Herbert, 6
Kyle, James H., 8, 23-26, 44, 115, 118, 120-121, 125, 157, 161

labor, 2, 57-58, 129
LaFollette, Robert, Sr., 28-30, 58-59
LaFollette, Robert, Jr., 152
Landon, Alfred, 11, 60
Lane, Rose Wilder, 6
Langer, William, 15-16, 124, 162
League of Women Voters, 58
Lee, Andrew E., 8, 25-27, 29, 45, 89-90, 93-95, 157
legislative campaign, 113
legislative caucus, 141
legislative powers, 98-100
Legislative Research Council, 92, 100, 135
legislative sessions, annual, 101
legislative strategy, 99
legislative voting behavior, 56, 108-109, 113, 130, 136, 161
legislators, 2, 100, 102-103, 105-107, 110, 114-115, 133, 140, 159
legislature, 2, 4, 7, 9, 11, 14, 15-16, 56, 98-114, 135, 141, 143
liberal and liberalism, 10, 32, 38, 54, 82, 85
Liberty ticket, 49
lieutenant governor, 12, 87, 89-90, 97, 102-103, 135
Lindley, John F., 42, 48
Lipson, Leslie, 163

liquor option, 98
local government, 143, 152
local officials, 119
local politics, 62-64
Lockard, Duane, 149, 153, 158,
    159, 163
Lodge, Henry Cabot, 61
Long, Norton, 154
Lorimer, William, 125
Loucks, Henry L., 22, 24, 27, 35
Lovre, Harold O., 39-41, 52, 115,
    117, 120, 124, 131
Lowden, Frank, 59-60
loyalty affidavits, 4
Lubell, Samuel, 73, 148
Lucas, William V., 24, 115, 117

McCarthy, Joseph R., 8, 15-16, 124
McGovern, George S., 8, 11, 19, 41-
    42, 45, 54-55, 116-118, 120-124,
    127-129, 131-132, 134, 152, 161
McKinley, William, 25, 27
McMaster, William H., 8, 10, 33-36,
    44, 89, 91, 95, 115-116, 118, 121-
    122, 126, 152, 162
McPherson county, 66, 85, 156

majority, the, 145
Mansfield, Mike, 124
Marsh, John O., Jr., 133
Martin, Eben W., 27-31, 44, 116-117,
    120, 124
Masonic lodges, 83, 85
masses, 137
Medicare, 57
Mellette, Arthur C., 21-24, 94-95
Mickelson, George T., 39-40, 45,
    59, 60, 91-92, 94-95, 103, 122, 157,
    158
midwest, 18, 44
migratory bird legislation, 125
Miller, A. C., 39, 42, 53
mining interests, 58
Minnehaha county, 66, 101
Minnesota, 5-6, 13-19, 21, 26, 43, 46,
    96, 136
minor party, 7, 48
minority representation, 21

Mississippi, 96
Missouri, 18
Missouri river, 5, 66, 79
monetary issue, 27
Montana, 5, 13-19, 26, 95-96, 136
Moody, Gideon C., 22-23, 115, 118,
    121, 161
moralistic political culture, 17
morality in government, 148
Morlan, Robert L., 32
Morton, Thruston, 61
Mt. Rushmore, 125, 162
Mundt, Karl E., 8, 19, 37-39, 41-45,
    55, 116-121, 123-124, 127-129,
    131-132, 134, 156, 158, 161, 162
municipal government, 64

National Association of Manufac-
    turers, 2, 57
National Farmers Organization,
    2, 57
National Farmers Union, 57, 62, 85,
    131
National Republican Progressive
    League, 30
natural resources, 122, 129
national-state relations, 116
national ticket, 14
Nebraska, 5, 13-16, 18-19, 26, 43, 93,
    96, 136
New Deal, 7, 9-10, 34, 38, 43, 45, 55,
    66, 87, 102, 126, 134, 154
New England, 18
New Hampshire, 112
New Mexico, 95
New York, 95-96
Nixon, Richard M., 3, 42, 61, 80-82,
    145, 156
nominations, 7, 41-42, 53, 86, 91, 154
nonpartisan, 14, 63-64:
    ballot, 147
    election, 7
    movement, 134
Nonpartisan League, 10, 32-34, 46,
    49
Norbeck, Peter, 7-8, 10, 13, 28-38,
    43-46, 49, 55-56, 60, 89, 91-95,
    115-116, 118, 121-126, 134, 152,

155, 157, 161, 162
Norris, George W., 45, 124-125, 152
North Dakota, 5-6, 13-16, 18-19, 26, 33, 46, 93, 96, 112
North Dakota Depressive Reaction, 6
Nye, Gerald, 152, 162

officials, 2, 3, 89, 138
Ohio, 18, 93, 132
oil companies, 151, 162
Old Guard, 30
Old South, 17
opinion, 83
organizational membership, 83-84

pacifism, 33, 125
Parker, William H., 28, 115, 117, 120
partisan activities, 140
partisan ballot, 63
partisan municipal government, 144
party, 2, 4, 17, 24, 47-64, 86, 107-108, 112-114, 139-143, 150; and issues, 53-56; control, 96, 140; elections, 153; endorsement, 7; hierarchy, 53, 86, 96, 135,136, 140, 157, 163; leadership, 49-51, 82, 88, 92, 138, 139, 144, 154; loyalty, 17, 81, 110-112; nominating process, 28; officials, 2, 48, 53, 56, 87, 113, 119, 138; organization, 55, 64, 82, 86-87, 134, 141, 144, 146, 163; platforms, 54-56, 142; responsibility, 141-142; strength, 12-17, 82, 85; system, 4, 138-140
patronage, 53, 125
Patterson, Samuel C., 148
Pecora, Ferdinand, 126
Pennington county, 66, 101
Pennsylvania, 18
petition, 52, 87
Pettigrew, Richard F., 8, 22, 24-25, 27-28, 44, 115, 118, 121, 124-125, 154, 155, 161, 162
pheasants, 2
Pickler, John A., 21-22, 24, 26, 116-117, 124

Pierre, 113, 137
Platt, George M., 101
policy, 1, 3, 58; and party control, 55; committees, 142; process, 45, 56, 113, 115, 140, 142
political ambition, 102
political careers, 88, 91, 115
political culture, 17-18, 148
political discussion, 56
political disposition, 14, 83-84, 86
political leaders, 54, 97, 137
political process, 4
political system, 9, 95-96, 144
"politico" (legislative role), 107, 160
popular democracy, 6
popular control, 50, 96, 136-137, 145
population, 5
Populism and Populist party, 7, 9, 13, 22-28, 43, 45, 48-49, 55, 89-90, 124-125, 134, 151
Populist-Democratic Alliance, 7, 27
power, 1, 32, 136, 153
diffusion of, 136, 143-144
structure, 136, 143
prairie, 5
precincts, 78-81, 85, 135, 148
President, 1, 12, 16, 50, 89, 92
Presidential elections, 13-14, 24, 73, 78, 81
Presidential electors, 32
Presidential nominations, 11, 24-25, 141
Presidential primary, 32, 37, 49, 58-60
press, 113-114, 116, 137
pressure (interest) groups, 2, 4, 47, 57, 58, 87, 96-97, 100, 107, 112, 119, 130-131, 136, 140-141, 143
Progressivism, 7, 13, 28-29, 34, 43, 45, 49, 54-55, 124-125, 134, 150
Progressive Republicans, 7, 10, 34, 38, 120, 151
prohibition, 21
Prohibition ticket, 25, 49
prosperity, 38
protest movements, 6
Protestant denominations, 85, 104

Public Utilities Holding Company
   Act of 1935, 126.
public utilities regulation, 58
public welfare, 129
Pyle, Gladys, 36, 52, 118, 161

radicalism, 7, 33, 46
radical policies, 26, 34
railroad (or public utilities) commissioner, 12
railroads, 27, 57-58
rangeland, 65, 73
Rapid City, 5, 93, 101, 106, 120,
   122, 137
reclamation, 122
referendum, 151, 159
reform, 7, 141-144, 146
registered voters, 48
registration laws, 53, 58
Reifel, Ben, 19, 41-42, 53, 116-117,
   120, 124, 128-129, 131-132
religion and religious affiliation, 81,
   84, 104-105
religious philosophy, 6
representation, 4
Republican strongholds, 85
responsibility, 3-5, 86, 138, 140, 143
Rice, Stuart, 148
Richards primary law, 154
Richards, R. O., 30-31, 33-35
Richland township, 81
rights of minority groups, 83, 85
Riker, William H., 148
Rockefeller, Nelson, 156
role perception, legislators, 107
Rolvaag, Ole, 6
Roosevelt, Franklin D., 13, 34, 36-37,
   39, 59-60, 81-82, 126, 147, 155
Roosevelt, Theodore, 10-11, 28, 30,
   34, 58-59, 125, 162
Rosenthal township, 81
rural cooperatives, 85
rural credits, 32, 34, 35
rural electrification, 57
rural recession, 125, 126
Russian-German counties, 66, 73, 85

sales tax, 2, 4

Saltonstall, Leverett, 123
Saunders, Phil, 41, 91
Scales of Justice party, 49
Schell, Herbert S., 6, 7, 157
Schlesinger, Joseph A., 19-20, 95-96
school districts, 12-year, 4
Scranton, William, 62
Seaton, Fred, 61
Securities Act of 1933, 126
Securities and Exchange Act of
   1934, 126.
seniority, 119, 152
service clubs, 85
Sharpe, Merrill Q., 39, 52, 91, 93-95,
   158
Sheldon, Charles H., 24, 94, 157
silver interests, western, 150
Silver Republicans, 8, 25, 27
silver, unlimited coinage of, 25
Sioux City, Iowa, 5
Sioux Falls, 5, 29, 93, 101, 106,
   120-122, 137
small state politicians, 43
Smith, Al, 35
Smoot, Reed, 126
South, 18, 44
South Carolina, 62, 96, 132
South Dakota Municipal League, 58
South Dakota Poll, 42
South Dakota State University, 104
Southwest, 18
socialism, 32, 86, 157
social isolation, 46
socialistic state ventures, 8
Socialist party, 27, 49, 59
speaker, South Dakota House, 103
special sessions, 92
Stalwart Republican faction, 10, 28,
   30, 55, 125, 134
Stassen, Harold, 39, 59-60, 124
statehood, 9, 21
state officers, 89-91
state ownership, 32, 86, 124
Sterling, Thomas, 23, 30, 32-34, 115,
   118, 121-122, 125, 152, 161
Stevenson, Adlai, 40-41, 61, 81-82,
   145
stock grower's association, 57-58

stock market investigation, 126
superintendent of public instruction, 12, 89
Supreme Court, South Dakota, 90, 92
Supreme Court, U. S., 102
survey data, 65

Taft, Robert A., 11, 40, 59-61
Taft, William Howard, 10, 30, 58-59, 125
tariffs, 126
tax structure, property basis of, 104
Temmey, Leo A., 39, 52
Tennessee, 96
tenure, 95, 120-121
terms of legislators, 100, 105-106
Teton National Park, 125
Texas, 96, 132
Thomas, J. Parnell, 123
Thomson, Keith, 15-16
Thorson, Thomas, 29
Tower, John, 132
traditionalistic political culture, 17
transportation, 122, 129, 137
tripartisan politics, 49
Truman, Harry S, 40, 59-60, 81-82, 126, 162
"trustee" (legislative role), 107, 160
Turner county, 66

Unemployment Compensation department, 90
unicameral legislature, 143
University of South Dakota, 30, 93, 120-121
upper midwest, 17
upper plains, 18
urbanization, 73

vacancies in elective public office, 53, 88, 90, 102, 157
Vermont, 93, 112
Vessey, Robert S., 28-29, 53, 94
veto, 92, 96
Viet Nam, 3, 152
voter registration, 56
voters, 4, 11, 50-51, 54, 82, 87, 113, 116, 135-136, 163
voting behavior, 65-85, 134
voting turnout, 53

Waggonner, Joe D., Jr., 133
Walker, Herman, Jr., and Peter L. Hansen, 152
Washington (state), 26
Weeks, I. D., 158
Weaver, James B., 24
Webb, Walter Prescott, 150
Werner, Theo B., 11, 36-37, 115, 117, 120, 124
West River, 21, 29, 66, 102, 108, 120-121, 135
Wheeler, Burton K., 124
Williamson, William, 33, 35-37, 44, 52, 115, 117, 120, 124
Willkie, Wendell, 38, 81-82
Wilson, Woodrow, 32, 59
Wisconsin, 13-19, 43, 93, 96, 112, 132
wisdom, 3, 145
Wood, Leonard, 59-60
workmen's compensation, 90
world affairs, 11
Wyoming, 5, 13-16, 18-19, 95-96, 125, 132

Yankee Puritan stock, 17

Zeller, Belle, 112

ABOUT THE AUTHOR

Alan L. Clem is Professor of Government and Associate Director of the Governmental Research Bureau at the University of South Dakota.

In the course of his varied career he has been an assistant to Senator Carl T. Curtis and Representative R. D. Harrison, a Fellow of the National Center for Education in Politics, an information specialist for the U. S. Department of Agriculture, a consultant of the American Enterprise Association, and a member of the city council of Vermillion, South Dakota.

He holds degrees from the University of Nebraska (B.A., 1950) and the American University (Ph.D., 1960).

He is the author of several political monographs and a contributor to such journals as the *Midwest Journal of Political Science,* the *Nebraska Law Review, Public Affairs,* and the *National Civic Review.*